THE SCHOOL HOUSE,
SUTTON COLDFIELD

THE EXCAVATIONS AT BABYLON

MACMILLAN AND CO., Limited
LONDON · BOMBAY · CALCUTTA
MELBOURNE

THE MACMILLAN COMPANY
NEW YORK · BOSTON · CHICAGO
DALLAS · SAN FRANCISCO

THE MACMILLAN CO. OF CANADA, Ltd.
TORONTO

COLOURED ENAMELLED VASE.—Page 236.

Frontispiece.

THE EXCAVATIONS
AT BABYLON

BY

ROBERT KOLDEWEY

TRANSLATED BY

AGNES S. JOHNS

WITH 255 ILLUSTRATIONS AND PLANS

MACMILLAN AND CO., LIMITED
ST. MARTIN'S STREET, LONDON
1914

COPYRIGHT

PREFACE

It is most desirable, if not absolutely necessary, that the excavation of Babylon should be completed. Up to the present time only about half the work has been accomplished, although since it began we have worked daily, both summer and winter, with from 200 to 250 workmen. This is easily comprehensible when we consider the magnitude of the undertaking. The city walls, for instance, which in other ancient towns measure 3 metres, or at the most 6 or 7 metres, in Babylon are fully 17 to 22 metres thick. On many ancient sites the mounds piled above the remains are not more than 2 or 3 to 6 metres high, while here we have to deal with 12 to 24 metres, and the vast extent of the area that was once inhabited is reflected in the grand scale of the ruins.

The gradual progress of the excavations, important and stimulating as it is for the explorers, appears of less interest to those who take little share in it or who look back on it after a lapse of years. As such an excavation never affords any guarantee of further continuance, those points must first be settled which appear to be of the highest interest in view of the results already attained. Accordingly the site of the excavations varies at different times in a manner which is rarely voluntary, and must generally be regarded as a logical development dictated by considerations of inherent necessity. Here we shall only deal with the external sequence of the principal events.

The excavations were commenced on March 26, 1899, on the east side of the Kasr to the north of the Ishtar Gate. At my first stay in Babylon, June 3–4, 1887, and again on my second visit, December 29–31, 1897, I saw a number of fragments of enamelled brick reliefs, of which I took several with me to Berlin. The peculiar beauty of these fragments and their importance for the history of art was duly recognised by His Excellency R. Schöne, who was then Director-General of the Royal Museums, and this strengthened our decision to excavate the capital of the world empire of Babylonia.

By the end of 1899 the Procession Street of Marduk was opened up as far as the north-east corner of the Principal Citadel and a cross-cut was driven through the north front of the Principal Citadel.

1900. The Temple of Ninmach was excavated, January–March; the centre of Amran, where we ascertained the site of Esagila, April–November; and the centre of the Principal Citadel, June–July. The south-east part of the Southern Citadel as far as the throne-room with the ornamental and enamelled bricks was begun in July and continued till July 1901, while the following up of the Procession Street in the plain continued till November 1902.

1901. A cross-cut over the ridge of mounds between Kasr and Sachn was effected, February–April; the south-west building of the Kasr was examined, April–May; and the excavations at Ishin aswad with the Ninib Temple carried out, July–December.

1902. The Ishtar Gate was excavated, February–November; the temple "Z," January–February; overlapping work at Borsippa, February–April; and Fara, June 1902–March 1903.

1903. The north-east corner of the Southern Citadel with the vaulted building was explored, December 1902–January 1904.

1904. The mounds of Homera were worked through

with the Greek theatre, January–April; and the inner city wall was begun in April. In the Southern Citadel the excavation was carried farther west, and the eastern portion of the palace of Nabopolassar was excavated, April 1904– February 1905.

1905. The inner city wall was partially opened up, January–March. The excavations, by order of the Turkish Government, were temporarily deferred, April 7–June 23; the two mud walls to the north of the Southern Citadel were commenced in June, and the Sargon wall with the beginning of the Arachtu wall was verified.

1906. The western boundary of the Southern Citadel with the two bastions on the north-west was excavated, and also the moat wall of Imgur-Bel, the Persian Building, and the south-west corner of the Southern Citadel, till June 1907.

1907. From the Persian Building a long exploration trench was carried through the western quarter, December 1906–March 1907; the eastern ends of the two mud walls in front of the Ninmach Temple were excavated, June– October, and a small piece of the outer wall near Babil, June–July. In October the southern quay wall of the canal south of the Kasr was followed up farther and the excavations in Merkes were begun, which with varying degrees of activity have been carried on up to the present time, May 1912.

1908. The main work lay in Merkes. It led *inter alia* to the uncovering of the earliest strata that have yet been reached and that belong to the period of the earliest Babylonian kings. In February, as a lengthy secondary piece of work, the opening up of Sachn was begun at the Tower of Babylon and lasted till June 1911. Also in July a cut was made through the quarter to the west of Sachn, which brought to light the Arachtu wall and the Nabonidus wall at this place.

1909. The main work still lay in Merkes, where the

strata of the dwellings of Nebuchadnezzar's period were laid bare in large connected areas.

1910. In January the main work was transferred to the north-east strip of the Kasr, where the northern ends of the two walls that flank the Procession Street were brought to light, that now — May 1912 — are almost finished. Here also the lengths of wall that project eastwards were opened up. As an additional piece of work the following up of the Arachtu wall from the Kasr to Amran was begun with the embankment walls of Nebuchadnezzar and Nabonidus that lay in front of it, April 1910–January 1911 ; this led to the discovery of the stone bridge over the Euphrates, August–November. The researches in Merkes were carried on with the opening up of more private houses and the Temple of Ishtar of Agade, November 1910–October 1911. Also, as a secondary piece of work, the outer walls of the temple of Esagila were identified, December 1910–July 1911.

1911. The main work on the north-east corner of the Kasr was continued, and the great stone wall with the inscription of Nebuchadnezzar emerged in April. The secondary work of the previous year was, as we have already said, carried farther ; for example, a considerable part of the network of streets in Merkes towards the south was traced.

1912. Besides proceeding with the digging at the north-east corner of the Kasr and at Merkes, the excavation was begun of the buildings with the great surrounding wall in the west of the Southern Citadel which had been cut by the exploration trench of 1907.

The digging is carried out by the general administration of the Royal Museums in Berlin, present Director-General His Excellency W. Bode, in conjunction with the Deutsche Orient-Gesellschaft, President His Excellency von Hollmann, under the patronage of H.M. the Emperor of Germany.

For many of the translations of inscriptions I am indebted to the kindness of Professor Delitzsch.

My scientific collaborators were : W. Andrae, March 26, 1899–February 1, 1903 ; B. Meissner, March 26, 1899–April 13, 1900 ; F. Weissbach, February 22, 1901–February 22, 1903 ; A. Nöldeke, May 8, 1902–January 11, 1908 ; F. Baumgarten, May 8, 1902–March 26, 1903 ; F. Langenegger, March 29, 1903–September 23, 1905 ; J. Jordan, March 29–August 3, 1903 ; G. Buddensieg, March 24, 1904, until now ; O. Reuther, October 16, 1905, until now ; F. Wetzel, December 15, 1907, until now ; J. Grossmann, December 24, 1907–January 10, 1908 ; K. Müller, May 13, 1909–February 29, 1912.

Among the earlier explorers who have dealt with the ruins of Babylon are the following : 1811, Rich (*Narrative of a Journey to the Site of Babylon in 1811*, London, 1839) ; 1850, Layard (*Nineveh and Babylon*, London, 1853) ; 1852–1854, Oppert (*Expédition scientifique en Mésopotamie*, Paris, 1863) ; 1878–89, Hormuzd Rassam (*Asshur and the Land of Nimrod*, New York, 1897).

It involves no depreciation of the labours of our predecessors when we say that they are superseded in almost every detail by the results of our many years of excavations, so far as the knowledge of the city ruins are concerned, and thus it would hardly be worth while to controvert expressly their numerous errors.

Further, my view of the purpose of the various buildings has altered during the course of the excavations, especially in relation to the literary sources. This is the natural result of gradual progress in research, never working with conclusive material.

In addition to the continuous reports of the excavations in the *Mitteilungen der Deutschen Orient-Gesellschaft*, the following have also been published in the *Wissenschaftliche Veröffentlichungen der Deutschen Orient-*

Gesellschaft: vol. i., Koldewey, *Die Hettitische Inschrift*, 1900; vol. ii., Koldewey, *Die Pflastersteine von Aibur-schabu*, 1901; vol. iv., Weissbach, *Babylonische Miscellen*, 1903; vol. xv., Koldewey, *Die Tempel von Babylon*, 1911; all published by Messrs. J. C. Hinrichs, Leipzig.

The Babylonian inscriptions which are of importance to us will be found in the above-mentioned works, and also for the most part in the *Keilinschriftliche Bibliothek* (E. Schrader), vol. iii. part ii. Berlin, 1890, and in the *Neu-babylonische Königsinschriften*, S. Langdon, Leipzig, 1912. The latter work I only met with after the close of this present volume, so that I have not been able to make use of it.

For the convenience of the reader, an appendix is added giving the principal statements of the classical authors so far as they refer to Babylon.

ROBERT KOLDEWEY.

BABYLON, *May* 16, 1912.

For the English translation special thanks are due to Dr. GÜTERBOCK for the trouble he has taken in reading the proofs, and the courtesy he has shown in suggesting alterations in the difficult architectural terms.

The use of the term "moat wall" has been decided on for the massive brickwork of the fosse in preference to the word revetment as more accurately expressing the nature of the construction, although the expression is not used in describing modern fortifications.

AGNES S. JOHNS.

CAMBRIDGE, *April* 1914.

CONTENTS

ILLUSTRATIONS

THE OUTER CITY WALLS

In the time of Nebuchadnezzar the traveller who approached the capital of Babylonia from the north would find himself where the Nil Canal flows to-day, face to face with the colossal wall that surrounded mighty Babylon (Fig. 1). Part of this wall still exists and is recognisable at the present time in the guise of a low earthen ridge about 4 to 5 kilometres in length. Up to the present we have only excavated a small part, so that it is only possible to give a detailed description of the most noteworthy features of these fortifications, that were rendered so famous by Greek authors.

There was a massive wall of crude brick 7 metres thick, in front of which, at an interval of about 12 metres, stood another wall of burnt brick 7.8 metres thick, with the strong wall of the fosse at its foot, also of burnt brick and 3.3 metres thick (Fig. 2). The fosse must have been in front of this, but so far we have not searched closely for it, and therefore the counterscarp has not yet been found.

Astride on the mud wall were towers 8.37 metres (about 24 bricks) wide, that projected beyond the wall on both its faces. Measured from centre to centre these towers were 52.5 metres apart. Thus there was a tower at intervals of about 100 ells, for the Babylonian ell measured roughly half a metre.

Owing to the unfinished state of the excavations it is not yet possible to say how the towers on the outer wall were constructed. The space between the two walls was

B

filled in with rubble, at least to the height at which the ruins are preserved and presumably to the crown of the outer wall. Thus on the top of the wall there was a road that afforded space for a team of four horses abreast, and even for two such teams to pass each other. Upon this crown of the wall the upper compartments of the towers faced each other like small houses.

This broad roadway on the summit of the wall, which was of world-renown owing to the descriptions of it given by classical writers, was of the greatest importance for the protection of the great city. It rendered possible the rapid shifting of defensive forces at any time to that part of the wall which was specially pressed by attack. The line of defence was very long; the north-east front, which can still be measured, is 4400 metres long, and on the south-east the ruined wall can be traced without excavation for a length of 2 kilometres. These two flanks of the wall certainly extended as far as the Euphrates as it flowed from north to south. With the Euphrates they enclosed that part of Babylon of which the ruins exist at the present time, but according to Herodotus and others they were supplemented on the other side of the Euphrates by two other walls, so that the town site consisted of a quadrangle through which the Euphrates flowed diagonally. Of the western walls nothing is now to be seen. Whether the traces of a line of wall to the south near the village of Sindjar will prove to have formed part of them has yet to be ascertained.

The excavations carried on up to the present time have yielded no surrounding walls beyond this fortification. The circuit extended for about 18 kilometres. Instead of this, Herodotus gives about 86 kilometres and Ctesias about 65 kilometres. There must be some error underlying this discrepancy. The 65 kilometres of Ctesias approximate so closely to four times the correct measurement that it may well be suspected that he mistook the figures representing the whole circumference for the measure of one side of the square. We shall later turn more in detail from the testimony of the ancient writers to the evidence of the ruins themselves. Generally speaking, the measurements given are not in accordance with those actually preserved, while the general description, on the contrary, is usually accurate. Herodotus describes the wall of Babylon as built of burnt brick. To an observer from without it would no doubt appear as such, as only the top of the inner mud wall could be seen from outside. The escarp of the fosse was formed of the square bricks that are so extraordinarily numerous in Babylon, that measure 33 centimetres and bear the usual stamp of Nebuchadnezzar. Those of the brick wall are somewhat smaller (32 centimetres) and unstamped. These smaller unstamped bricks are common previous to the time of Nebuchadnezzar, but nevertheless they may very well date from the early years of his reign, as we shall see farther on. To what period the mud-brick wall may be assigned we do not yet know, it is certainly older. It apparently possessed an escarp, of which there are some scanty remains within the great brick wall. It

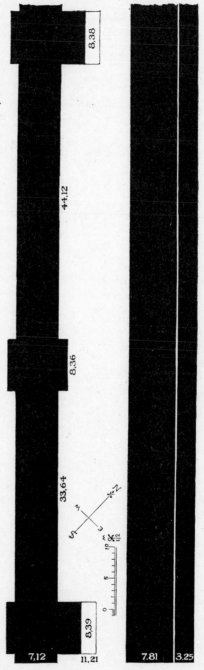

FIG. 2.—Part of the outer city walls ; ground-plan.

appears to have been cut through on the outside by the latter.

Up to the present we have found about 15 of the towers on the mud wall only. They are the so-called Cavalier towers, and project both at the front and the back, thus placed astride on the wall. They were, of course, higher than the walls, but we can get no clue from the ruins as to the height of walls or towers, as only the lower parts remain. The towers are 8.36 metres wide and are placed 44 metres apart. Thus on the entire front there were about 90, and on the whole circumference—provided the town formed a square—there must have been 360 towers. How many there were on the outer wall we do not know. Ctesias gives the number as 250. No gateway has yet been found, which is not surprising, considering the limited extent of the excavations.

During the Parthian period these lines of fortification can have been no longer in a condition to afford protection. On the town side of the mud wall there are Parthian sarcophagi, inserted in holes dug in the wall itself.

While the foundations of the brick wall are below the present water-level, the mud wall stands on an artificial embankment. As a general rule mud walls were not provided with deep foundations. The mortar employed for the mud wall was clay, and for the brick wall bitumen was used. The same method of construction can be recognised in other parts of the city, where it is better preserved and can be more satisfactorily studied.

At the northern end of our line of wall, which encloses the mound of ruins, called " Babil," with a hook-like curve, the inner wall also was built of brick. This appears, at least, from the two deep trenches left by plunderers which occur here, but it must be inferred pending excavation. The digging for the valuable bricks which occurred in recent times has left deep traces in the otherwise smooth surface of the ground which we do not find in the attempted demolitions of more ancient times.

For this reason, with the exception of the portion near Babil there is nothing to be seen of the burnt-brick wall without excavating, while the mud wall, which has merely suffered from the ravages of time, has left behind a clearly marked line of ruins of some height. The town wall of Seleucia on the Tigris, likewise a mud wall, stands out similarly above its mounds of debris to a considerable height. It cannot therefore be said that a burnt-brick wall of 480 stadia, the gigantic dimensions recorded by Herodotus, must necessarily have left considerable and unmistakable traces, and it is not this consideration that leads us to doubt the existence of an encircling wall of such dimensions, which has been accepted as an established fact since Oppert's excavations in Babylon. Neither does the immense size of itself demand dismissal as fantastic. The great wall of China, 11 metres high and 7.5 metres broad, with its length of 2450 kilometres, is just 29 times as long as that of Herodotus. There are other overwhelming considerations which we shall investigate later. In any case the city, even in circumference, was the greatest of any in the ancient East, Nineveh itself not excepted, which in other respects rivalled Babylon. But the period in which the fame of Babylon's vast size spread over the world was the time of Herodotus, and then Nineveh had already ceased to exist.

A comparison with modern cities can scarcely be made without further consideration. It must always be remembered that an ancient city was primarily a fortress of which the inhabited part was surrounded and protected by the encircling girdle of the walls. Our great modern cities are of an entirely different character, they are inhabited spaces, open on all sides. A reasonable comparison can, therefore, only be made between Babylon and other walled cities, and when compared with them Babylon takes the first place, both for ancient and modern times, as regards the extent of its enclosed and inhabited area.

Nebuchadnezzar frequently mentions this great work in his inscriptions. The most important passage occurs in his great *Steinplatten*[1] inscription, col. 7 l. 22-55: " That no assault should reach Imgur-Bel, the wall of Babylon ; I did, what no earlier king had done, for 4000 ells of land on the side of Babylon, at a distance so that it

---

[1] Usually called in England The East India House Inscription.

(the assault) did not come nigh, I caused a mighty wall
to be built on the east side of Babylon. I dug out its
moat, and I built a scarp with bitumen and bricks. A
mighty wall I built on its edge, mountain high. Its broad
gateways I set within it and fixed in them double doors
of cedar wood overlaid with copper. In order that the
enemy who devised (?) evil should not press on the flanks
of Babylon, I surrounded it with mighty floods, as is the
land with the wave-tossed sea. Its coming was like the
coming of the great sea, the salt water. In order that no
breach should be made in it, I piled up an earthen
embankment by it, and encompassed it with quay walls of
burnt brick. The bulwark I fortified cunningly and made
the city of Babylon into a fortress" (cf. H. Winckler,
Keilinschriftliche Bibliothek, vol. iii. 2, p. 23). It can
hardly be expected that we can yet reach absolute certainty
as to the meaning of all the details here given. That can
best be afforded by a complete excavation, which is
urgently to be desired.

II

THE MOUND BABIL

FOLLOWING the ridge of the ruined city wall from the
excavated portion farther to the north-west, one reaches a
gap in the wall where it was ruthlessly broken down by
later canals, now themselves dried up (Fig. 3). They
were forerunners of the present Nil Canal. The Arabic
word *nil* denotes the blue colour which is generally
produced by indigo, and has given its name to various
watercourses on Arab soil; the name of the Egyptian
Nile is probably connected with it. The Nil Canal runs
to-day a few hundred metres to the north-east along the
city wall and roughly parallel with it. The embankments
of these canals, which in places are of immense height,
intersect the plain with a sharp line. The contrast with
the plain is most striking when they are seen on the

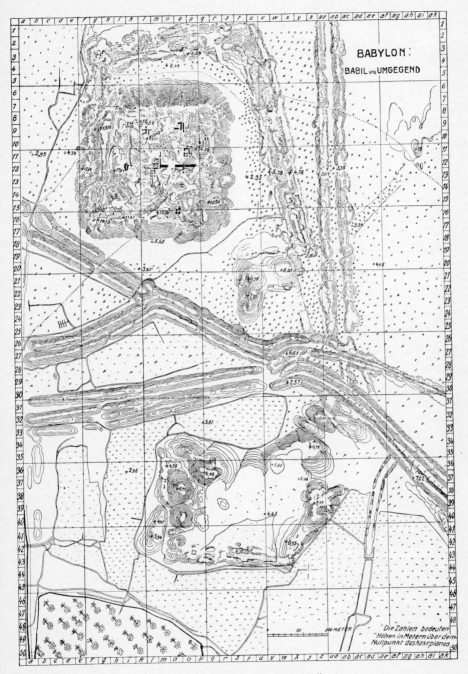

FIG. 3.—Plan of the mound "Babil."

horizon, where the mirage comes to their aid and makes them look like hills of some importance. At first sight, also, they appear to be entirely out of proportion with the small amount of water that flows so slowly through the canal. That, however, is only the case where the canal has been in use for some long time. When the canal is first constructed each embankment, under normal circumstances, consists of no more than half of the earth which is dug out, as these irrigation works, wherever the lie of the ground permits, are so arranged that the surface of the water may be higher than the surrounding plain. Only in this way would it be possible with comparatively small expenditure, and without special machinery for raising water, to provide the field with a gentle supply of the

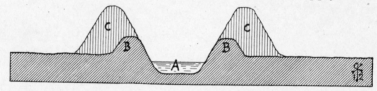

FIG. 4.—Section of a canal when newly constructed (B), and after long use (C).

fructifying moisture. But the Euphrates at the period of high water, when the irrigation takes place, bears a quantity of material in suspension that is specially valuable for agriculture. If the water stands quiet for long, as it does in a lake, it becomes clear as glass, and is no longer suitable for irrigation, it is "dead," as the Arabs say. As the water flows slowly through these canals it deposits this precious material in the canal-beds, and especially sand and mud in great quantities. Thus it is necessary every year to clear out the canals, and the material thrown out on to the embankments continually raises them in height (Fig. 4). Obviously there must come a moment in the history of each canal when it is more expensive to clear it out than to construct a new one, and thus every canal bears within it the germ of its own destruction. The sanding up of the canal-bed is naturally more insistent in portions nearest the river, and hence it is that this canal displacement occurs so frequently in the neighbourhood of the river-course. On the way from Bagdad to Hilleh

in the neighbour-
hood of the Euph-
rates, one crosses
extraordinarily
numerous groups
of abandoned
canals, most of
which are noth-
ing else than the
older courses of
the same irriga-
tion system that
is in use to-day.

This explana-
tion must be borne
in mind when be-
wildered by the
first sight of these
ruined canals,
either in reality
or on a plan. As
one approaches
the mound Babil
from the north or
the east — the
mound, by the
way, which alone
has preserved its
ancient name to
the present day
—one encounters
the annoyance of
this ruthless dis-
turbance of the
ground; it is
hardly possible
to see the mound
till one has
climbed the em-
bankment nearest

FIG. 5.—View of the mound "Babil."

to it, but the impression is then all the more striking (Fig. 5).

The mound rises with a steep slope to the height of 22 metres above the plain. Its area forms a square of about 250 metres, and this hill, consisting of broken brick or clayey earth, is pierced by deep ravines and tunnels, while on the north and south-west remains of walls of very considerable height are still standing, with courses of mud brick held together by layers of well-preserved reed stems. They date from a later period, and may have belonged to a fort which was erected in Sassanide or Arabic times on the already ruined Babylonian building.

The astoundingly deep pits and galleries that occur in places owe their origin to the quarrying for brick that has been carried on extensively during the last decades. The buildings of ancient Babylon, with their excellent kiln bricks, served even in antiquity, perhaps in Roman times, certainly in Parthian days, as a quarry for common use. Later centuries appear to have done less to destroy the ruins, but in modern times the quarrying for bricks has assumed far more important dimensions. About twenty years ago, when the Euphrates first began to pour its life-giving waters into the Hindiyeh, a side branch somewhat farther above Babylon, near Musseyib, an attempt was made to head back the river into its old bed by building up a dam, the *Sedde*, which with us has a somewhat evil reputation. Building was carried on year after year without interference at this dam, as long as the height of the water permitted, and that with bricks from Babylon. Quite recently this outrage has been checked by the powerful influence of Halil Bey, Director-General of the Ottoman museums, and of Bedri Bey, the Turkish Commissioner on the excavations; so now there is a well-grounded hope that the ruins of the most celebrated city of the East, or perhaps of the world, shall go down to posterity without further injury. Soon after the commencement of the excavations I had interested myself in checking this spoliation, but that was possible only for the Kasr, at Babil it still went on. Even at the Kasr I had to drive these workers out of their pits, and we set the people to

work in our diggings, as the Arab is entirely indifferent
as to the method by which he earns his scanty wage.   The
only objectors were the contractors, through whom the
materials for the Sedde building were sold.   Very recently
the latter also made an attack on the tower of Borsippa,
but their barbarous attempt was promptly stopped by the
action of the Turkish Government.

The robbers carried away the walls layer after layer,
carefully leaving the adjoining earth untouched, as the
trench grew daily deeper, since a downfall would render
it inaccessible.   This enables us to make some instructive
observations in the interior even before beginning our
excavations at this place.

It was a building consisting of many courts and chambers, both small and large, a palace upon a substructure
about 18 metres in height.   The latter is so constructed
that the building walls throughout are continuous and of
the same thickness above and below, while the intermediate
spaces are filled up to the height of the palace floor with
earth and a packing of fragments of brick.   As on part of
the Kasr, the floor consists of sandstone flags on the edge
of which is inscribed, " Palace of Nebuchadnezzar, King of
Babylon, son of Nabopolassar, King of Babylon."   There
are also many portions of a limestone pavement that
consists of a thick rough under stratum, and a fine upper
stratum half a centimetre thick, and coloured a fine red or
yellow.   This pavement is similar to those of the best
Greek period, and it may be considered to be an addition
of the time of the Persian kings, or of Alexander the
Great and his successors.   All the bricks stamped with the
name of Nebuchadnezzar, of which we learn more when we
turn to the Kasr, were laid either in asphalt or in a grey
lime mortar, both of which also occur at the Kasr.

All these things considered, it is impossible to doubt
that Babil was a palace of Nebuchadnezzar's.   The
parallel passage in his great inscription very probably
refers to it (*K.B.* iii. 2, p. 31), col. 3 l. 11-29: "On the
brick wall towards the north my heart inspired me to
build a palace for the protecting of Babylon.   I built
there a palace like the palace of Babylon of brick and

bitumen. For 60 ells I built an *appa danna* towards
Sippar; I made a *nabalu*, and laid its foundation on the
bosom of the underworld, on the surface of the (ground)
water in brick and bitumen. I raised its summit and connected it with the palace, with brick and bitumen I made
it high as a mountain. Mighty cedar trunks I laid on it
for roof. Double doors of cedar wood overlaid with copper,
thresholds and hinges made of bronze did I set up in its
doorways. That building I named ' May Nebuchadnezzar
live, may he grow old as restorer of Esagila ' " (translated
by H. Winckler). Various expressions remain extremely
obscure, and their explanation awaits the excavation of
the building. Especially should we like to know what
was meant by the *appa danna*. These words in
Babylonian mean a " strong nose," which taken absolutely
literally is nonsense. In this connection, however, as
the appendage of a palace they recall so strongly the
apadana with which the Persian kings in Persepolis
denoted their palaces that one can hardly be mistaken in
thinking there must be some esoteric connection. An
apadana in Persia had the ground plan of a many-fronted
Hilani (see Fig. 77), and it would be very interesting and
of the highest importance in the history of architecture
to discover what a building of Nebuchadnezzar's in
Babylon looked like, that at any rate, bore a name so
exactly similar in sound. It is only excavation that can
give the long-delayed answer to that question.

III

GENERAL VIEW OF THE CITY

THE heights of Babil afford a fine view (Fig. 6) over the
entire city, especially towards evening when the long purple
shadows cast on the plain throw up the golden yellow outlines of the ruins in high relief. No human habitation is
in sight. The villages on the left bank of the Euphrates—

FIG. 6.—General view of Babylon, seen from the north-west.

Kweiresh, where our house is, and Djumdjumma farther
south—are so buried among the green date palms that one
can scarcely catch a glimpse of even a wall. On the other
bank are Sindjar and Ananeh also concealed in the same
way, although the latter village with the farm of Karabet
stands forward somewhat more clearly. The Euphrates is
fringed with palms which cluster more thickly near the
water. To the south above their ornamental crowns the
minaret of Hilleh gleams, and in the blue distance can be
seen a somewhat pointed hill surmounted by a jagged wall,
the ruin of E-ur-imin-an-ki, the tower of Borsippa. Due
east is the mound of Oheimir, where are the ruins of the
ancient Babylonian Kish (?), towards the north the palms
of Khan Mhauil are to be seen, and, when the weather is
favourable, Tell Ibrahim, the ancient Kutha. With these
exceptions all that is visible is the sombre dun-coloured
desert. The cultivated stretches are diminishing in extent
and are only noticeable for those few weeks in the year
when they are clothed with green.

To those accustomed to Greece and its remains it is a
constant surprise to have these mounds pointed out as
ruins. Here are no blocks of stone, no columns : even in
the excavations there is only brickwork, while before work
commenced only a few brick projections stood out on the
Kasr. Here in Babylonia mounds form the modern representatives of ancient glories, there are no columns to bear
witness to vanished magnificence.

The great mound, the Kasr or castle, forms the centre
of the city. It is the great castle of Nebuchadnezzar that
he built for a palace, completing the work of his father,
Nabopolassar. The modern name Kasr thus expresses
the purpose for which it was built. By Greek historians
it was called the Acropolis, by Romans the Arx. In area
it is three or four times as large as Babil, but it is
not so high, and when observed from that hill the greater
part is hidden by palms. This Acropolis, built on what
is called the *Irsit Babylon* (*Steinplatten* inscription, col. 7
l. 40), the piazza or town square of Babylon, is actually
the original Babylon, the *Bab Ilani*, the Gate of the
Gods. It commanded the approach to the greatest and

most renowned sanctuary of Babylonia, the temple of
Marduk called Esagila. This lies somewhat farther to
the south, buried 20 metres deep under the great hill,
the third of the three great mounds of Babylon, Amran Ibn
Ali, a name acquired from the sanctuary which is upon
it, the tomb of Amran the son of Ali. It is 25 metres
high, the highest of all the mounds, and owes this to
the fact that after all the other sites were abandoned it
was occupied for habitation right up to the Middle Ages,
under Arab rule. Close by to the north lies the rectangular
ruin of the tower of Babylon, E-temen-an-ki, on a small
plain called Sachn, that represents its sacred precincts.
Due east of the Kasr a smaller but unmistakably higher
mound rises from the plain, called from its red colour
Homera. It conceals no buildings, but from top to bottom
it consists of brick fragments. We shall return to it later.
Close by, almost due north and south, extends the low
ridge of ruins of the inner city wall that encircled the
inner portion of the city in a line not yet fully traced.
Between Homera and Amran, as well as to the south of
the latter, and between the Kasr and Babil, we see the
plain broken by a number of low mounds distributed in
groups. Here clustered the dwellings of the citizens of
Babylon, and the recollection of them has so far survived
to the present day that one of these groups south-east
of the Kasr is called by the Arabs Merkes, the city or
centre of the dwellings. It is here that the dwellings and
streets of the city of the time of the Persian kings, and
as far back as that of the earliest Babylonian kings,
have survived in the mass of ruins. Externally these
remains present the appearance of mountainous country in
miniature; heights, summits, ravines, and tablelands are
all here. At Merkes there is a sharp hill visible from a
distance, due to an excavation previous to our expedition
when the rubbish dug out was collected there. There are
also public buildings buried in the ruins. Thus between
Homera and Merkes there is a Greek temple, on Merkes
itself is a temple, and there are two in the so-called Ishin
aswad, the district south-east of Amran.

Where there are no mounds, husbandry is carried on

to some extent. In the eastern corner, in the angle of the
outer wall, the overflow of water collects in a lake during
the period of irrigation. But even in this low quarter of
the city there were once dwellings, which the course of
centuries has covered with the enveloping shroud of the
shifting and levelling sands.

IV

THE EUPHRATES AND ITS COURSE

ALTHOUGH the Euphrates lies for the greater part of the
year shrunken in its arid bed (Fig. 7), yet at the commencement of our expedition its full flood covered the
entire bed from 100 to 200 metres wide (Fig. 8). In comparison with its boisterous relative the Tigris, it appears
very sluggish, but it entirely fulfils its mission as an alluvial
river. At each bend it removes the superfluous matter from
one bank to deposit it as a valuable asset on the other bank
lower down, and by this assiduous and steady work it
gradually alters its course. As far back as the time of
Nebuchadnezzar its general direction was from north to
south, but not precisely as to-day. Its course took it close
by Babil, which commanded its entrance into the city, and
it certainly washed the west front of the Kasr exactly where
the village of Kweiresh stands to-day. From here we
can trace its ancient course in the long, shallow depression
that runs close under Amran. Here we have found the
stone bridge mentioned by Greek authors as spanning the
river. The Kasr lay then, as now, on the left bank of
the Euphrates, but there was a period under the Persian
and Greek kings when it lay on the right bank, and its
north, east, and south sides were more or less washed by
those waters.

It is easy to understand that the continuous shifting
of the river must have altered both its bed and its level.
To-day, when very little water comes into the river, ground
water is reached 1 or 2 metres lower than 10 years ago,

Fig. 7.—The Euphrates in 1911.

Fig. 8.—The Euphrates, seen looking north from the Expedition House in 1907.

C

when it was at about the same level as in the time of
Nebuchadnezzar, but it must have been considerably lower
under the first kings of Babylon, when the houses in
Merkes were built, as these now stand below water-level.

These variations are comparatively trifling.   There are
more important ones arising from other causes.   As the
river-bed rises, the banks also rise.   This is brought about
by the more luxuriant vegetation and the activity of the
husbandmen in the neighbourhood of the banks, as well
as by an occasional overflow, when naturally the largest
share of sediment is deposited near the river.   Thus the
river flows over what may be termed an artificially raised
bed between two raised banks; the surface of the water
is actually higher than the plain beyond the banks, a
difference which the unaided eye can scarcely detect as
it deals with a rise of only a few metres over an extent of
several hundred.   At a specially high flood, however, or
owing to carelessness in dealing with the canals, the river
bursts its banks, rushes out over the lower plain, and, un-
hindered by any obstacles, makes its way lower down into
its ancient bed.   This happened in modern times in
Musseyib, when the Euphrates left its ancient bed, from
Musseyib to Samaua, and transferred itself to the western
Hindiyeh branch.   It appears to have flowed appreciably
more to the west in the neighbourhood of Divaniyeh in
ancient times.   According to a plan of the city found on
the spot, Nippur seems to have lain on the Euphrates.
Fara also, the ancient Shuruppak, where the Babylonian
Noah built his ark, and which we have excavated, is represented on the border of the river, though it now lies 12 hours
from Divaniyeh.   These great shiftings of the river must
have altered the geographical and topographical aspect of
the country to an extraordinary degree in the course of
hundreds and thousands of years.   When we attempt to discover the reason for selecting a particular site for an ancient
town we are confronted by the difficulty of not knowing
where the ancient canals lay.   The ruined canals of to-day
go back, perhaps without exception, to the Middle Ages of
Arab rule.   The great " Habl Ibrahim " is on the whole
no older than this.   Whether an ancient canal of similar

extent ran in its immediate neighbourhood we do not know ; there are no remains of one.   Certain ancient water-courses, as those at Nippur or Farah, can no longer be recognised on the surface.   The river-bank at Fara was first brought to light by excavation.

The walk from Babil to Kasr along the river - bank takes one entirely among characteristic Babylonian scenery. Gardens, palms, and fields are sometimes all grouped together, forming a scene of rich luxuriance.   It is, how-ever, no more than a strip about 600 metres wide.   For the first year after their planting the palms require regular watering, after that they grow of themselves and the roots of a fully grown tree are supposed to reach ground water. Gardens and fields must be watered, since we are in the almost rainless subtropical zone, and have scarcely 7 centi-metres of downfall in the whole year.   The canals are not directly available for the irrigation of the river-banks as the level of the water rarely rises to their height.   Here artificial elevators, the *djird*, are required.   A huge leather bag is raised to the top of a short incline of about 30 grades by an ox, where its funnel end, closed during the ascent by a cord at the top, automatically empties itself into the irrigating channel.   The cord on which the leather bag is suspended works over a cylinder supported on two projecting palm trees laid horizontally.   Its rotation produces a resounding noise which penetrates the solemn stillness of the palm grove.   Each djird possesses a characteristic melody of its own, to which the Arab attendant adapts his own song.   These djirds are always under the shade of a mulberry tree, which is often of gigantic size (Fig. 9).   The *na'ura*, the water-wheel so common on the upper Euphrates, is never used here as the stream is not sufficiently powerful.   The *dolab*, a chain pump driven by a whim, is occasionally used, and the motor pump has been recently introduced by certain up-to-date farmers.

It is clear that this continual watering, together with the shifting of the river and the flooding of the land, must raise the level of the ground, but it is difficult to estimate to what extent.   Our only opportunity of observing it is among ruins, and there the process of elevation is, of course, far more rapid owing to the continual demolition of the buildings. In historical times, which we may here reckon

FIG. 9.—A djird, opposite Kweiresh.

as beginning with the invention of writing somewhere in the fourth millennium B.C., the measurable rise of the land has certainly been only slight. With regard to the totally unknown period of the prehistoric culture, it may safely be affirmed that the entire level of the land probably rose many metres.

The entire method of irrigation, particularly that of the

djird, bears a distinctly ancient character, it cannot have changed much since the time of Nebuchadnezzar ; neither

FIG. 10.—Arab at work on a canal, in the neighbourhood of Babylon.

can the fashion in which the people divide their land by low embankments into rectangles and then lay them under water by alternately piercing and closing up the trenches

FIG. 11.—The hooked plough in Babylon.

(Fig. 10) ; the primitive hooked plough (Fig. 11) and the trampling in of corn by animals must be equally ancient. All these seem to carry one back many thousands of years.

At the bend of the Euphrates, between Babil and Kasr, lie the ruins of the former village of Kweiresh, whose population migrated elsewhere a hundred years ago. The walls of mud brick still overtop the heaps of debris.

FIG. 12.—Doorway of the Expedition House in Kweiresh.

The modern village of Kweiresh lies close to the Kasr, to which we must now turn our attention. The most northerly house of Kweiresh is the headquarters of our expedition (Fig. 12), called by the Arabs " Kasr abiad."

V

THE KASR. THE ASCENT AND PROCESSION STREET

THE Kasr presents so many different aspects that it is not easy to give a clear representation of it (Fig. 13).

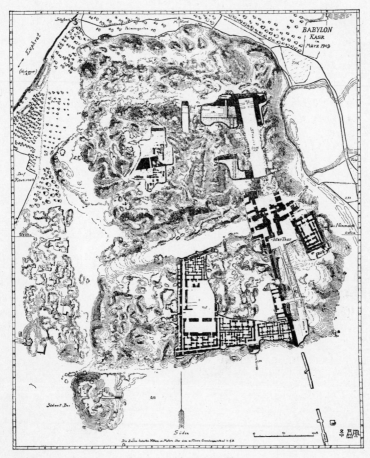

FIG. 13.—Plan of the Kasr.

We will first traverse the whole of it and try to give some account of what is to be seen there, before classing together the buildings of different periods. Almost all that is visible at a first glance is of the time of Nebuchadnezzar, who throughout his reign of 43 years must have been unremitting in his work of building and extending his castle.

The ascent was from the north in the north-east corner. All uncertainty on this point has been removed by our recent excavations. Here we had to uncover walls of great extent and deeply buried, and discover their connection with each other. To do this, almost the whole of our men were set to work on the site. We regularly employ from 200 to 250 men, divided into gangs. The leader breaks up the ground with a pickaxe, and 16 men carry away the earth in baskets which are filled by three men with broad axes. This is the usual method, which is necessarily varied according to circumstances. The leader receives 5 piastres daily, the basket-fillers 4, and the carriers 3, as wages. At the diggings we adopt various methods according to the nature of the site and the object aimed at.

Here the workmen descend abreast in a broad line down a slanting incline to the prescribed verge. Having reached it, they draw back to a distance of 5 metres and recommence work. In this way sloping layers of earth are successively peeled off and the walls gradually emerge. By means of a field railway the earth is removed some distance to a site which provisionally we decide to be unimportant. When one of these slopes reaches the lowest level, which is generally the water-level, the workmen face in the opposite direction and remove the remainder in a similar fashion, only leaving a portion of the slope on the edge of each excavation available for transport.

At this point the ends of two parallel walls came to light running south, which we shall describe later with the fortification walls. Between them is a broad street or roadway, which leads direct to the Ishtar Gate (made by Nebuchadnezzar as a processional road for the God Marduk, to whose temple of Esagila it eventually leads. It still possesses the brick pavement covered with asphalt which formed a substratum for the immense flagged pavement. The central part was laid with mighty flags of limestone measuring 1.05 metres each way, and the sides with slabs of red breccia veined with white, 66 centimetres square. The bevelled edges of the joints were filled in with asphalt. On the edges of each slab (Fig. 14), which, of course, were not visible, was an inscription, " Nebuchadnezzar, King of Babylon, son of Nabopolassar, King of Babylon, am I. The Babel Street I paved with blocks of shadu stone for the procession of the great Lord Marduk. Marduk, Lord, grant eternal life.") On the flags of breccia the word *Turminabanda*, breccia, has been substituted for *Shadu*, mountain. The fine hard limestone may have been brought from the neighbourhood of Hit or

FIG. 14.—Paving block of the Procession Street.

Anah, where a similar stone is quarried, and transport by river would present little difficulty; of the provenance of the turminabanda I have not been able to acquire any knowledge. The great white paving-stones give the impression of being intended for wheeled traffic, but those that are still *in situ* do not show the slightest traces of being used for any such purpose, they are merely polished and slippery with use.

The Kasr roadway lies high, 12.5 metres above zero,[1] and slopes gently upwards from the north to the Ishtar Gateway. A later restoration, possibly of the Persian (?) period in brick, rendered it horizontal. Before the time of Nebuchadnezzar it was considerably lower, but as he placed the entire palace on a level higher than that of its predecessor, he was forced also to raise the roadway. In consequence of this we can to-day enjoy the glorious

[1] See p. 167.

view over the whole city as far as the outer walls. It is clearly of this work of his that Nebuchadnezzar speaks in his great *Steinplatten* inscription (col. 5): " From Dul-azag, the place of the decider of fates, the Chamber of Fate, as far as Aibur-shabu, the road of Babylon, opposite the gateway of Beltis, he (Nabopolassar) had adorned the way of the procession of the great lord Marduk with turminabanda stones. Aibur-shabu, the roadway of Babylon, I filled up with a high filling for the procession of the great lord Marduk, and with turminabanda stone and with shadu stone I made Aibur-shabu, from the Illu Gate to the Ishtar-sakipat-tebisha, fit for the procession of his godhead. I connected it together with the portions that my father had built and made the road glorious " (trans. by H. Winckler). Ishtar-sakipat-tebisha is the Ishtar Gate, and from this we find that the inscription does not refer to the whole of the Kasr Street, but only to part of it, either that which adjoined the Ishtar Gate on the north or on the south.

The fine view now obtainable from the street of Kasr was certainly not visible in antiquity, for the roadway was bordered on both sides with high defensive walls. They were 7 metres thick and formed the junction between the northern advanced outworks and the earlier defences, of which the Ishtar Gateway is part. They guarded the approach to the gate. Manned by the defenders, the road was a real pathway of death to the foe who should attempt it. The impression of peril and horror was heightened for the enemy, and also for peaceful travellers, by the impressive decoration of long rows of lions advancing one behind the other with which the walls were adorned in low relief and with brilliant enamels.

The discovery of these enamelled bricks formed one of the motives for choosing Babylon as a site for excavation. As early as June 1887 I came across brightly coloured fragments lying on the ground on the east side of the Kasr. In December 1897 I collected some of these and brought them to Berlin, where the then Director of the Royal Museums, Richard Schöne, recognised their signifi-cance. The digging commenced on March 26, 1899, with

FIG. 15. — Beginning of the excavations on March 26, 1899, with the pavement of the Procession Street on the east side of the Kasr.

a transverse cut through the east front of the Kasr
(Fig. 15). The finely coloured fragments made their
appearance in great numbers, soon followed by the discovery of the eastern of the two parallel walls, the pavement of the processional roadway, and the western wall,
which supplied us with the necessary orientation for further
excavations.

The tiles represented lions advancing to right or to
left (Fig. 16) according to whether they were on the
eastern or the western wall. Some of them were white
with yellow manes, and others yellow with red manes, of
which the red has now changed to green (see p. 106)
owing to decomposition. The ground is either light or
dark blue, the faces, whether seen from the left or the
right, are all alike, as they have been cast in a mould.
None have been found *in situ*. The walls were plundered
for brick, but they were not so completely destroyed as to
prevent our observing that they were provided with towers
that projected slightly and were obviously placed at
distances apart equal to their breadth. Black and
white lines in flat enamel on the edges of the towers
divided the face of the two walls into panels, defining
the divisions made by the towers in the two long friezes
of 180 metres, the plinth was decorated with rows
of broad-leaved rosettes. As the lions are about
2 metres long, it is possible that each division contained two lions. That would give 60 lions at each side,
a total of 120 that agrees well with the number of
fragments found.

We must now consider the reliefs and their colouring.
For the reliefs a working model must first have been
obtained of which the several parts could be used for
making the mould. The most natural method would be
to build a temporary wall the size of one of these lions
with bricks of a plastic clay, and with a strong mortar
compounded with sand, on which the relief could be
modelled. The jointing was carefully considered, for it is
so arranged as not to cut through the figures too obviously,
and each brick bears a considerable share of the relief.
The joints serve an actual purpose in regulating the pro-

FIG. 16.—THE LION OF THE PROCESSION STREET.

portions, and take the place of the squaring lines with which Egyptian artists prepared their work.

With the help of these models, moulds could be made for each separate brick. They were probably of burnt pottery similar to the moulds made for the abundant terra-cottas of Babylonia. The mould would form one side of the frame in which the brick was struck, and, according to the regular method of bonding, a course of whole bricks (33 × 33 centimetres) would be followed by a course of half bricks (33 × 16½). Thus the ground of the reliefs and the wall surface were actually identical, and there is not even a projecting base on which the paws of the great beasts might appear to rest, as would be the case with stone reliefs. This is art in clay, a specialised art, distinguished from all other kinds of relief. The edges of the figures do not project more or less squarely as they do in Assyrian alabaster reliefs (Fig. 17 A), but in an obtuse angle (Fig. 17 B). Also there are no even upper surfaces as there are on Assyrian stone carvings. Both peculiarities would considerably facilitate the withdrawal of the tile from the mould.

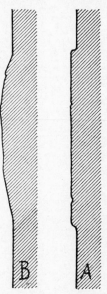

FIG. 17.—Cross-section of a lion relief (B) and of an Assyrian relief (A).

The same conception of art influenced the marvellous, highly developed, glyptic art of Babylonia. The style of the gem reliefs during the time of Hammurabi was also transferred to stone, while the older Babylonian stone reliefs distinctly show their direct derivation from the previous flat bas-reliefs, to which Assyrian art of the later period still adhered. Previous to our excavations no example of the plastic art of the time of Nebuchadnezzar was known.

The brick when moulded and before it was enamelled was burnt like any ordinary brick; the contours were then drawn on it with black lines of a readily fusible vitreous composition, leaving clearly marked fields. These were filled with liquid coloured enamels, the whole dried and then fused, this time apparently in a gentler fire. As the black lines had the same fusing-point as the coloured portions they often mixed with the colours themselves, thus giving the work that marvellous and harmonious brilliancy and life which we admire to-day. With the Persian enamels which we shall meet with in connection with the Persian buildings these black lines have a higher melting-point and therefore remain distinct and project above the coloured enamels after the firing.

The bricks had then to be arranged according to the design. In order to facilitate this and to ensure an accurate distribution of them on the building site, the bricks were marked on the upper side in rough glaze with a series of simple signs and numerals. The sign on the side of a brick and on that which was to be placed next it are identical. We shall learn more of the system in the Southern Citadel, where it was employed in the enamelled decorations of the great court.

A complete study of these details could not be made in Babylon as we were cramped for space and could not spread out the pieces. The chemical preservation of them was carried out in Berlin with great care under the able direction of Professor Rathgen. The antiquities from the ruined sites, more especially the pottery, were completely permeated with salts, saltpetre, and the like. These materials, owing to long exposure to air, had formed hard crystals on the surface, which had to be removed by long-continued soaking. Here in Babylon also we numbered each piece so that we could be certain at what part of the Processional Street each fragment had been found. The transverse cut in the wall u 13 of the plan of Kasr (Fig. 13) gives an excellent insight into the method of construction. Over every course of brick is a thin layer of asphalt, and above this an equally thin layer of mud and then another course of bricks. The joints of the course, which are from 1 to $1\frac{1}{2}$ centimetres thick, are also formed of asphalt and mud. In every fifth course a matting made of reeds, the stalks of which have been split and rendered flexible by beating, is substituted for the mud. The matting itself has rotted, but the impression left on the asphalt is still perfectly fresh and recognisable. In appearance it corresponds exactly with the ordinary matting in use in the neighbourhood to-day.

A determined and very remarkable effort was obviously made to separate the courses, to prevent their adhering to each other, overlaid as they were with asphalt. This separation occurs in other parts of the city effected by reed straw instead of mud. Only in some few detached instances were the bricks laid immediately on the bitumen, where they fitted together as firmly as a rock, as in the wall 17 metres thick which in *k* 13 runs through the great Principal Citadel, in the southern strongest part of the Ishtar Gateway, and also in the postament of the cella in the temple of Borsippa. We may add that asphalt and mud, or asphalt and reed straw are regularly used for joints throughout the period of the Babylonian kings. Only in his latest buildings, the Kasr, the Principal Citadel, and Babil, did Nebuchadnezzar change to lime mortar, while Nabonidus for his Euphrates wall turned once more to asphalt. The later builders, Persians, Greeks, and Parthians, employed mud for mortar.

The asphalt mortar in the great defensive walls of Babylon and the inserted mats are mentioned by Herodotus (i. 179): he records that after every 30 courses of bricks a plaited mat was inserted. So large a number has not yet been observed by us. The lowest number is 5, the highest 13. In the Babylonian inscriptions on buildings, especially on those of Nebuchadnezzar, asphalt is very often mentioned in connection with burnt brick, but never mud, lime, or reeds.

VI

THE ISHTAR GATE

THE magnificent approach by way of the Procession Street corresponds entirely with the importance, the size, and the splendour of the Ishtar Gate. With its walls which still stand 12 metres high, covered with brick reliefs, it is the largest and most striking ruin of Babylon and—with the exception of the tower of Borsippa which, though now shapeless, is higher—of all Mesopotamia (see ground-plan on Fig. 46).

It was a double gateway. Two doorways close together,

FIG. 18.—Eastern end of the mud-brick wing, at the Ishtar Gate, from the north.

one behind the other, formed into one block by short connecting walls, lead through the walls of crude brick (Fig. 18), which are equally closely placed. At a later period the latter formed a transept which stood out square across the acropolis and afforded special protection to the inner part, the Southern Citadel (cf. the restored view, Fig. 43). Apparently these walls were originally connected directly with the inner town wall still extant at Homera, for inscriptions found there prove conclusively that to it belonged the name Nimitti-Bel, while the Ishtar Gate is itself frequently spoken of in other inscriptions as belonging to

FIG. 19.—General view of the Ishtar Gate from the north.

D

both Imgur-Bel and Nimitti-Bel. Imgur-Bel and Nimitti-
Bel are the two oft-mentioned celebrated fortress walls
of Babylon, of which we shall presently speak (p. 150
et seq.).

Of each of the two gateways two widely projecting
towers close to the entrance are still standing (Fig. 19),
and behind them a space closed by a second door.
This space, which is generally called the gateway court,
although it was probably roofed in, shows clear signs that
its primary object was to protect the leaves of the double

door which opened back into
it from the weather, and also
that it strengthened the pos-
sibilities of the defences. In
the case of smaller gates
which do not possess these
interior chambers, the leaves
of the doors were inserted
in the thickness of the wall,
which afforded a protection ;
an embrasure which is absent
in the gateways. On the

FIG. 20.—Gold plaque from grave in the
Nabopolassar Palace (scale 3 : 1).

northern gate the gateway chamber lies transversely, on the
southern it extends along the central axis. Here also it is
enclosed with walls of such colossal thickness that it may
be supposed to have supported a central tower of great
height, but nothing remains in proof of this. This
assumption is delineated in Fig. 21, while in Fig. 43 it
is taken for granted that the gateway chamber was commanded by the towers. Here, as in all the other buildings,
we have little to guide us as to the superstructure. Among
the ornaments in a grave in the Southern Citadel was a
rectangular gold plate (Fig. 20) which on the face represents
a great gateway. On it, near the arched door, we see the
two towers overtopping the walls, while on their projecting
upper part triangular battlements and small circular loop-
holes can be seen. Of the latter we found thick wedge-
shaped stones under the blue enamelled bricks, and also
part of the stepped battlements in blue enamel which, on
the whole, may have had an appearance of triangles.

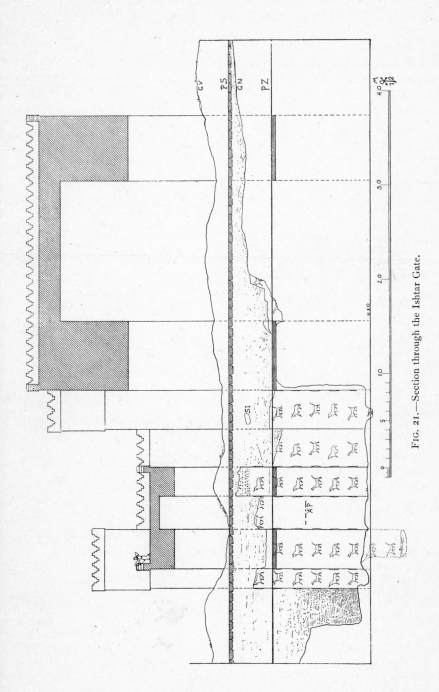

FIG. 21.—Section through the Ishtar Gate.

The gateway itself was not placed immediately in the mud wall, but between four wing-like additions of burnt brick, in each of which was a doorway. Thus the Ishtar Gate had three entrances, the central one with fourfold doors, and one to right and left, each with double doors. The foundations of the main building are so deep that, owing to the present high water-level, we could not get to the foot of them (Fig. 21). The gateway wings are not carried down so far, and the walls that stretch northward still less. It is conceivable that those parts of the wall where the foundations are specially deep do not sink so much in the course of time as those of shallower foundations, and settlement is unavoidable even with these, standing as they do upon earth and mud. Thus where the foundations are dissimilar there must be cleavages in the walls, which would seriously endanger the stability of the building. The Babylonians foresaw this and guarded against it. They devised the expansion joint, which we also make use of under similar circumstances. By this means walls that adjoin each other but which are on foundations of different depths are not built in one piece. A narrow vertical space is left from top to bottom of the wall, leaving the two parts standing independent of each other. In order to prevent any possibility of their leaning either backwards or forwards, in Babylon a vertical fillet was frequently built on to the less deeply

FIG. 22.—Grooved expansion joints at the Ishtar Gate.

FIG. 23.—View of the Ishtar Gate from the west.

rooted wall, which slid in a groove in the main wall
(Fig. 22). The two blocks run in a guide, as an engineer
would call it. In the case of small isolated foundations,
the actual foundation of burnt brick rests in a substructure of crude brick shaped like a well, filled up with earth,
in which it can shift about at the base without leaning
over, which gives it play like the joints of a telescope.
In this way the small postament near the eastern tower
of our gate is constructed, and also the round one which
stands to the westward of it on the open space in front of
the gate (Fig. 23). On these postaments and on similar
ones in the northern gateway court and in the intermediate court must " the mighty bronze colossi of bulls
and the potent serpent figures" have stood which Nebuchadnezzar placed in the entries of the Ishtar Gate
(*Steinplatten* inscription, col. 6).

Where the southern door adjoined its western buttress
there were some remarkable and rather considerable.
ancient cavities in the wall, for which I cannot discover
any certain explanation. They were filled with earth, and
had not been meddled with in modern times. Later than
these, but also of ancient times, there is a well hewn out in
the northern wing. A narrow staircase led down to it, and
could only be reached by a passage 50 centimetres wide
cut through the wall, which opened on to the space in
front of the gate. The exit was hidden away in a corner,
and almost entirely concealed.

VII

THE WALL DECORATIONS OF BULLS
AND DRAGONS

THE decoration of the walls of the Ishtar Gate consisted
of alternated figures of bulls and dragons (*sirrush*). They
are placed in horizontal rows on the parts of the walls
that are open to observation by those entering or passing
(Fig. 24), and also on the front of both the northern

FIG. 24.—The two eastern towers of the Ishtar Gate.

wings, but not where they would be wholly or partially invisible to the casual observer. The rows are repeated one above another; dragons and bulls are never mixed in the same horizontal row, but a line of bulls is followed by one of sirrush. Each single representation of an animal occupies a height of 13 brick courses, and between them are 11 plain courses, so that the distance from the foot of one to the foot of the next is 24 courses. These 24 courses

FIG. 25.—Enamelled reliefs at the Ishtar Gate, beginning of the excavation, April 1, 1902.

together measure almost exactly 2 metres, or 4 Babylonian ells, in height. As these bricks change their standard when in use as binders or stretchers at the corners, the reliefs on one side of a corner are invariably either one course higher or lower than on the wall on the adjoining side.

From top to bottom of the wall there are 9 rows of these animals visible in relief. The two lowest rows are frequently under the water-level, which has risen so considerably in recent years. In 1910, however, it was possible

to penetrate as low as some of these reliefs.   Above there
was a row of bulls in flat enamels, a good portion of which
was found *in situ* on the south-east pier of the north gate
(Fig. 25).   Above this must have been at least one row of
sirrush and one of bulls in flat enamels, and a row of
sirrush in enamel reliefs; the whole ruin was bestrewn
with an extraordinary number of fragments from these
upper rows.   Those fragments have recently been brought
to Europe, and it now remains to determine from them the
actual numbers of the figures, so far as they can be counted.
When this is done, we shall be able to decide whether or
not there were more of these rows.   The succession of the
rows in the meantime may be schematized thus :—

Row 13. Sirrush in enamelled relief.
  „   12. Bulls in enamelled relief.
  „   11. Sirrush in flat enamel.
           Upper level of pavement of shadu and turmina-
             banda stone.
  „   10. Bulls in flat enamel, the top row of those found
             still *in situ*.
  „   9. Bulls in brick relief, carefully worked.
           Older road pavement of burnt brick.
  „   8. Sirrush in brick relief.
  „   7. Bulls in brick relief.
           Traces of an older pavement (?).
  „   6. Sirrush in brick relief.
  „   5. Bulls in brick relief.
  „   4. Sirrush in brick relief.
  „   3. Bulls in brick relief.
  „   2. Sirrush in brick relief, in 1910 only above water-
             level.
  „   1. Bulls in brick relief, in 1910 only above water-
             level.

Each of the 8 lower rows contained at least 40 animals,
and the upper 5 rows 51 animals.   For in the latter there
were certainly 5 more on the south-eastern angle of the
northern gateway court and 6 more on the front of the
northern wings.   This gives a minimum number of 575
animals.   After the excavations 152 pieces were to be seen

still in position, and about as many more may yet be discovered in the part not yet uncovered.

The whole of this collection of creatures was certainly at no period visible at the same time and from the same point of view. The level on which the Ishtar Gate stood was repeatedly raised by artificial means. The traces of the two last heightenings can be seen between the 10th and 11th and the 8th and 9th rows. The traces of a pavement between the 6th and 7th rows are not clear. It is possible that when the gate was first built the roadway lay at the same level as the surrounding plain, but there is no proof of this. It may also be surmised that, for some time at least, the lower part of the gate was used as such, but in any case with the successive heightenings of the road the lower part of the building gradually disappeared below the surface. The filling-up shows the existence of great foresight, and of most scrupulous care expended on the work. The reliefs were carefully smeared over with mud, and those of the 8th row were actually covered with a fine clean white stucco. On the irregular surface of this covering the marks of the smearing hands are clearly visible. The white plaster so catches the eye that at first I imagined it to be the remains of a coating intended to be painted and to ensure a more perfect moulding of the form and outline of the animal; the obvious roughness of the work, however, precluded any such conclusion.

Below the 8th row, that is below the older roadway, an unusual neglect of the wall surface appears. The bricks are often reversed and laid irregularly backwards or forwards, and thus in places the reliefs are not fitted together (Figs. 26, 27). The asphalt often protrudes from the joints and has run in thick black streaks over ground and figures alike. None of these defects occur in the 9th course. The field of the reliefs, on the contrary, is carefully smoothed to a fine surface with some polishing instrument, and the animal figures are worked over with a rasp. This seems to point to the conclusion that the lower rows were not intended to stand out free and meet the eye, at any rate not for any considerable length of time; and this also shows that when the gate was built, it was intended

Fig. 26.—THE BULL OF THE ISHTAR GATE.

FIG. 27.—A bull, not enamelled.

from the first that the Procession Street and the level of the
old pavement should be raised. Even in the lowest courses
we find the 3-lined stamp that is characteristic of the latter
half of Nebuchadnezzar's reign. No traces have been found
of an earlier building, though Nebuchadnezzar speaks of one.

In the great *Steinplatten* inscription, col. 5 and 6,
the king says : " . . . Ištar-sâkipat-têbiša of Imgur-Bel

FIG. 28.—Inscription from the Ishtar Gate.

and Nimitti-Bel—both entrances of the town gates had
become too low owing to the filling up of the street (sulû)
of Babil. I dug out that town gate, I grounded its
foundations facing the water strong with bitumen and
baked bricks, and caused it to be finely set forth with baked
bricks of blue enamel, on which wild oxen and dragons
(sir-ruš) were pictured. I caused mighty cedars to be laid
lengthways for its ceiling. Door leaves of cedar covered
with copper, thresholds and hinges of bronze I fitted into
its gates. Lusty (?) wild oxen of bronze and raging (?)
dragons I placed at the thresholds. The same town gateways I caused to be made glorious for the amazement of
all peoples " (trans. by Delitzsch).

Fig. 29.—ENAMELLED WALL LENGTH OF THE ISHTAR GATE.

Between the two doorways, at the level of the topmost pavement, a great block of limestone was found bearing the consecration inscription of the Ishtar Gate (Fig. 28) which, with another lying by it, must have belonged either to the jambs or the soffit of the door. The inscription runs thus : "(Nebuchadnezzar, King of Babylon, son of) Nabopolassar

Fig. 30.—The enamelled piece of wall.

(King of Babylon am I). The gate of Nana (Ishtar . . . I built) with (blue) enamelled bricks . . . for Marduk my lord. Lusty bulls of bronze and mighty figures of serpents I placed at their thresholds, with slabs (?) of limestone (and . . .) of stone I . . . the enclosure of the bulls (. . . ?) Marduk, exalted lord . . . eternal life . . . give as a gift" (trans. by Messerschmidt).

The expression "uknû," which here and in other inscriptions is used for enamelled brick, properly denotes

lapis lazuli. It corresponds in fact, and possibly in derivation, with the Greek "kyanos." The technique of the
enamel, the reference marks of the bricks, and the varied
colourings are precisely the same as we have already
observed with the lions (Figs. 29, 30).

The lion, the animal of Ishtar, was so favourite a subject
at all times in Babylonian art that its rich and lavish
employment at the main gate of Babylon, the Ishtar Gate,
is by no means abnormal. With the bull, and still more
with the sirrush, the case is different. The bull is the
sacred animal of Ramman, the weather god. A pair of
walking bulls often form the base on which his statue
stands, or his emblem the lightning is frequently placed
on the back of a recumbent bull. Similar representations
point to the sirrush as the sacred animal both of Marduk
and of Nabû. In the Babylonian pantheon of Nebuchadnezzar's time, Marduk occupied a very prominent position.
To him belonged Esagila, the principal temple of Babylon,
and to him Nebuchadnezzar consecrated the Procession
Street and the Ishtar Gate itself. His animal, the sirrush,
frequently appears on carvings of this period, such as the
seals and boundary stones. This "dragon of Babylon"
was the far-famed animal of Babylon, and fits in admirably
with the well-known story in the Apocrypha of Bel and the
Dragon. One may easily surmise that the priests of
Esagila kept some reptile, probably an arval, which is found
in this neighbourhood, and exhibited it in the semi-darkness
of a temple chamber as a living sirrush. In this case there
would be small cause for wonder that the creature did not
survive the concoction of hair and bitumen administered to
it by Daniel.

The artistic conception of the sirrush (Figs. 31 and 32)
differs very considerably from that of the other fabulous
creatures in which Babylonian art is so exceedingly rich.
Although not free from impossibilities, it is far less
fantastic and unnatural than the winged bulls with human
heads, or the bearded men with birds' bodies and scorpions'
tails, and similar absurdities.

As indicated by the Babylonian name it is a "walking
serpent." A striking feature is the scaly coat and the

Fig. 31.—THE SIRRUSH OF THE ISHTAR GATE.

FIG. 32.—A sirrush, not enamelled.

great tail of a serpent's body. The head with the forked tongue is purely that of a serpent, and is in fact that of the horned viper, so common in Arabia, which bears the two erect horns, of which, as in the case of the bulls, only one is visible in the purely profile attitude. Behind lie two spiral combs similar to those so generously bestowed on the heads of the frequently represented Chinese dragon. The tail ends in a small curved sting. The legs are those of some high-stepping feline animal, probably a cheetah. The hinder feet are those of a strong rap-torial bird (Fig. 33) with powerful claws and great horny scales. But the tarsal joint is not that of a bird but of a quadruped, and the metatarsals are not anchylosed, or only very slightly at the distal end. It is remarkable that, in spite of the scales, the animal possesses hair. Three corkscrew ringlets fall over the head near the ears, and on the neck, where a lizard's comb would be, is a long row of curls.

FIG. 33.—Leg of a sirrush and of a raptorial bird.

This conjunction of scales and hair, as well as the marked difference between the front and hinder extremities, is very characteristic of the prehistoric dinosaur. Also the small size of the head in comparison with the rest of the body, the carriage and disproportionate length of the neck, all correspond with the distinctive features of this extinct lizard. The sirrush is a proof of an unmistakable self-creative genius in this ancient art and far exceeds all other fantastic creatures in the uniformity of its physiological conceptions. If only the forelegs were not so emphatically and characteristically feline, such an animal might actually have existed. The hind feet of a lizard are often very similar to those of birds.

VIII

THE PROCESSION STREET SOUTH OF THE ISHTAR GATE

THE street pavement extended through the Ishtar Gate, and in the southern gateway court the older pavement is still in place. Here there are three layers of bricks set in asphalt, which curve upward near the walls, forming a shallow trough (visible in Fig. 19). Its purpose must have been to prevent the collected water soaking into the joints of the walls. Similar curves in other places are the result of the unequal settling of the lighter material of the filling below the pavement and of the unyielding walls of baked brick, while a curve in the opposite sense can often be remarked on the flooring of buildings of crude brick, because the closely compressed mud wall settled with greater force than the slightly compressed filling under the pavement.

On leaving the Ishtar Gate we cross the substructure of the threshold, which rested on many layers of brick and must itself have been of stone. On the south of the gate some later insignificant buildings, perhaps Parthian, have clustered round it. These leave the entrance free, and Nebuchadnezzar's great paving-blocks of the upper roadway, over which Nebuchadnezzar, Daniel, and Darius must frequently have passed, are still in position. Farther on only the lower pavement remains. It extends parallel with the east front of the Southern Citadel as far as the end of the mound, where it surrounds an altar (?) of mud brick.

A branch of the street leads to the principal entrance

E

of the Southern Citadel. A great number of limestone and turminabanda paving-stones found in the southern portion originally formed part of the destroyed upper pavement. It appears that during the Greek or Parthian periods balls for projectiles were made out of this lime-stone, as many have been found here. They divide into groups of various weights (Fig. 34). Some measure 27.5 centimetres in diameter, and weigh 20.20-20.25 kilos : others 19 centimetres, and 7-7.75 kilos ; and others again 16 centimetres, and 4-4.5 kilos.

South of the Citadel the street crosses a watercourse, which apparently varied at different periods both in width

FIG. 34.—Limestone projectiles.

and in name. In the time of Nebuchadnezzar it was perhaps the canal " Libil-higalla," while in Persian and Greek times it was the Euphrates itself that flowed here. We dug a ditch here that extended from the mound to the recommencement of the street, and which clearly showed the stratum to have been formed by the deposit of water. The strata contain no ruins with the exception of a canal, which in places is barely 3 metres broad. This canal is constructed in later fashion with the ancient bricks of Nebuchadnezzar, the best outside, the fragments inside, and all laid in mud. To the east it soon comes to an end and disappears in the banked-up watercourse. To the west it first widens out into a basin of three times its breadth, where narrow steps lead down the embankments to the level of the water (Fig. 35), and then once more narrows to its ordinary width. Farther to the west we know nothing of it. At the narrow portions, at about the height of the ancient water-level, courses of squared limestone of considerable size were laid. In the western part the northern bank contained a square opening many brick courses deep. The whole conveys the impression of a kind of sluice, which perhaps served to connect a watercourse in the east, of high water-level, with another in the west of lower level. This construction may date from the time of Neriglissar, when throwing a bridge across the canal to carry the Procession Street presented no difficulty. In earlier times the street appears to have been carried on a dam with walled embankments, which latter still exist below the walls of the canal.

FIG. 35.—Canal to the south of the Kasr.

The eastern canal, Libil-ḫigalla, was restored by Nebuchadnezzar, according to *K.B.* iii. 2, p. 61 : "Libil-ḫigalla, the eastern canal of Babylon, which a long time previously had been choked (?) with downfallen earth (?), and filled with rubbish, I sought out its place, and I laid its bed with baked bricks and bitumen from the banks of the Euphrates up to Ai-ibur-šabû. At Ai-ibur-šabû, the street of Babylon, I added a canal bridge and made the way broad for the procession of the great lord Marduk " (trans. by Winckler and Delitzsch). Neriglissar also says of himself (*K.B.* i. 1, p. 75): "The eastern arm, which an earlier king (indeed) dug, but had not constructed its bed, (this) arm I dug (again) and constructed its bed with bricks and kiln bricks; beneficent, inexhaustible water I led to the land" (trans. by Winckler).

To the north of the Citadel there is a similar canal constructed after the same fashion, of which the vaulting still exists. My opinion is that this canal conveyed to the east the water of the Euphrates, which was probably still called "Arachtu" there, and that possibly it flowed round the Kasr in somewhat irregular fashion, even in the Neo-Babylonian period. This easterly body of water would then return to the Euphrates by means of the canal just described. At the south-west corner of the Kasr buildings, where they joined the wall of Nabonidus, the openings through which the water escaped are still preserved in this wall.

To the south of our water-channel the street appears once more, but at a much lower level. It is paved with brick, plastered with asphalt, and is of the same breadth as the southern Kasr Street. It passes between the houses of Merkes and the sacred peribolos of Etemenanki, keeping close to the latter, but at a sufficient distance from the secular dwellings of the Babylonians. The first part of the street, as far as the great gate of Etemenanki, had a flooring of kiln bricks overlaid with paving-stones of turminabanda, which still lie undisturbed on the branch leading to the gate (Fig. 36). They bear the same dedicatory inscription as that on the Kasr: some of them, however, have in addition on the underside the name of Sennacherib, the bloodthirsty Assyrian who while still well disposed to the city often beautified it, only at last to destroy it utterly, as he emphatically states in his Bavian inscription.

Nebuchadnezzar makes no reference to this work of one of his predecessors, he only refers to that of his father Nabopolassar (*Steinplatten* inscription, col. 5, 12): "From Du-azag, the place of the deciding of fates, the chamber of fate, to Aiburšabu, the street of Babylon, opposite the 'Lady' Gate, he (Nabopolassar) had paved

the Procession Street of the great lord Marduk splendidly
with paving-stones of breccia" (trans. by Delitzsch). Of
these paving-stones of Nabopolassar there are certainly
no remains that can be identified with certainty. Just
as Nebuchadnezzar made use of the blocks of Sennacherib
for his new building, so doubtless he would appropriate
those of his father.

In addition to digging out the street on the east side
of the peribolos we also excavated a portion of it on the
south side. Here we could trace it between the peribolos

FIG. 36.—View of Procession Street, east of Etemenanki.

and Esagila as far as the (Urash?) gate in the Nabonidus
wall and the Euphrates bridge there. In this whole
length, several superimposed pavements of baked brick,
separated from each other by shallow layers of earth,
occurred rather frequently; all the upper ones bear the
stamp of Nebuchadnezzar, the bricks of the lowest pavement are unstamped and smaller (32 centimetres): these
may date from Nabopolassar, but not necessarily. North
of the Ishtar Gate we only find Nebuchadnezzar's brick
stamps. Consequently the above-quoted passage seems
to refer to the section of the street between Esagila and
the Kasr. If so, the "Lady" Gate (bâb bilti) must be
sought on the eastern front of the Kasr, and Du-azag

either in Esagila or in the peribolos of Etemenanki. The Procession Street on the Kasr was called Aiburshabu. To this latter section only the above-quoted passage applies (*Steinplatten* inscription, col. 5, 38).

We found a brick, although not *in situ* (Fig. 37), with an inscription that refers to the construction of the street by Nebuchadnezzar, with a number of fragments of similar content: "Nebuchadnezzar, King of Babylon, he who made Esagila and Ezida glorious, son of Nabopolassar, King of Babylon. The streets of Babylon, the Procession Streets of Nabû and Marduk my lords, which Nabopolassar, King of Babylon, the father who begat me, had made a

FIG. 37.—Inscription referring to the Procession Street.

road glistening with asphalt and burnt bricks: I, the wise suppliant who fears their lordship, placed above the bitumen and burnt bricks a mighty superstructure of shining dust, made them strong within with bitumen and burnt bricks as a high-lying road. Nabû and Marduk, when you traverse these streets in joy, may benefits for me rest upon your lips; life for distant days and well-being for the body. Before you will I advance (?) upon them (?). May I attain eternal age" (trans. by Weissbach).

Here and there on the street, and also below the procession pavement, are Babylonian graves. The adults are in large jars, the children in shallow elliptical bowls of pottery. We have observed no traces of monuments above ground, nor could we expect to find any in such a position on the street, nor yet in the other usual places of burial—the streets and squares of the city, on the fortification walls, and in the ruins of fallen houses.

IX

THE TEMPLE OF NINMACH

PASSING out of the Ishtar Gate, we find ourselves on a high open space before the east front of the Southern Citadel, where stood its great portal. Like the street and the palace itself, it is raised to the same level as the rest of the Citadel by means of artificial piling up of materials in several distinct stages. In the north-east corner stands the temple of Ninmach, " the great mother " (Fig. 38). Its entrance façade faces the north, immediately opposite one wing of the Ishtar Gate, to which it is joined by a short wall containing a doorway. At the south-east corner a mud brick wall begins, which also has a gate, and which probably was intended to form the boundary of the temple square, but of which only a short piece now remains. In this manner the secular area was entirely excluded from the sacred precincts.

Immediately in front of the temple entrance was a small altar of mud brick surrounded by an area of kiln brick, the edge of which was defined by tilted bricks fixed edge-ways in the ground.

The temple, like all others hitherto found by us, is composed of mud brick, but we must not judge of its original appearance by the present condition of the ruins ; its walls were covered with a white plaster that gave it the appearance of marble. The designs employed in laying out this temple were borrowed from military architecture. Towers in close proximity to each other are placed on the walls and especially beside the gateways. None of their upper portions now exist, but we believe we have sufficient evidence to prove that, like those of fortifications, they were crowned with the usual stepped battlements. In addition, these sacred buildings possessed a very characteristic form of decoration which is absent in fortresses and other secular buildings. This consists of vertical grooves carried from top to bottom of the walls, either rectangular in section or stepped, as here in the temple of Ninmach. In other temples, as at Borsippa or

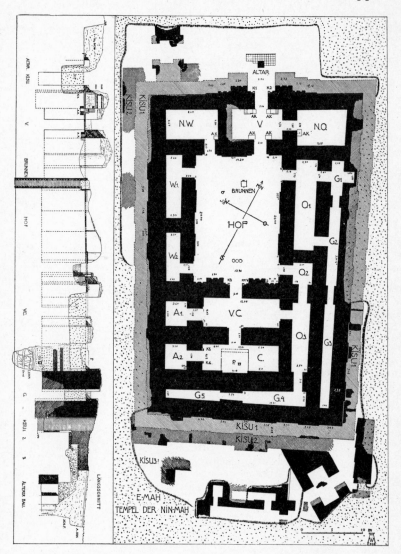

FIG. 38.—Ground-plan and section of Ninmach Temple.

the earliest Esagila, in place of the grooves there are
semicircular fillets. Cornices, friezes, and the like, as well
as columns or entablatures, are entirely absent in Babylonia.

In the gateway the three upper floorings lie super-imposed and separated from each other by layers of earth. They are very instructive and show that they pertain to the last three raisings of the temple-level. That the temple was raised twice previously we learn from the cella. Under each pavement at the gate there is a channel which carried off the rain-water from the building, and on each side of the entrance, also under the pavement, is one of those remarkable structures formed of six bricks placed together which we found in connection with almost every doorway of any importance in the temples. One of these was empty, but in the eastern one was deposited a bird in earthenware, and with it a fragment of pottery with an almost illegible inscription. Such deposits may probably be termed offerings, and every one of these small caskets which is now empty certainly contained gifts which in course of time have perished and disappeared. The exact significance attached to them by the Baby-lonians we do not know; the in-scriptions found on some of the clay figures on other sites do not make this clear.

FIG. 39.—Bronze ferrule of doorpost, Emach.

The entrance was fitted with double doors. The base of the doorposts stood in a bronze ferrule (Fig. 39), and turned in stone sockets of considerable dimensions. The brick cavities in which these sockets were inserted are well preserved, the stone sockets themselves have disappeared, as in most other cases. The two blocks of brickwork by which the old pivot sockets were partially covered were in some way which cannot now be clearly recognised used as foundations for the stone sockets of the later, higher pavement. The door could be very strongly barricaded, apart from the bolts which we may safely take for granted, by a beam that was propped against it from the inside. For the admission of this beam there was a slight depression in the pavement and also a stone which rose slightly above its level exactly as at the Urash Gate, and at the Citadel gateway at Sendjirli.

The usual method of fastening was undoubtedly by beams which could be drawn out of the wall, as we shall see them in the ancient gate of the Southern Citadel. The prop was intended merely to strengthen the fastenings in troubled times and enable the priests of Emach to defend their sanctuary as a stronghold. The towers and parapets of the external walls may also have helped in this case.

When we leave the vestibule, as we may well name

FIG. 40.—Court in Ninmach Temple.

the first chamber at the gateway, we find ourselves in the court, which was proportionately large and certainly open to the sky, and which gave more or less direct access to the remaining chambers. Immediately opposite lies the entrance to the cella (Fig. 40), indicated by towers decorated with grooves. From here it must have been possible to behold through the open cella-doors beyond, in the mystic twilight of the Holy of Holies, the cultus image on its pedestal. To the right was a brick-lined well which must have played an important part in the service of the cult. Immediately in front

of the entrance to the cella, in the asphalt covering
of the pavement, three circular depressions may be
observed, in which metal vases, now lost, appear to have
stood. Similar cavities may also be seen near the centre
of the court. One would expect incense-burners, thymi-
ateria here, but of these we have no knowledge.

At the time of the final raising of the floor-level,
the mud façade of the cella was provided with a slight
dressing of kiln bricks, of which there are now only
scanty remains. The caskets for offerings at each side
of the entrance are there. Originally rectangular, they
are much distorted by the settling down of the walls:
this also caused a curvature of the pavement, which has
been re-levelled in the corners by means of asphalt and
broken brick.

The cella had an ante-chamber of similar size, and both
have a small side chamber. This side chamber we have
termed the Adyton, without any further ground for doing
so than the analogy with Greek temple cellae. It appears
probable that the secular folk were not allowed to penetrate beyond the ante-chamber. Access to the cella was
evidently intentionally rendered difficult by the postament,
which projected almost as far as the door—a peculiarity
which we shall find with most of the cellae. The postament of the upper floor-level is no longer there. Its
principal adjustments could still be traced on the floor and
by the fragments of asphalt that cling to the niche in the
hinder wall. Below, and almost beneath it, are two postaments lying one above another of burnt brick and bitumen
which bear witness to two earlier periods during which the
temple was in use. These postaments always rose very
slightly above the floor-level, and had a low step in front.
Still farther down, at the edge of the foundation, below
the postament was the casket of burnt brick usual in this
position and containing a small pottery figure of a man
holding a slender gold staff in his hand. In other temples
we shall see this better preserved. At a still greater
depth the excavations reached a natural stratum of alternate sand and mud, as though water had flowed here
for some considerable time.

In the Adyton at the end of the foundations at one corner lay the foundation cylinder of Sardanapalus (Fig. 41). This was surrounded by sand, and near by lay tablets of the time of Nebuchadnezzar. Thus the cylinder cannot have been found in the place where it was deposited by Sardanapalus, though certainly not far off. For Nebuchadnezzar must have read the four last lines of this document with the same awe with which we read it to-day : "Who with cunning deed shall destroy this record of my name . . . bring to the ground, or alter its position, him may Ninmah before Bel, Sarrateia bespeak to evil, destroy his name, his seed in the lands!" (trans. by Delitzsch).

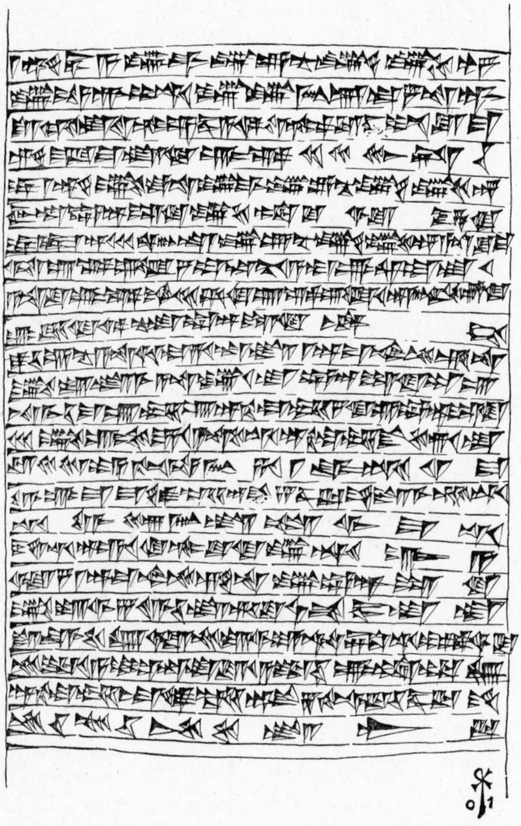

FIG. 41.—Emach cylinder inscription of Sardanapalus.

Sardanapalus refers to the founding of the temple in line 13 : "At that same time I caused E-mah, the temple of the goddess Ninmah in Babil, to be made new." It can no longer be proved whether and how far the lower part of the walls date back to the time of Sardanapalus. The two lower postaments have no stamp on their bricks, nor has the upper pavement. That the raising of the pavement that Nebuchadnezzar considered necessary was his work is proved by tablets bearing his name which have been found below, and especially by the stamps of the burnt-brick wall which the king caused to be erected round the temple.

This " Kisu," as the wall is named on the inscriptions, was built with the object of strengthening the external walls of the building as the floor-level was heightened. The mass of new material brought in for this work must have pressed very seriously on the outer walls, and rendered such strengthening necessary. We find the same method adopted for several monumental buildings as they were raised in height. It was a special delight to the Babylonians to seize the opportunity afforded by rebuilding to raise the level. To build higher and yet higher always on the same ground plan is the characteristic tendency of all restorers of buildings.

FIG. 42.—Kisu inscription of Emach.

In the debris of the Kisu, which was largely destroyed by early plunderers, we have found a considerable number of inscribed bricks that refer to the rebuilding of the temple, and to the Kisu (Fig. 42) : " Nebuchadnezzar, King of Babylon, son of Nabopolassar, King of Babylon, am I. E-mah, the temple of Ninmah in Babylon, have I built anew to Nin-mah the Princess, the Exalted, in Babylon. I caused it to be surrounded with a mighty Kisu of bitumen and burnt brick," etc. (trans. by Winckler). The inscription is identical with that on small cylinders now in various museums, but of which we have found none (*K.B.* iii. 2, p. 67). We see here what Nebuchadnezzar meant by "mighty" : it is a wall 2.02 metres thick.

The heightening of the floor-level involved also the raising of the immediate surroundings, apparently to about the same level. The upper floor lies at about the same height as the old Procession Street.

Round this older Kisu, which exactly follows the outer lines of the temple with all its projections, there runs a later one, which has only large tower projections in some places. It is built with Nebuchadnezzar's bricks, and its foundations are not so deep as those of its predecessor. Towards the south there appear to be remains of a third Kisu of still shallower foundation.

In the south behind the temple, as low down as the ancient Kisu, are buildings of mud brick which we have not sought further. They show that the Citadel square was formerly occupied by buildings of a private character.

To whom the two upper pavements which still remain in the entrance doorway may be ascribed cannot be stated with certainty. In this case we cannot place much reliance on the Nebuchadnezzar stamps. On the upper pavement stood an entirely unimportant construction of Nabonidus bricks.

This building in later years was demolished and levelled above the upper pavement, and on it was erected a building of mud brick on the lines, however, of the ancient temple. So little of it now remains that it is impossible to make out its purpose with any certainty.

In order to secure more strength for the building, wooden clamps were inserted about half-way between the bottom of the foundations and the main flooring, which reached from the outer walls to those opposite. We found the holes left by them in the walls of the north-east room, and in chamber W 2.

At about each 8th course there is a thick layer of reeds laid crossways over each other, which have now rotted to a white powder. They were certainly intended in some way to strengthen the walls, but it is now difficult to estimate the length of time for which they served this purpose.

The angles of the walls at the gates were secured by the insertion of pieces of wood washed over with tar. A plank of wood, the height of a brick course, lay in the jamb, and another, one course higher on each side, thus forming a frame, which probably also served as an attachment for the door or door casing.

We should, of course, wish to give a clearer explanation of the object and use of the various parts of the building, but this is a difficult matter. We have very little information as to the usages of the cult connected with the temple. It is therefore of great importance that in Babylon we have not only one, but a series of four temples, in which the arrangement of the chambers is clearly repeated. From these we can conclude with certainty that for a temple the towered façade, the vestibule, the court, the cella with its postament in the shallow niche, were regarded as indispensable. It is not difficult to recognise the small side-chamber near the cella as the storeplace for the various requirements of the cult. The chamber next the vestibule can be identified with some certainty as either a waiting-room or the porter's lodge. The long narrow passages near the cella are remarkable; others exactly similar have been found in other temples. They would be well adapted to enclose the ramps or staircases that led to the flat roof, and some part of them may, in fact, have been used for that purpose. But it is by no means easy to understand why two such arrangements so completely alike as G 1, G 2, G 3 and O 3, G 4, G 5 should have been placed close together. I might provisionally suppose that these passages represent the remains of a more ancient and certainly an unknown type of ground-plan. The whole arrangement gives an impression that the original Babylonian house was essentially a four-sided walled enclosure, inside which opposite the entrance, separated from the enclosing wall by a narrow intermediate space, stood a detached house of one room. In course of its development other single chambers were added, which were built near the other sides of the enclosing wall. The intermediate space would make it possible to guard the main house from any danger from robbers who might break through the outer walls. But this, as we have said, is all hypothetical, and entirely depends on the result of further research.

No cultus image has been found. In many temples the postaments are supported on gigantic and deep foundations although their height above the flooring is invariably very slight. We may conclude from this that they were intended to bear heavy weights. Herodotus (i. 183) states that the seated statue of Marduk in the temple Esagila with its accessories weighed 800 talents of gold, and speaks of another sacred statue 12 ells high in massive gold. It is obvious that such costly statues could not survive to a later period. Their immense value was their certain ruin. Thus if we attempt to form an idea of the appearance of a temple statue we must have recourse to the terra-cottas. They are found by many thousands over the entire city area. Only a few of these are uninjured, by far the largest number are in small fragments. These, however, even when they are very small, can be recognised as belonging to a well-known type. Great as is the number of these terra-cottas, the number of different types is proportionately small. They appear to have been used as a species of household gods, and they are all of the same modest size, about 12 centimetres high. They are moulded, and the design is only on the front, the back is smooth and merely rounded; thus they are absolutely full face. The men are clothed, but the women are nude until the Greek times, when the woman with a child in her arms appears for the first time draped. All other female types remain unclothed up to the latest period. With regard to technique, in the later Greek period a slight change was introduced, and a mould was made for the back as well as for the front of the figure; the two edges must have been fastened together, leaving the inside hollow. These terra-cottas now show only the yellowish, or occasionally reddish, colour of the burnt clay, but originally they were painted, as we learn from some few better-preserved specimens. Of the time of Nebuchadnezzar and earlier there are some that appear to be glazed in one colour; but the glaze is always so much decayed that it is impossible to say whether or not the figures were originally glazed in a variety of colours.

The characteristic form of each of these somewhat rare types of divinities occurs with such convincing similarity in the numerous examples of each type that the cultus image of the respective gods in their temples must have had the same form. Now, if we find in, or near, one temple a considerable number identical in type, we are, in some measure, justified in forming from them a conjectural restoration of the divine image. We must bear in mind, however, that coincidence may here play a part. In any case, I am quite prepared later to modify the conclusions here put forward with regard to each temple, in favour of what may be thought more solid and more probable considerations.

The terra-cottas of the Ninmach temple (cf. Fig. 202) show the type of a standing female figure, with hands laid in one another and folded in the Babylonian fashion, with well-dressed hair, a necklet, and several anklets. The figure is thoroughly symmetrical, the face round and full, and exactly in accord with the Arab ideal of feminine beauty.

The tablets found in the temple contain lists of the delivery of building materials, of workmen, and of others who did not work. Also the name of an architect, Labashi, occurs.

Emach, as this temple of Ninmach was called, has provided us with the type of the Babylonian temple which, previous to our excavations, was entirely unknown. The consideration of all the other temples will be much more quickly accomplished, as it will only be needful to bring forward the individual peculiarities of each temple.

X

THE SOUTHERN CITADEL

THE southern, most ancient part of the Acropolis of Babylon we have been accustomed to distinguish as

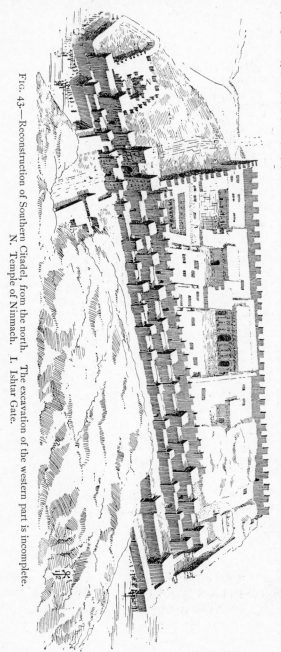

FIG. 43.—Reconstruction of Southern Citadel, from the north. The excavation of the western part is incomplete. N. Temple of Ninmach. I. Ishtar Gate.

the Southern Cita-del (Figs. 43, 44). This also was not all built at one time but at successive periods. The oldest part lies between the squaring lines *i* to *m* of the Kasr plan (cf., for the squares, Fig. 13). Here apparently stood a palace of Nabopolassar, which Nebuchad-nezzar preserved in order to dwell there during the building of the eastern portion. This eastern side in front of the ancient palace, which was origin-ally unoccupied or only built upon with private houses, was en-closed by a fortifi-cation wall of which certain of the more ancient parts still remain, such as the arched door on the eastern side. Nebuchadnezzar's first work consisted in rebuilding the surrounding walls of the eastern part

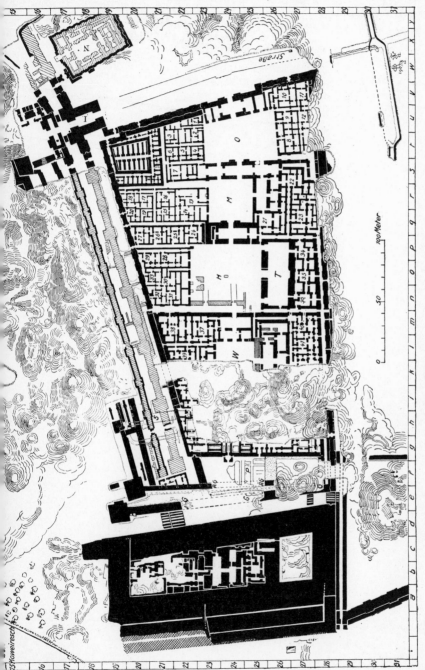

FIG. 44.—Complete plan of Southern Citadel. N. Ninmach Temple. I. Ishtar Door.

of this fortress with burnt brick, raising the whole square
to a higher level, and placing on it a new palace. The
new part was connected for a time with the older, lower
portion by ramps (Fig. 67), which have been discovered
uninjured beneath the pavement. The second building
period of Nebuchadnezzar also renewed the ancient palace,
raised it to the same height, and extended the western
boundary as far as the squaring line g of the Kasr plan.
Thus the whole formed a connected uniform building of
quite unusual size. The further and later important
enlargement of the palace by Nebuchadnezzar, which
extended to the north and the west of the Southern
Citadel, we will consider later. In the meantime we will
turn to the inspection of the Southern Citadel, which
presents itself as being uniformly the work of Nebuchadnezzar. Neriglissar's work consisted of a restoration of
the upper parts of the western portion. Nabonidus
repaved the great court with fine large bricks, many of
which still remain in position, and Artaxerxes built an
Apadana against the west front, of which the foundations, as well as enamelled bricks and fragments of marble
pillars and inscriptions, have been found (f 25 in plan).
(Cf. p. 127 et seq.)

XI

THE EAST FRONT OF THE SOUTHERN
CITADEL

THE east front consists of a defensive wall that ran
parallel with the Procession Street (cf. Fig. 44). It is
guarded by cavalier towers placed at short intervals,
and the principal entrance is a doorway inserted in a
shallow recess and flanked as usual by two towers. The
recess is shallower on the north than on the south side.
The wall itself does not run exactly north to south, which
is the direction of the greater part of the palace, and care
has evidently been taken to render this deviation as little

noticeable as possible. This doorway is perhaps that of Beltis (*Steinplatten* inscription, col. 5, 17).

Fig. 45.—Arched doorway in Southern Citadel.

To the south near this gateway is an older piece of

wall which in many respects is different from the rest. The bricks are smaller (31.5 × 31.5 × 7.5), the joints are formed of asphalt and reeds, the asphalt is laid flush with the face of the wall and has oozed out over it, giving it a blackish appearance, in marked contrast with the neighbouring wall of Nebuchadnezzar's time, which is lighter in colour, as the asphalt does not show on the surface. This piece of wall contains an arched gateway (Fig. 45), with a threshold that lies about 6 metres below the street pavement. This gate, which is generally known as the arched doorway, was blocked up with mud bricks during the general raising of the ground. It seems, however, that during a later period a door of secondary importance was placed here, of which a small part of the frame still exists. It must have led into the palace that lay behind it. It had two doors, one directly behind the other, as we may infer from the rebates that project by one brick both on the inner and outer sides of the wall. The inner door could only be opened by any one who wished to enter after he had entered the small chamber and had closed the outer door behind him. The outer door could be fastened by a large wooden bolt which pushed backwards and forwards in a cavity in the northern wall.

Very interesting, and very characteristic both of this time and of its art, is the construction and the external appearance of this arch. It consisted of a series of three ring courses one above another, each of them covered by a flat course. The lower ring of the outside is destroyed and has disappeared completely. The bricks of our arch are of the usual form, not wedge-shaped. The laying is so slightly radial that at the vertex an actual three-cornered gap remains filled in with chopped brick. The central bricks were covered with asphalt before being laid, the lower ones are laid in mud and asphalt. The inner imposts are bound together by clamps made of poplar wood soaked in asphalt on a system which can no longer be clearly worked out. The lower ring alone formed an actual arch, each of the two higher rings begin some courses higher than the last and follow only a part of the semicircle, thus forming a segment. They begin nevertheless with a brick laid horizontal and not sloping. It is obvious that the planning of this arch construction is very faulty and inconsistent in comparison with Roman stone vaulting.

The wall stands throughout on a level foundation bed. On the outside it is perpendicular, but on the inside the courses recede a little one behind the other, causing a slight slope and rendering the walls somewhat thicker below than they are above. This batter of the walls never occurs in buildings that are indisputably of the time of Nebuchadnezzar.

On to this old piece of wall, with its three towers to the north and the south, the later walls are built with grooved and tongued expansion joints (see p. 36), for which purpose the old wall was hacked out as far as necessary. The later wall is plain; it formed, however, only a foundation for the now destroyed upper part, which certainly must have been furnished with towers. By this new building the old wall appears to have been strengthened within as by a Kisu, to which the palace walls are closely fitted by means of plain expansion joints.

The lower part of the long northern portion with its seven towers is similar both in age and style of building to the arched door. The upper part is contemporary with the Citadel Gate, and of course the tongued expansion joints are employed throughout, and a powerful strengthening is added on the inside; according to the principles of the ancient architects it was not permissible to rest the footings of this inner strengthening on the lowest level of the foundations, and accordingly there remained in the mesopyrgia narrow spaces that were filled up by small independent walls only one brick thick. Nebuchadnezzar's architects were very consistent on these points. The gate on the north corresponds with the arched door and is closed with later brickwork. The door in the angle abutting on the Ishtar Gate afforded the entrance to the area enclosed by the two mud walls of the Ishtar Gate. In order to leave this door clear the Citadel wall here in the corner is set back.

The other sides of the Citadel wall we will observe later. The palace must now be studied in detail.

THE EASTERN COURT OF THE SOUTHERN CITADEL

THROUGH the Beltis door we first enter the usual gateway court, out of which open two rooms with large doorways. These are well adapted for the use of the castle guard and afford access to the court. Two other chambers close by may be regarded as waiting-rooms.

To the north and south of the eastern court (Fig. 46, O), accessible by passages or alleys, were the houses of the officials employed here, similar to those found in other courts. Here they are of smaller dimensions than in the other courts, where they are clearly built in accordance with their degree of importance. The largest dwellings are always placed on the south side of the courts. The chambers of these houses are invariably grouped round a small court, which can easily be distinguished from the chambers by its square ground-plan. The smaller houses have only one court, while the larger ones have two or more. Thus 1, 2, 3, 6, 10 have only one court; 4 with 5, 8 with 9, and 11 with 12 have two. Owing to the curtailed space below the wall the latter is slightly out of the square. It appears that a royal manufacture of flasks was established here. A very large number of those graceful vases, which in Greek art are called alabastra (Fig. 47), were found here, especially waste products of the manufacture. For the purpose of hollowing them out a crown-bit was used first of all, which cut out a cylindrical piece and afforded room for other boring instruments. Masses of these cylindrical cores were found here.

The house 8 with 9 had two large rooms which opened on the great court (O), but had no direct communication with the other rooms. They thus possess the characteristics of offices open to the public from the great court, while the official could enter them by a small passage from the open court in front of his own rooms. As in all

FIG. 46.—Eastern part of Southern Citadel.

the great courts the largest buildings lay to the south, so
in each of these houses the principal chamber lay on the
south side of the court; and this must have been the
pleasantest part of the whole house, as it lay in shadow
almost all day.   Owing to the peculiar climate of Babylon
it is obvious that in laying out a house, only the summer
and the heat would be taken into consideration.   The

summer lasts 8 months, from the
middle of March to the middle
of November, and during June,
July, and August the temperature is at times abnormally high.
We have observed a maximum
of $49\frac{1}{2}$ grades Celsius in the
shade, and 66 in the sun, and
the heat lasts for many hours
of the day.   It begins in the
morning by 9 o'clock, and only
at 9 o'clock in the evening does
it begin to abate : the minimum
heat is in the early hours of the
morning after sunrise.   The
months of December and February correspond on the whole,
with our autumn and spring. The
only cold weather is in January,
if the sun does not shine, and
sometimes there are night frosts.

FIG. 47.—An Alabastron.

Frosty days can be counted on the fingers of one hand,
and the unaccustomed body feels these cold days very
keenly.   Rain is very scanty.   I believe if all the hours
in the whole year in which there were more than a few
drops of rain were reckoned up, they would barely amount
to 7 or 8 days.   The annual downfall has been registered
by Buddensieg at 7 centimetres, in North Germany Herr
Hellmann informs me it is 64, and in places in India 1150
centimetres.   Naturally there are exceptional years.   The
winter of 1898 was severe and long, the thorn bushes of
the desert were thickly frosted over, and the breath of a
rider froze as he rode.   In 1906 hundreds of palms were

frozen in the neighbourhood of Babylon, and in 1911 the snow lay ankle deep all over the plain between Babylon and Bagdad for a whole week. But these are exceptions, and then people usually pretend that such a thing has not happened for 100 years. The result of this fine climate is that for the greater part of the year all business is carried on in the open air, in the courts, or at any rate with open doors.

Windows do not appear to have existed. None have ever been found, and the evidence of the ground-plans bears out this presumption. The evenings and nights were spent on the flat roofs. Thus the chambers were used very much as refuges or store chambers, with the exception of the principal rooms, where in any case as a matter of business the official must have installed himself. He may, however, have often done his business in the court in front of his office.

In the south-east corner of the Kasr the earliest brick stamps of Nebuchadnezzar occur, and the king appears to have begun his new building here. These stamps have six lines of inscription, ending with the words "am I," *anaku* (Figs. 48, 51). In general the legends on these different varieties of stamps are the same: "Nebuchadnezzar, King of Babylon, fosterer of Esagila and Ezida, son of Nabopolassar, King of Babylon." There are 6-lined, 4-lined, 3-lined, and 7-lined stamps, and one single specimen is 5-lined. The 4-, 3-, and 7-lined stamps substitute for the old simple "son," *maru*, the more detailed "first-born son," *aplu ašaridu*, after which the name of the father that follows is introduced with *ša*, which does not occur on the 6-lined stamps.

We can distinguish three methods by which the working stamps were produced. In the first the original inscription was produced in terra-cotta, in which the signs were most carefully and beautifully written, and the strokes show the regular three-cornered section. From this original inscription the working stamp could then be struck in clay and baked. These we call "pottery stamps." In them the rows of cuneiform writing are separated from each other by ruled lines. In the second sort the signs were cut out separately

in wood, joined together in one block, and then moulded
in sand. From this mould the working stamp was apparently cast in bronze. The strokes of these are of roundish
section. Of this "metal stamp" the impressions are fine
and deep, but, on the other hand, the ground between the
strokes easily becomes clogged during the stamping, and
thus on the bricks the signs frequently appear only in
outline, while the wedges are confused and flattened. Lines
between the rows of writing in these metal stamps are

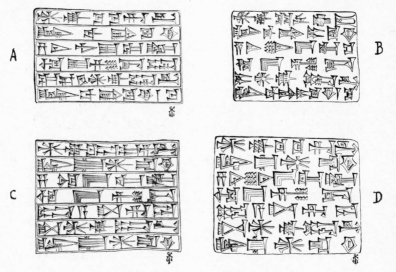

FIG. 48.—Brick stamps of Nebuchadnezzar.

rare, and it is possible there was some difficulty in producing
them. With the third method the original inscription is
produced in stone, undoubtedly by grinding. In this way
the wedges acquire a scratched appearance, as is more
especially the case with the stone objects bearing votive
inscriptions of the time of the Kassite kings. The working
stamp made from this may have been taken either in bronze
or in pottery. We have found no actual working stamp,
but this is not surprising, considering that in the course of
our excavations we have not yet met with a brick-kiln,
and it is of course possible that the method of production
was very different from what I have suggested. In the

meantime it is important to describe the technical characteristics of the different kinds of stamps as they exist, and to
give a concise name to each of them. The 6- and 7-lined
stamps occur both as pottery and metal stamps, never
as " Kassite," the 4-lined are almost exclusively pottery,
and the 3-lined are never metal, but either pottery or
" Kassite."

The orthographical differences also arrange themselves

FIG. 49.—Stamped brick of Nebuchadnezzar, omitting his father's name.

with the same distinctness in clearly defined groups.
On the 6-lined stamps *Ba-bi-lu* or *Ba-bi-i-lu* is written
for Babylon, while on the 7-, 4-, and 3-lined stamps it
is exclusively called *Ka-dingir-ra*. The term *Tin-tir*,
which is by far the most usual on stone inscriptions,
only occurs once on a 3-line and once on a 4-line
stamp on bricks. Very rare is a 4-line stamp on which
the father's name is omitted (Fig. 49), and as a curiosity
7-line metal stamps occur on which the order of the
lines has been reversed. What elsewhere is the 7th line is
here the 1st. We have no wish to decide whether this is
mere carelessness. We must, however, remember in this
connection that we have Assyriologists of repute who
read the cuneiform writing from above downwards, with

which its historical development certainly agrees. The
literature of the tablets for the ordinary right-handed man
was written from left to right, but were the scribe left-
handed he would be forced to write from above downwards,
and many of the archaic stone inscriptions indeed convey
the impression that they should be read in this fashion.

FIG. 50.—Brick stamp of Evil-Merodach.

All will agree that the later writings must be read
from left to right. It is quite possible that Nebuchadnezzar, who so greatly preferred the archaic characters
which were so highly decorative, also made an attempt to
employ the ancient method of arranging them vertically.
The stamps are all inscribed with these monumental, early
Babylonian characters.

The 6-lined stamp gives *Nabu-ku-dur-ru-u-ṣur* or
Nabu-ku-dur-ri-uṣur, the 7-lined gives either the latter

or *Nabu-ku-du-ur-ri-uṣur*. The 4-lined is exclusively characterised by the use of *ap-lam* instead of *tur-uš*, which is universally used elsewhere.

It may be advisable at this juncture to consider the stamps used by Nebuchadnezzar's successors. Of Evil-Merodach we have found only two examples (Fig. 50), one of 3 lines, exactly analogous to the stamps of Nebuchadnezzar. Neriglissar (Fig. 51 G) has 3- and 4-lined stamps, with the text, "Neriglissar, King of Babylon, fosterer of Esagila and Ezida, who accomplishes good deeds." Of Nabonidus (Fig. 51 H) are 3- and 6-lined stamps, with the text, "Nabonidus, King of Babylon, the chosen one of Nabu and Marduk, son of Nabubalatsuikbi, the wise prince, am I,"

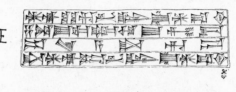

E

F

G

H

FIG. 51.—Brick stamps of Nebuchadnezzar (E, F), of Neriglissar (G), and Nabonidus (H).

and "Nabonidus, King of Babylon, fosterer of Esagila and Ezida, son of Nabubalatsuikbi, the wise prince." So far no stamp has been found of Labashi-Marduk. All these stamps bear general texts, applicable to any building. In contrast to them are the special stamps, which like the inscribed bricks refer to individual buildings, for which they were exclusively intended. We have such of Nabopolassar, Sardanapalus, Esarhaddon, Sennacherib, and

Sargon, and shall speak of them when we come to the buildings to which they refer.

In addition, a fair number of stamps are found in Aramaic, either alone or in conjunction with cuneiform (Fig. 52). Of these no convincing translation has yet reached me ; they appear to be names sometimes abbrevi-

ated. The name of Nabonidus is easily recognised, as it often occurs in Aramaic in conjunction with his cuneiform stamp. ?HI*ℓ (Fig. 53) appears to be an abbreviation of the canal name Libil-ḥigalla, and in *g ʾ* we may recognise the initial letters of Nimitti-Bel.

FIG. 52.—Aramaic addition on Nebuchadnezzar brick.

Among other signs more symbolic in character are the lion, the double axe, and the symbol of Marduk, a triangle on a shaft, either alone or combined with other stamps.

The manufacture of these bricks was carried on as it is with us at the present day. The fairly pure clay was well kneaded and pressed into a rectangular wooden frame laid on a rough reed matting. Nebuchadnezzar's bricks almost invariably show the impress of the matting on one side, while the bricks of the other monarchs appear to have been made without this underlay. The frames were frequently grooved on one or more of their inner sides, which caused corresponding ridges on the narrow edges of the bricks. We can thus distinguish bricks with 1, 2 (see Fig. 71), or even 7 of these ridges. In Nebuchadnezzar's first building period the bricks had no ridges, then only one, while in his latest buildings, such as the Principal Citadel, there are seven. It thus happens that no 7-ridged brick has a 6-line stamp, as by that time they were disused. Besides their number, the ridges vary in breadth, depth, and position. The sign of early manufacture is that they are placed in the centre of the side, and are of greater breadth, while later they are placed near the corners. Thus we have ample material for dividing them, not only

FIG. 53.—Aramaic addition on Nebuchadnezzar brick.

according to the places where they were made but also as to their age. In the course of the 43 years' reign of Nebuchadnezzar, it is obvious that with the gradual multiplication of brick factories the necessity of being able to distinguish between their several productions increased in like measure. The bricks are not always accurately separated from each other in the buildings, according to their marks, but on the whole the stamps, in addition to the ridges on the sides, enable us to distinguish the relative ages of the various walls.

It is evident from the bricks themselves that the burning was done in ovens, which can scarcely have differed

G

materially from the brick-kilns used to-day both here and in Bagdad. They are built outside the town, where the clay is good and fuel—the low bushes of the desert—is abundant. They form great fantastic groups of buildings, to which the people attach tales of horror. With the Persians it was a favourite method of execution to throw persons into these heated ovens, and when one sees the flickering glare from their mouths rising up against the evening sky of Babylon, one is unconsciously reminded of the striking account in the third chapter of Daniel of the three men, Shadrach, Meshach, and Abednego, in the fiery furnace. Herodotus states that the manufacture of bricks for the town walls was always carried on close to the site where they were to be used. This may have been done in exceptional cases, but ordinarily the ovens were certainly farther outside.

The whole of the walls of the Southern Citadel have been pillaged by brick robbers even below the pavement, the level to which our excavations usually extend (Fig. 54). Everywhere we have laid the walls bare as far as the bricks still remain in position. Here in the south-east corner we have gone still deeper and have dug down to the foundation fillings, reaching nearly to water-level. The fillings consist almost exclusively of sand and clayey earth, river settlement with occasional patches of ancient building material, rubbish, charcoal and ashes, bones and some broken pottery. Possibly the sediment was taken from the watercourse that flowed past the southern side of the Citadel, and which would then be considerably deepened and widened. The footings are carried down almost to water-level, of the same even thickness without any broadening. At this depth the soil is interspersed with the remains of a very ancient settlement, characterised, as in other quarters of the city, by pipe wells and much pottery. Thus in the foundations everything is avoided that could prevent the settlement of the walls, and they are perfectly free to sink vertically. In laying the foundations the doorways were left open. Hence there are separate blocks of buildings, which doubtless even before the floor-level was reached settled independently of each other during the course of

FIG. 54.—Excavations in Southern Citadel, from the north.

erection. In order to bind these blocks together across the door spaces, beams of poplar wood soaked in tar were inserted at intervals and fixed in the wall head with short transverse pieces, thus forming huge ⌐-rivets.

The jointing of the brick courses can be clearly observed at this point. It is very simple, owing to the square shape of the bricks that necessitates two-handed manipulation. The cross-joints run straight through the walls, and if in one course a whole brick—a binder—lies at one corner, the next course has a half brick—a stretcher. At the edges and in the corners the sequence of the series changes. When on occasion the change does not occur owing to some irregularity, a quarter brick was employed at the edge, and in the corner a whole brick with its corner cut out was used, or one wall penetrated to the depth of half a brick into the adjoining wall, with a vertical joint extending from top to bottom. This is to be seen at this part of the Citadel. The care bestowed on applying these building regulations sometimes leaves much to be desired. The vertical joints are of uneven thickness, the walls were patched with inserted fragments, and in thick walls the regularity is frequently broken by small channels that extend transversely or lengthways through the wall, of the height and breadth of a course, and are only closed on the outer surface by an inserted fragment; they appear to have been constructed to secure the dryness of the building. In the Arachtu wall of Nabopolassar, and in his palace, as well as in the ascent on the north-east angle of the Kasr (*t* 4), an exceptional feature occurs, a border series in which, within the same course, a half brick laid behind a whole one is regularly alternated with a whole brick laid behind a half one, so that the whole mass of the wall is joggled together by this border series. This is another instance of the false principles of construction which are found throughout antiquity far more frequently than enthusiastic admirers would credit.

In the house court, *v* 27, we found a brick built into the wall low down, bearing a 6-lined inscription (Fig. 55), which ran thus: "Nebuchadnezzar, King of Babylon, son of Nabopolassar, King of Babylon, am I. The palace, the dwelling of my kingship on the soil of Babylon (or "the place Babil" [Delitzsch]), which is in Babylon, I built. Mighty cedars from the mountain of Lebanon the splendid forest, I brought, and for its ceiling I laid them. Marduk the compassionate god who hears my prayer: the house

FIG. 55.—The six-lined Lebanon inscription from Southern Citadel.

that I built, may it satisfy him by its delights; the Kisu that I constructed, may its decay be renewed; in Babylon may my walks therein be continued to old age; may my posterity for ever rule over the blackheads" (trans. by Weissbach). Thus the palace was ceiled with cedars of Lebanon, and with exceptions to be dwelt on later, it was

FIG. 56.—The eight-lined standard inscription from Southern Citadel.

not vaulted. By the Kisu the king must have meant the strengthening wall that we have already seen on the eastern side, and that we shall see on other parts of the surrounding walls. These 6-lined inscribed bricks, of which we have found 80, were principally in the eastern part of the Southern Citadel, but few are in position. Strewn over the whole of the Southern Citadel, more especially in the central part, was a second kind of inscribed brick, the 8-lined legend on which ran much like the previous one (Fig. 56), but the cedars of Lebanon are not mentioned : "Nebuchad-nezzar, King of Babylon, the fosterer of Esagila and Ezida, son of Nabopolassar, King of Babylon, am I. The palace, the dwelling place of my Majesty I built on the Babil place (irṣit Babil) of Babil. I grounded its foundations firm on the bosom of the underworld, and with asphalt and baked bricks I raised it mountain high. By thy behest, wise one of the gods, Marduk, may I be satisfied with the fullness of the house that I have built, along with my posterity. May my posterity bear rule in it for ever over the blackheads" (trans. by Delitzsch, cf. *K.B.* iii. 2, p. 69). Of these 8-lined bricks we have found altogether 412, many of them in the foundations of the great hall of the Principal Court and of its great gateway. Here they were frequently laid in the same course (Fig. 57), only separated by a few uninscribed bricks. The script is Neo-Babylonian, and always very good and carefully executed. The arrange-ment of the lines is always the same ; they almost convey the impression that a certain rhythmic utterance was intended, which was expressed by the arrangement, for while in some lines the signs are placed so far apart as to produce considerable gaps, in others the signs are crowded together. The lines of inscription are separated by dividing lines which appear to have been made by a 2-ply cord stretched across and pressed into the pottery. Such numerous and monotonous repetitions are very vexatious for the ex-cavator. He would be better pleased if the texts varied on the different bricks, and afforded him an opportunity of acquiring more details of building achievements, and their nomenclature and purpose. But this desire for information on the part of later scholars was evidently not foreseen by the King of Babylon. The principal object was to preserve the name of the king as the promoter of mighty works, and the hundreds of inscribed bricks, and the millions of stamped bricks do in fact form an enduring monument to the king, which it would be difficult to surpass.

According to these inscriptions the Southern Citadel stands on the "Babil place," and in my opinion that is the site of the earliest settlement, which was named Babilu or Babilani, the gate of god or gate of the gods. At that time Esagila was separate from Babylon. It was later, though at a very early date, that both were united in one great Babylon. Later on, however, Esarhaddon, on one of the bricks found by us, says (No. 38940) that he built "Babylon and Esagila" anew, and on the numerous bricks

FIG. 57.—Inscribed bricks *in situ*, Southern Citadel.

of his Arachtu wall (No. 30522) Nabopolassar calls himself "the restorer of Esagila and Babylon." The measurements of 190 metres broad by 300 metres long are amply sufficient for those very ancient cities. The acropolis of Tiryns, with its length of 150 metres and breadth of 50 metres, could be placed inside the eastern part of the Southern Citadel, which comprises the eastern court with its two gateways, and stretches from the northern to the southern wall. The 6th level of Troy, the Mycenæan level, is also considerably smaller than the southern acropolis, with its 130 × 180 metres; its two ancient encircling walls measure only 80 × 110 metres and 100 × 110 metres. Thus on the *irṣit* of Babylon there is certainly sufficient room for an ancient settlement of the size usual at that very remote period. Esagila lay 800 metres away, and therefore we must not imagine that from the beginning Babylon and Esagila formed a combined township. On the other hand, it is quite possible that when they were first founded, the entrance to the sacred place Esagila was completely dominated by the fortress Babil, and that it was only through this *god's door* that access could be obtained to Esagila.

These conditions may have been modified quite early, possibly by the beginning of the historical times. In Merkes, as far back as Hammurabi, we certainly find fully developed houses in straight streets, which we have excavated and which show a remarkably wide expansion of the town. The Hammurabi period, the 3rd millennium, is the oldest so far attained by our excavation. Of the prehistoric existence of Babylon we only find the evidence of flints and other stone implements, which owing to the continuous occupation of this site and the frequent disturbance of the soil, have been raised to the levels accessible to us.

We will once more return to the Southern Citadel and examine the Eastern Court. It is paved with Nebuchadnezzar's bricks, which became chipped and damaged, and was then restored. The level was slightly raised above the old pavement, which was covered with an even wash of asphalt, and on the piled-up material a new flooring was laid of fine tiles almost exactly 50 centimetres square, that bear Nebuchadnezzar's stamps on one edge. The vertical joints are filled with gypsum-mortar and no asphalt is used. Thus the pavement could be sprinkled and kept pleasantly moist, for the burnt tiles absorb the moisture readily while the underlying wash of asphalt prevented its penetrating to the foundations.

Whether the walls of the court were left uncovered, or whether they had a coat of plaster, we do not know. We know that the gateways at any rate were decorated with the coloured enamelled bricks with lions, which are found in

all the courts. The inner chambers were covered with a
fine plaster of pure gypsum laid on over a thicker coating
of gypsum. In the chamber of the eastern gateway there
is still a piece of this remaining, where the ancient wall is
protected by the accumulated earth of the raised level of
the floor.

In the court we found the base of a column (Fig. 58)
and a capital of fine white limestone. The base has the
same bowl-shaped form and the circular leaf ornament,

FIG. 58.—Base of column, Southern Citadel.

with a contour of fillets, as the base of Kalach (Nimrud).
The capital is severely damaged, but the circular drum can
still be recognised, as well as two projecting masses which
appear to be the remains of two bulls' heads, similar to
those on the capitals of Persepolis. The fragments lay on
a pile of rubbish 1 metre high, and must therefore have
been removed here after the palace was destroyed. It is
possible that the base belonged to the round circular
pedestal in front of the Ishtar Gate near the north-west
bastion. In the court itself there is no place whatever for
a column. It is in the vaulted building (see p. 99) alone
that we can imagine columns to have been used.

THE CENTRAL COURT OF THE SOUTHERN CITADEL

THE central court (M on Fig. 46) is entered by a doorway, similar to the eastern gate. Here, however, both the adjoining rooms have a side-chamber connected with them by a wide opening without any door, and with the large adjoining houses by a door. Here we see clearly the idea of a government bureau. These gateway chambers I am disposed to regard as courts of justice, where the judge occupied the side-chambers, which could only be reached from the house, while the litigants made use of the gateway chambers, which could be reached both from the courts and from the gateways. In the Old Testament the gateways are represented as places for administering justice. We have no proof, however, of a similar use of our gateway chambers.

Here, again, the southern house is exceptionally spacious, with its two courts (21 and 22) and a large hall opening on the central court. It must certainly have belonged to the highest state officials. Behind the great hall there are three chambers, much like courts, which with their respective side-chambers may have served for the administration of public business. From here, as well as from the adjoining house, which also comprised a number of rooms round 23, there was direct communication, only interrupted by many doors, with the royal private offices on the western side.

On the north was a house with two courts (13 and 14) and two business offices opening on to the central court, and six one-court houses (15, 16, 17, 18, 19, 20). Unfortunately we do not know the purpose of the long large chamber near court 13. In the adjoining office there is a walled well, an unusual feature in a house.

The paving of the court is similar to that already

described, even to the repaving by Nabonidus, who
covered the older flooring with his stamped paving blocks
50 centimetres broad.

XIV

THE VAULTED BUILDING

FROM the north-east corner of the central court a wide
passage leads to a building in the north-east corner of the
Southern Citadel, which from every point of view occupies
an exceptional place among the buildings of the Citadel and
even of the whole city—one might almost say of the entire
country.

Fourteen cells, similar in size and shape, balance each
other on the two sides of a central passage, and are
surrounded by a strong wall. Round this slightly irregular
quadrangle runs a narrow corridor, of which the far side to
the north and east is in large measure formed of the outer
wall of the Citadel, while other ranges of similar cells abut
on it to the west and south. In one of these western cells
there is a well which differs from all other wells known
either in Babylon or elsewhere in the ancient world. It
has three shafts placed close to each other, a square one
in the centre and oblong ones on each side, an arrangement for which I can see no other explanation than that
a mechanical hydraulic machine stood here, which worked
on the same principle as our chain pump, where buckets
attached to a chain work on a wheel placed over the
well. A whim works the wheel in endless rotation. This
contrivance, which is used to-day in this neighbourhood,
and is called a *dolab* (water bucket), would provide a
continuous flow of water. We will speak later of the
use to which we presume it to have been put.

The ruin (Fig. 59) lies completely below the level of
the palace floor, and is the only crypt found in Babylon.
It was approached from the upper passage by steps of

FIG. 59.—The Vaulted Building, from the south-west.

crude brick faced with burnt brick that led into one of the southern chambers.

All the chambers were vaulted with circular arches (Fig. 60). The arches consist of numerous ring courses, separated from each other by level courses (Fig. 61), exactly as in the eastern door of the Citadel.

We must here observe the difference that exists between arches, underground vaulting, and outstanding vaulting. The wall in which the arch is placed provides

FIG. 60.—Arches of the Vaulted Building.

it with the necessary abutments; there are no difficulties to encounter in its construction, and we meet with it in the earliest times, at Nippur and Fara as early as the invention of writing. In Fara there is an underground canal which consists of actual arches placed close together; in Babylon and Assur there are underground vaults which certainly date back to the year 1000. Such vaultings are easily constructed, for the earth in which they are buried affords the necessary abutments. But the case is very different when the vaulting has to be carried from one free standing wall to another. Then the building has to be so constructed that the thrust of the vaulting is counter-balanced by the walls themselves. This distinct advance appears to have been first attempted, or at any rate planned, in Mesopotamia by Nebuchadnezzar. Certainly, no house vaulting older than ours on the Southern Citadel has been found in Mesopotamia, roofing as it does a huge connected complex of chambers. The vaultings asserted by Place to be over the chambers at Khorsabad are, without exception, absolute inventions. Sargon was only acquainted with the arch in the wall, which, as we have already seen, is not a noteworthy achievement, and with the sloping courses employed in forming the arched roofing of a canal. Those Assyrian - Babylonian palaces were entirely roofed with wooden beams, like the cedars of Lebanon of our

FIG. 61.—Abutments of arches of the Vaulted Building.

Southern Citadel. It is possible that the throne-room of the principal court was vaulted, but that is not certain. The vaulted building shows clear signs of tentative and inexperienced work in the arrangement of the vaulting. It consists merely of simple barrel-vaults, and there is, of course, no cross vaulting, cupola, or any arrangement of the kind. The thrust of the central chambers is on the north against the strong Citadel wall, and on the south against the outer row of chambers vaulted in the other direction (Fig. 62).

Further observation of the ground-plan shows that the central chambers with the same span as the outside row have thicker walls. The only explanation for this must be that the former were more heavily weighted than the latter, a supposition which is corroborated by the expansion joints that surround them, by which the vaulting itself is disconnected from the wall surrounding it on all four sides. Owing to this the whole of the 14 barrel-vaultings could move as freely upwards or downwards within the enclosing quadrangle as the joint of a telescope. In this respect the vaulted building is unique among the buildings of Babylon, and in another respect also it is exceptional. Stone was used in the building, as is proved by the numerous fragments, shapeless though they now are, that are found in the ruins. In excavating this makes a far deeper impression than the mere report can do.

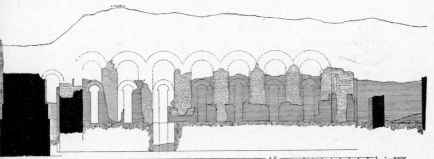

FIG. 62.—Section through the Vaulted Building.

There are only two places where hewn stone occurs in any large quantity—in the Vaulted Building and on the north wall of the Kasr, and it is remarkable that in all the literature referring to Babylon, including the cuneiform inscriptions, stone is only mentioned as used in two places, in the north wall of the Kasr and in the hanging gardens. The Street and the Euphrates bridge, where stone was also used, do not come under consideration here. Add to this, that the ruins themselves, as well as the written evidence, only speak of one single building that differed from the others to a striking extent, the vaulted building of the Kasr and the κρεμαστὸς κῆπος ; and therefore I consider them to be identical.

That the identification when studied in detail bristles with difficulties, will surprise no one who has more than once had to bring ancient statements of facts into accord-

ance with discoveries of the present day. We can always
rejoice when they agree in the main points. For the
convenience of readers I will here give extracts from
the ancient writers who describe the hanging gardens.

1. Berosus in Josephus, *Antiq. Jud.* x. 11 : Ναβουχο-
δονόσορος . . . τειχίσας ἀξιολόγως τὴν πόλιν καὶ τοὺς πυλῶνας
κοσμήσας ἱεροπρεπῶς προσκατεσκεύασε τοῖς πατρικοῖς βασιλείοις
ἕτερα βασίλεια ἐχόμενα αὐτῶν· ὧν τὸ μὲν ἀνάστημα καὶ τὴν
λοιπὴν πολυτέλειαν περισσὸν ἴσως ἂν εἴη λέγειν, πλὴν ὡς ὄντα
μεγάλα καὶ ὑπερήφανα συνετελέσθη ἡμέραις πεντεκαίδεκα. Ἐν δὲ
τοῖς βασιλείοις τούτοις ἀναλήμματα λίθινα ἀνοικοδομήσας καὶ τὴν
ὄψιν ἀποδοὺς ὁμοιοτάτην τοῖς ὄρεσι καταφυτεύσας δένδρεσι παντοδαποῖς ἐξειργάσατο, καὶ κατεσκεύασε τὸν καλούμενον κρεμαστὸν
παράδεισον, διὰ τὸ τὴν γυναῖκα αὐτοῦ ἐπιθυμεῖν τῆς οἰκείας
διαθέσεως, ὡς τεθραμμένην ἐν τοῖς κατὰ Μηδίαν τόποις.

2. Ktesias in Diodorus, ii. 10 : Ὑπῆρχε δὲ καὶ ὁ
κρεμαστὸς καλούμενος κῆπος παρὰ τὴν ἀκρόπολιν, οὐ Σεμιράμιδος
ἀλλά τινος ὕστερον Σύρου βασιλέως κατασκευάσαντος χάριν
γυναικὸς παλλακῆς· ταύτην γάρ φασιν οὖσαν τὸ γένος Περσίδα
καὶ τοὺς ἐν τοῖς ὄρεσι λειμῶνας ἐπιζητοῦσαν ἀξιῶσαι τὸν
βασιλέα μιμήσασθαι διὰ τῆς τοῦ φυτουργείου φιλοτεχνίας τὴν τῆς
Περσίδος χώρας ἰδιότητα. (2) Ἔστι δ᾽ ὁ παράδεισος τὴν μὲν
πλευρὰν ἑκάστην παρεκτείνων εἰς τέτταρα πλέθρα τὴν δὲ πρόσβασιν ὀρεινὴν καὶ τὰς οἰκοδομίας ἄλλας ἐξ ἄλλων ἔχων, ὥστε τὴν
πρόσοψιν εἶναι θεατροειδῆ. (3) Ὑπὸ δὲ ταῖς κατεσκευασμέναις
ἀναβάσεσιν ᾠκοδόμηντο σύριγγες, ἅπαν μὲν ὑποδεχόμεναι τὸ
τοῦ φυτουργείου βάρος, ἀλλήλων δὲ ἐκ τοῦ κατ᾽ ὀλίγον ἀεὶ
μικρὸν ὑπερέχουσαι κατὰ τὴν πρόσβασιν· ἡ δ᾽ ἀνωτάτη σύριγξ
οὖσα πεντήκοντα πηχῶν τὸ ὕψος εἶχεν ἐφ᾽ αὑτῇ τοῦ παραδείσου
τὴν ἀνωτάτην ἐπιφάνειαν συνεξισουμένην τῷ περιβόλῳ τῶν
ἐπάλξεων. (4) Ἔπειθ᾽ οἱ μὲν τοῖχοι πολυτελῶς κατεσκευασμένοι
τὸ πάχος εἶχον ποδῶν εἴκοσι δύο, τῶν δ᾽ ἐξόδων ἑκάστη τὸ
πλάτος δέκα · τὰς δ᾽ ὀροφὰς κατεστέγαζον λίθιναι δοκοί, τὸ
μὲν μῆκος σὺν ταῖς ἐπιβολαῖς ἔχουσαι ποδῶν ἑκκαίδεκα, τὸ δὲ
πλάτος τεττάρων. (5) Τὸ δ᾽ ἐπὶ ταῖς δοκοῖς ὀρόφημα πρῶτον
μὲν εἶχεν ὑπεστρωμένον κάλαμον μετὰ πολλῆς ἀσφάλτου, μετὰ
δὲ ταῦτα πλίνθον ὀπτὴν διπλῆν ἐν γύψῳ δεδεμένην, τρίτην
δ᾽ ἐπιβολὴν ἐπεδέχετο μολιβᾶς στέγας πρὸς τὸ μὴ διικνεῖσθαι
κατὰ βάθος τὴν ἐκ τοῦ χώματος νοτίδα. Ἐπὶ δὲ τούτοις

ἐσεσώρευτο γῆς ἱκανὸν βάθος, ἀρκοῦν ταῖς τῶν μεγίστων δένδρων ῥίζαις· τὸ δ᾽ ἔδαφος ἐξωμαλισμένον πλῆρες ἦν παντοδαπῶν δένδρων τῶν δυναμένων κατά τε τὸ μέγεθος καὶ τὴν ἄλλην χάριν τοὺς θεωμένους ψυχαγωγῆσαι. (6) Αἱ δὲ σύριγγες τὰ φῶτα δεχόμεναι ταῖς δι᾽ ἀλλήλων ὑπεροχαῖς πολλὰς καὶ παντο-δαπὰς εἶχον διαίτας βασιλικάς· μία δ᾽ ἦν ἐκ τῆς ἀνωτάτης ἐπιφανείας διατομὰς ἔχουσα καὶ πρὸς τὰς ἐπαντλήσεις τῶν ὑδάτων, ὄργανα δ᾽ ὧν ἀνεσπᾶτο πλῆθος ὕδατος ἐκ τοῦ ποταμοῦ, μηδενὸς τῶν ἔξωθεν τὸ γινόμενον συνιδεῖν δυναμένου. Οὗτος μὲν οὖν ὁ παράδεισος, ὡς προεῖπον, ὕστερον κατεσκευάσθη.

3. Strabo xvi. 1, 5 : διόπερ τῶν ἑπτὰ θεαμάτων λέγεται καὶ τοῦτο (*i.e.* the walls of Babylon) καὶ ὁ κρεμαστὸς κῆπος, ἔχων ἐν τετραγώνῳ σχήματι ἑκάστην πλευρὰν τεττάρων πλέθρων· συνέχεται δὲ ψαλιδώμασι καμαρωτοῖς, ἐπὶ πεττῶν ἱδρυμένοις κυβοειδῶν ἄλλοις ἐπ᾽ ἄλλοις· οἱ δὲ πεττοὶ κοῖλοι πλήρεις γῆς, ὥστε δέξασθαι φυτὰ δένδρων τῶν μεγίστων, ἐξ ὀπτῆς πλίνθου καὶ ἀσφάλτου κατεσκευασμένοι καὶ αὐτοὶ καὶ οἱ ψαλίδες καὶ τὰ καμαρώματα. ἡ δ᾽ ἀνωτάτη στέγη προσβάσεις κλιμακωτὰς ἔχει, παρακειμένους δ᾽ αὐταῖς καὶ κοχλίας, δι᾽ ὧν τὸ ὕδωρ ἀνῆγον εἰς τὸν κῆπον ἀπὸ τοῦ Εὐφράτου συνεχῶς οἱ πρὸς τοῦτο τεταγμένοι. ὁ γὰρ ποταμὸς διὰ μέσης ῥεῖ τῆς πόλεως σταδιαῖος τὸ πλάτος· ἐπὶ δὲ τῷ ποταμῷ ὁ κῆπος.

4. Curtius Rufus, *Hist. Alex.* Vɪ : Super arcem, vulgatum Graecorum fabulis miraculum, pensiles horti sunt, summam murorum altitudinem aequantes multarum-que arborum umbra et proceritate amoeni. Saxo pilae, quae totum opus sustinent, instructae sunt, super pilas lapide quadrato solum stratum est patiens terrae, quam altam iniciunt, et humoris, quo rigant terras : adeoque validas arbores sustinet moles ut stipites earum VIII cubitorum spatium crassitudine aequent, in L pedum altitudinem emineant frugiferaeque sint, ut si terra sua alerentur. Et cum vetustas non opera solum manu facta, sed etiam ipsam naturam paulatim exedendo perimat, haec moles, quae tot arborum radicibus premitur tantique nemoris pondere onerata est, inviolata durat, quippe XX [pedes] lati parietes sustinent, XI pedum intervallo distantes, ut procul visentibus silvae montibus suis inminere videantur. Syriae regem Babylone regnantem hoc opus esse molitum memoriae proditum est, amore

H

conjugis victum, quae desiderio nemorum silvarumque in
campestribus locis virum conpulit amoenitatem naturae
genere hujus operis imitari.

It would lead us too far afield were I to attempt here
to emphasise all the points that weigh for or against my
contention; I may safely leave the decision to time.
According to Berosus, the hanging gardens must have
been on the Kasr, as he places them in a formal and
detailed manner in the area of the buildings by which
Nebuchadnezzar enlarged the palace of Nabopolassar.
The Principal Citadel may also be taken into consideration in this connection, and the question can only be
settled by excavation. A difficulty that is apparently
serious lies in the length of the side of the quadrangle,
which is given by Strabo and Diodorus as 4 plethra (about
120 metres). On examining the central building we find
this is exactly four times its actual measurement, and any
one who holds fast by these figures will naturally reject
my hypothesis. I have been too often misled by ancient
statements of measurements to treat this information as
conclusive, and as in the case of Herodotus' statements
with reference to the town walls, I consider it possible
that the length and breadth have been confused with the
circumference. The central building rested on the 16
walls that supported the vaults, and on the 4 walls surrounding them, 20 in all. Thus a non-philologist might readily
conclude that the text of Curtius quoted above, "Haec
moles . . . durat, quippe XX lati parietes sustinent," can
be correct without the addition of "pedes" inserted between
XX and *lati*. The 10- to 11-foot span of the vaults can be
seen to-day in the ruins in approximate accordance with
the statement of Diodorus and Curtius. I would attach
little importance to any of these details, and lay stress
only on the main facts. Our authors here speak of a
building, with characteristics completely different from all
others, and precisely similar to those of the vaulted building.
It is possible to reconstruct what has perished from their
description and from the evidence of the ruins in more
than one way.

Either the central portion towered high above the upper storey which, in any case, we must suppose to have been above the outer series of vaulted chambers, or else the vaulted roof of the central chambers directly bore the layer of earth in which the trees were planted, thus forming an inner garden court on the ground level. In the latter case the surrounding corridor wall can be regarded as having served as the foundation for the columns or pillars of which the base found in the Eastern Court (p. 89) may have formed part. A court planted with trees, connected with pillared halls, would show such a striking analogy with the festival house of Assur (*M.D.O.-G.* No. 33, Fig. 8) that one might be tempted to recognise in the vaulted building *E-sigiši* the "house of offerings for the exalted festival of Marduk, lord of the gods" (*Steinplatten* inscription, 3, l. 7), were it not that some difficulties seem for the present to forbid it. The practical result of the whole arrangement was, no doubt, to neutralise to the greatest possible extent the oppressive heat of summer.

The entire building was roofed over, and the central part corresponds with the courts of other houses except that it is ceiled. The roof is protected by an unusually deep layer of earth. The air that entered the chambers, the διαίτας βασιλικάς of Diodorus, through the leaves of the trees must have been delightfully cooled by the continuous watering of the vegetation. Possibly the palace officials did a great part of their business in these cool chambers during the heat of summer. At the present time, in the Turkish government offices, the window is hung with a frame composed of two pieces of wide-meshed trellis work of palm leaves between which a layer of *agul* is fixed. Agul is a prickly desert plant with a great power of retaining water. This is continually sprinkled, and as the wind blows through it, cools the room to a very remarkable degree, at the same time darkening it, but this is not objected to by the clerks, as especially in summer the people are contented with very little light.

In any case the building was intended to be much in use, for two doors in the south wall lead to it, and the passage from the central court is unusually wide. The crypt below shared fully in the advantage of security from heat. The remains of the vaulted portions show that at all times it must have been very dark, and can therefore hardly have been used except as a storehouse for all manner of goods, a use for which the numerous uniform chambers are well adapted. The large number of tablets found in the stairway chamber on the south side also point to this use, as the inscriptions on them relate to grain.

The protection of the roof from the permeation of moisture, as described by Greek and Roman authors, agrees well with what we know of the practice of the ancient architects. A layer of reeds and asphalt was placed over a strong roofing of hewn stone, part of which has been found in the ruins, and above this rested two courses of bricks laid in mortar. A lead covering again separated these from the deep layer of earth placed on the top.

These hanging gardens have aroused the wonder of the world for centuries and indeed for millenniums. Their legendary connection with the name of Semiramis has largely contributed to this, although it was directly denied by Diodorus. Also the expression "hanging" has no doubt heightened their fame, although the terms κρεμαστός and *pensilis* conveyed no such marvellous ideas to ancient scholars as they do to us. *Pensilia* are the balconies of the Romans, and were nothing out of the common for them. The reason why the hanging gardens were ranked among the seven wonders of the world was that they were laid out on the roof of an occupied building.

XV

THE PRINCIPAL COURT (H)

The gate leading to the Principal Court (Fig. 63) is considerably larger than the two previous ones; it is more spacious and the walls are stronger, and therefore must have been carried higher. Here also we find the

0   50   100 Meter

FIG. 63.—The central part of the Southern Citadel.

two side-chambers.   In the northern one there are the
foundations of an ascending stairway, which led to an upper
storey, or to the roof.   It is one of the very few examples
of its kind to be found in Babylon, and with the outside
steps in the canal wall on the south-east of the Kasr, at the
well, and on the transverse wall of the Ishtar Gate, the
ascent to the north-eastern bastion of the Kasr affords
evidence of the way in which these stairways were constructed.   The long narrow passages in the temples may
quite possibly have contained the staircases.   In private
houses we never find similar passages, and yet we can feel
certain that during the long summer heat the people must
have had some means of access to the roof, that exceedingly delightful and important part of the house.   We can
therefore only imagine that in private houses they used
some wooden contrivance, made in the simplest fashion
(see Fig. 238).   The villagers of to-day often use a palm
tree with steps roughly cut in it, which they lean against
the wall.   This total absence of staircases bears on the
question of whether or not the Babylonian house consisted
of many storeys.   Herodotus (i. 180) speaks of houses of
three or four storeys.   Such do not now exist, and the mud
walls of the private houses in the town are scarcely strong
enough to support even one upper storey.   The burnt-
brick walls of the houses in the Southern Citadel, or at any
rate many of them, could undoubtedly have carried several
storeys.   We cannot at present decide the question, but
we shall not be far wrong if we assume that the ordinary
house was on one floor.   Certain dwellings, on the contrary,
may have had upper storeys, in which case wooden steps
may have formed the means of communication.

The Principal Court occupies an imposing site 55
metres broad by 60 metres long.   Like the others, it was
paved with tiles, and towards the close of the Sassanide
period it was used for burials.   Endless shallow coffins
either of trough or slipper shape, made of terra-cotta, and
frequently in blue glaze, were deposited in the soil as low
as the earliest floor-level, and frequently one above another.
The brick robbers have left them displaced and smashed
to pieces.

Exactly in the centre is a somewhat small basin for water. It has been cut through the brick pavement, and may therefore date back only to the Persian period and not to Nebuchadnezzar. An outflow channel led the water into the drain of the western passage; there are no signs of an inflow. The sides are constructed of upright bricks, and the inside is washed over first with asphalt and then with gypsum mortar. Gypsum decomposes in water, but only very slowly. When our Expedition House was built at Assur, the necessary reservoirs for water were made with gypsum mortar, and the gypsum wash on the walls, the roof, and balustrades of our house at Babylon has already lasted perfectly for twelve years. The basin corresponds with the indispensable "Hudeh" of modern Persian houses, in which everything employed for eating and drinking, and much besides, is washed.

To the north lies a house of two courts (28 and 29) and one of four courts (30, 31, 32, and 33); the bureau that adjoins the first is connected with it by a door, while the two bureaus in front of the second house are only accessible from the court. In the north-east corner two parallel passages lead northwards. In one are the entrances to 28 and 29, in the other are those to the eastern houses. These open separately on to the passage, but the three northern houses are also connected with each other by doors, and it thus appears that they could be used if necessary either as separate dwellings or as one large one. This passage, like the one yet farther to the east, led to a door in the Citadel wall. In order to separate the two entrances to the Principal Court as completely as possible, the dividing wall is reinforced by an additional block that projects into the court.

To the south lies the largest chamber of the Citadel, the throne-room of the Babylonian kings. It is so clearly marked out for this purpose that no reasonable doubt can be felt as to its having been used as their principal audience chamber. If any one should desire to localise the scene of Belshazzar's eventful banquet, he can surely place it with complete accuracy in this immense room. It is 17 metres broad and 52 metres long. The walls on the longest side are 6 metres thick, considerably in excess of those at the ends, and lead us to suppose that they supported a barrel-vaulting, of which, however, there is no proof. A great central door and two equally important side doors open upon the court. Immediately opposite the main door in the back wall there is a doubly recessed niche in which doubtless the throne stood, so that the king could be visible to those who stood in the court, an arrangement similar to that of the Ninmach temple, where the temple statue could be clearly seen from the court. The pavement does not con-sist in the usual manner of a single layer of brick, but of at least six, which were laid in asphalt and thus formed a homogeneous solid platform which rested on a projecting ledge built out from the walls. As we have already seen from the east gate, the walls of these chambers were washed over with white gypsum.

The façade of the court was very strikingly decorated with richly ornamented enamelled tiles (*M.D.O.-G.* No. 13). On a dark blue ground are yellow columns with bright blue capitals, placed near together and connected by a series of palmettos. The capitals with the bold curves of their double volutes remind us of the forms long known to us in Cyprus (Fig. 64). Above was a frieze of white double palmettos, bordered below by a band of squares, alternately yellow, black, and white. The various colours of the decora-tion were effectively heightened on the dark background by means of white borders. This fantastic representation of a pillared building, such as the king and his followers would naturally have seen in their military expeditions, must have appeared strangely foreign to the Babylonian countryman, who was unaccustomed to either capitals or entablatures.

The technique is similar to that of the flat enamels of the Ishtar Gate; each colour is outlined in black, and the position marks are also employed here in the same manner. They can be better studied here than elsewhere, for the greater number of the bricks were found in their original connection. After the destruction of the wall by brick robbers the outer coating fell towards the north, and we could take them up, one piece after another, as though no accident had befallen them. The system of signs can be

FIG. 64.—DECORATION OF THE THRONE ROOM.

seen best on the capitals (Fig. 65). Here the markings consist of numerals combined with dots. They are marked on the upper edge of the bricks with a poor, somewhat blackened, glaze. The signs that distinguish the courses are in the centre, those for the lateral arrangement are close to the vertical joints. Each of the latter signs is a

FIG. 65.—Position marks on the enamelled bricks.

counterpart of the sign near the vertical joint of the brick adjoining it. Of the central signs that mark the courses the top course of the upper row of volutes has one stroke, the second has two, and so on up to seven. The seven courses of the lower row of volutes are numbered in the same way, but the groups of strokes are preceded by a dot to distinguish them from those of the upper series. For the sequence of the bricks one of the intermediate ornaments forms a single unit with the capital adjoining it on the right. All the bricks that belong to the same unit bear the same number of strokes. The counting runs from left to right. The numerals are crossed by a transverse stroke, which, in order to mark the direction of the signs, has a dot attached to it. This direction line is parallel to the vertical joint on the central ornament, and parallel with the front of the brick on the volutes. It is quite probable that the separate groups were first provisionally built together, at any rate for the purpose of drawing the design, which is still visible in red colour under the enamel, so as to secure that boldness and freedom of outline which delights us with its beauty at the present time. But when once the process of enamelling began—the transportation of the bricks, the drying, the burning, and all the unavoidable processes that had to be carried through before the bricks could be placed in the wall —it would be impossible to keep them apart. The marks would then afford the only means of placing them correctly on the walls, and rendering it easy to deliver them in groups to the respective masons.

In order to close the joints completely the bricks are slightly wedge-shaped. The joints between the courses are laid in mud over asphalt, which, as we observe in other careful building, does not extend to the front of the building but stops at a distance of half a brick, thus avoiding any blotching of the face of the wall.

In addition to the black outline and the dark blue ground, the colours employed are white, light blue, yellow, and red. The red now has everywhere the appearance of green, but where this colour is thickened, as for instance where drops have trickled down, a core of brilliant red is found coated with green, which must be the result of a superficial change of colour that has occurred during the course of ages. We have also some large pieces of enamel from ancient breakages in which we can observe this same fact. The green coating extends to a depth of 2 to 3 millimetres, which in the ordinary enamel on the brick would entirely supersede the original red colouring. This is an important point, because the manufacture of opaque red enamel has been attended with considerable difficulty even in recent times, while transparent red glaze is made with ease at the present time. Thus in forming a judgment on the sense of colour of the ancient Babylonian it must not be forgotten that this fine red was included in their scheme. We can well imagine a red-haired, but not a green-haired lion (see above, p. 28).

Beside the decoration already described we find other designs which belonged to a floral frieze. This was undoubtedly placed on the façade of the throne-room, but nothing definite has so far been found to show its exact position. It must always be remembered that an exhaustive study of these bricks and of other similar objects found in Babylon requires far more space than our Expedition House can afford; the things must be spread out, and that cannot be done here. We have always to be careful to pack away the finds as quickly as possible, and that renders them inaccessible for any further comparison, however desirable it may be. The conditions of our work are by no means easy, and in dealing with small objects such as terra-cottas, cylinder seals, implements, ceramics and the like, I have experienced serious and unavoidable difficulties.

As the purpose of the principal hall is unusual, so also the chambers behind differ considerably from the usual arrangement, but they show some similarity to the inner chambers near the great hall of the central court. They are three lofty chambers or courts each provided with a side-chamber on the south side, which can also be entered from the open passage behind the wall of the Citadel. The side courts are connected with the throne-room by an inter-mediate chamber, and with the side corridors by another apartment, while they communicate with each other through the central court 35. In each of the two chambers that abut on the rear wall of the throne-room there is a circular walled well, and each of these chambers is completely walled in from the floor down to water-level with broken brick, asphalt, and mud. The wells in each case lie in the south-west corner of the chamber. The object of this solid walling-off of the wells must have been to secure absolutely pure water for the use of the royal household. The river water would naturally be well filtered by the earth through which it passed before reaching the wells. A peculiarity of this country at the present time is the fine distinction made between the various kinds of drinking water, as a natural result of the climate. The people distinguish the various kinds of water, such as sweet, salt, flat or brackish, much as we distinguish our alcoholic drinks, and as we speak of light or heavy beer, so the Oriental speaks of light or heavy water. The water of the Euphrates is famed, and is considered lighter than the water of the Tigris. One of the earlier governors of Bagdad drank Euphrates water exclusively, and had it sent daily from Musseyib. Another travelled from Bagdad to Constantinople with a large supply of Euphrates water stored in leather bottles, just as a celebrated modern traveller drank nothing but champagne during a long journey to Haïl in Central Arabia. Nowadays the water in most of the wells on the town site of Babylon, as in many other ruined sites, is brackish or salt and not good. I still do not understand fully why this should be the case; it certainly was not so in early times, otherwise it would be difficult to explain the number of wells found in all the ruins, where the soil is now so salt that the Arabs in early summer collect the upper crust of earth and from it obtain salt for cooking and saltpetre for gunpowder. As a result of this the ruins are extremely bare of vegetation, and stand out grey and barren in contrast with the surrounding plain, which is green, at any rate during the spring-tide, when there is some slight rainfall.

At a later period, apparently during Persian times, two pillars formed of two roughly hewn palm stems were set up in court 36 to support a roof constructed either half way or completely over the court. They stood on the brick pavement, which here as in the adjoining chambers is composed of tiles measuring 40 × 41 centimetres. The lower end of the pillars was encased in a socket of brickwork covered with plaster (Fig. 66). The interior of this base still retains the impressions of the palm stems, the upper portion of which was also plastered. Strabo describes this kind of pillar (xvi. 1, 5): "διὰ δὲ τὴν τῆς ὕλης σπάνιν ἐκ φοινικίνων ξύλων αἱ οἰκοδομαὶ συντελοῦνται καὶ δοκοῖς καὶ στύλοις· περὶ δὲ τοὺς στύλους στρέφοντες ἐκ τῆς καλάμης σχοινία περιτιθέασιν, εἶτ᾽ ἐπαλείφοντες χρώμασι καταγράφουσι, τὰς δὲ θύρας ἀσφάλτῳ." Nothing now remains of the reed rope that was twisted round the palm stems, but it is fairly certain that the stems were plastered over.

The rear wall of the group of chambers behind the throne-room is toothed in a peculiar fashion. Since the wall joins the building at an oblique angle the series of rooms must either have been oblique, or, if the architects insisted on making them rectangular, the inner face of the

FIG. 66.—Bases of late columns in court 36, Southern Citadel.

wall could not have been parallel with the outer face. The latter could only have been effected by inserting wedge-shaped portions in the single brick courses, which would have imperilled the cohesion of the bricks and would have been very clumsy workmanship. If, on the contrary, the wall were built in retreating steps, the inner chambers could be rectangular and the rows of bricks laid straight, thus ensuring good bonding of the wall. This very character-istic feature of the outside of the building completely dominated the whole of the secular Babylonian architecture of the later period (cf. Fig. 156). All the streets of the town excavated by us in Merkes show these walls faced with remarkable one-sided projections, a method which was still adhered to in the later Graeco-Parthian period, when so much building was done with broken brick, although it was not then justified by technical considerations. It must not, therefore, be regarded as a mere requirement of the workmen, but as a model arising from the technique of an early art, unusual but very characteristic.

In the houses 28, 29, 30, a large chamber is interposed between the court and the usual principal room lying to the south of it. This additional chamber is a hall that opens with a wide arch on to the court. This must have been a very pleasant room in summer, for the entrance lies all day in shadow. These halls opening with wide arches into the court played a prominent part in Parthian and Sassanide times in the ground plans of Ktesiphon, Hatra, Assur and other towns of that period, especially in the palaces; and as *liwan* they now play an important part in modern oriental architecture. Visitors to Mossul, Aleppo, and many other cities have a vivid recollection of them.

Here in Babylon the idea shows itself tentatively and timidly. The houses 13, 14, and 16 have similar rooms. In 25, 26, 27, the entrance hall opens in *liwan* fashion on to the court. We can here observe the uncertainty that attends a new idea, which only after the course of centuries, and not without reiterated fertilisation from the west, has at last emerged into glorious fruition.

In the north-west corner of the Principal Court a broad passage guarded by a series of three arched doorways leads to a gate in the city wall. Here the eastern portion of the Citadel wall, with its closely set towers, adjoins the western portion, of which only the foundations remain which show no traces of towers. In the passage is a large drain, roofed over with corbelled brick courses, which carried off the surface water from the Principal Court through the door in the wall past the palace and then farther west to the Euphrates. The same drain also branched off to the south, down through the southern wall of the Citadel, where, as the wall was already in existence, an outlet was cut for it. Thus it had a fall to the north and another to the south.

The entire west front of the Principal Court was

occupied by the façade of the earliest part of the palace, which extended from north to south, the building named by us the Nabopolassar Palace. This palace on its older

Fig. 67.—Ramps between the Nebuchadnezzar and Nabopolassar Palaces.

and lower level was still in use when the newer eastern portion on its higher level was completed. In order, however, not to render communication between the two buildings unnecessarily difficult, the following method was adopted: the Principal Court was shut off on the west by a mud wall, which left an intermediate space between it and the old palace, of the same breadth as the northern passage, and a second one lying at the same level as the old palace. A wide doorway, which later was narrowed, led through the mud wall. Ramps led up to the higher levels (Fig. 67). At first they were constructed in the shape of shallow funnels which led upwards from the doorways in all directions. With the first relaying of the pavement, however, they were ingeniously enclosed on both sides with walls of mud brick. Finally, the old palace itself was raised to the same level as the later one, the ramps were filled up, and overlaid with fine large tiles bearing Nebuchadnezzar's stamp on the side. As a consequence of this the two ramps with their ancient pavement of roughened limestone flags are in a state of perfect preservation. The mud wall still remained and was only demolished on a further raising of the pavement. This last pavement, which again had the usual bricks with Nebuchadnezzar's stamps, is almost destroyed owing to its later use as a burial-place.

Such is the palace which Nebuchadnezzar in the Grotefend cylinder (*K.B.* iii. 2, p. 39, col. 3 l. 27) specially designates as a palace intended both for government and for administration, in these words: " In those days I built the palace, the seat of my kingdom, the bond of the vast assemblage of all mankind, the dwelling-place of joy and gladness, where I . . . the gifts, in Babylon anew, laid its foundations on Earth's wide breast with bitumen and bricks, mighty trunks of cedars I brought from Lebanon, the bright forest, for its roofing, I caused it to be surrounded with a mighty wall of bitumen and brick, the royal command, the lordly injunction I caused to go forth from it " (trans. by Winckler and Delitzsch).

XVI

THE PALACE OF NABOPOLASSAR

So far we have traced the eastern, official portion of the palace, which is quite distinct from the private part on the western side of the Principal Court. Here the lowest part represents the earliest palace of those we can recognise on the Kasr. We have named this the palace of Nabopolassar, without, however, having found written authority for it on the site itself. Our grounds for the hypothesis are as follows. In the great *Steinplatten* inscription, 7, 34, Nebuchadnezzar says: "In Babil, my favourite city, that I love, was the palace, the house the marvel of mankind, the centre of the land, the shining residence, the dwelling of Majesty, upon the Babil place in Babil, from Imgur-bel to the eastern canal Libil-ḫigalla, from the bank of the Euphrates to Aiburšabû, which Nabopolassar, King of Babylon, my father, my begetter, built of crude bricks and dwelt in it—in consequence of high waters its foundations had become weak, and owing to the filling up of the street of Babil the gateways of that palace had become too low. I tore down its walls of dried brick, and laid its corner-stone bare and reached the depth of the waters. Facing the water I laid its foundation firmly, and raised it mountain high with bitumen and burnt brick. Mighty cedars I caused to be laid down at length for its roofing. Door leaves of cedar overlaid with copper, thresholds and sockets of bronze I placed in its doorways. Silver and gold and precious stones, all that can be imagined of costliness, splendour, wealth, riches, all that was highly esteemed I heaped up within it, I stored up immense abundance of royal treasure within it" (trans. by Delitzsch). Nebuchadnezzar undoubtedly speaks here of the whole Southern Citadel. We need not infer from this, however, that the palace of Nabopolassar was of the same extent, for the ancient kings were not too exact with regard to such statements (cf. the inscription of Neriglissar).

I

The walls of mud brick of which the ancient palace consisted can of course no longer be found, as Nebuchadnezzar
states that he destroyed them, but the foundations remain,
which he improved and strengthened, and which therefore
must have been built of burnt brick and not of crude brick.
This method adopted by Nabopolassar of building a wall
of crude brick on a foundation of burnt brick is actually
seen on the north-west corner of his Arachtu wall, and
appears also in the houses in Merkes that date from
the time of Hammurabi. It is my opinion that these
burnt brick foundations of Nabopolassar still exist on
the western part of the Southern Citadel, and if so
Nebuchadnezzar made use of them without any altera-
tion in laying out his new building.

We have dug out the ancient building to a considerable
depth, especially on the north and south sides. The bricks
are of the small size (32×32 centimetres), and·bear no
stamp. They are laid in asphalt and reeds and are crushed
and split in every direction. The wall surfaces are daubed
over with asphalt, which also covers the split and damaged
portions, and thus we have ample evidence of the handiwork of the restorer. On the north side Nebuchadnezzar
added to the foundations of the chambers a strengthening
length of rubble wall laid with asphalt and reeds, which
faced the north front for a breadth of about 10 metres.
The ancient wall rises to a height of about 7 metres
above zero (see p. 167). Above this lie the usual 33-centi-
metre bricks with Nebuchadnezzar's 4-lined stamp, also
laid in asphalt and reeds, with the border courses laid in
mud. In the lower courses of the later building a number
of tiles measuring $44 \times 44 \times 6$ centimetres are built into the
wall, which can be recognised with certainty as having been
previously used as flagstones by the fragments of gypsum
mortar that still adhere to their joints, and show that
Nebuchadnezzar very naturally took up the pavement of
Nabopolassar, and used it in part as material for the
walls. His new pavement consists of ten courses of
brick laid in asphalt alone, covered with a layer of brick
rubble, over which paving-stones measuring $38·5 \times 38·5$
are laid. Of this pavement, however, we have found little

more than a small piece, which still remains in the southern
chambers.   This later pavement was apparently higher
than the old one, but 7 metres lower than that in the great
eastern portion.   Of the final alterations that brought the

FIG. 68.—Space between the Nabopolassar Palace and Citadel wall, on the south.

whole up to one and the same level there are only traces,
for instance, the building by which the principal hall adjoining the Western Court (W) was enlarged.

The ancient palace comes to an end at the squaring-
line *i* of Fig. 44.   Originally it extended farther, and the
wall that faces west was here chipped off, when the portion

farthest to the west was added. On the south, on the contrary, the ancient palace wall still stands and is distinctly escarped (Fig. 68). Here Nebuchadnezzar jointed his brickwork with a grid-like insertion of beams of poplar wood laid lengthways and crossways to strengthen it. The foundations of the adjoining chambers have also a filling of broken brick to the east and of mud brick to the west.

Of the eastern side nothing is visible except on the north. Here we see that the pillars of the doors of the three arches of the broad passage-way do not exist below in the ancient building, as was only to be expected, as the eastern building was not yet in existence at that time. Near the corner is a groove forming an expansion joint for the wall that originally joined it at this place, the fortification wall of Nabopolassar, which must have united here with the line of the palace wall. Nebuchadnezzar, however, substituted for it a brick wall of his own, which he pushed farther to the north.

The north front is in good preservation at this point and is very remarkable (Fig. 69). It is treated in the stepped or toothed fashion that we have already met with. As the deviation from the line of the walls of the building is very considerable, the steps are short, and on the façade, which is 80 metres long, there are 80 of these vertical steps, which give a unique appearance, to be met with in no other order of architecture. The stepped wall rests on a level foundation at the height at which Nabopolassar's pavement must originally have been laid. At the same level a grid of poplar wood is inserted in the brickwork, and a beam is placed on each long side and another on the short side of each projection. This can be clearly seen in the photograph. Where the doorway leads to the passage to the court, the step is made larger in order to afford convenient space for the door.

A large part of the ground-plan is still buried under rubbish, which up to the present time has prevented our gaining a clear idea of the general arrangement. The entrance from the east consists of a three-chambered building, which differs somewhat in arrangement from the usual plan of a gateway building. The towers that are

FIG. 69.—North wall of the Nabopolassar Palace.

found elsewhere at the sides of gateways of any importance are absent here. The first room, which is unusually spacious, affords access to the double house 37 and 38. Two doors lead to the chamber near the court, and two more direct to the court. At these doors there are still the great stone sockets of the hinges. Owing to uneven setting they became much distorted, but they were already in this condition when they were washed over with gypsum mortar.

The houses of this part of the palace are remarkable for the strength of their walls and the admirable regularity with which they are laid out. Court 38 is reached by a passage-way from the Western Court and also by the wide passage from the Principal Court, the latter through a hall which, as in the case of 25, 26, and 27, opens with three doors on to court 38. Between the doors, pillars project from the walls, and correspond with others on the opposite side. They must have served as piers to support arches for the ceiling, although it is difficult to make out clearly what was the object of this structure. In this house, as in the neighbouring one and in the house farther east, the irregularity of the floor space has been utilised to form an alcove or niche, and these rooms may safely be regarded as sleeping chambers. In one of the doorways we found a statuette of Papsukal, such as we have elsewhere found only in the temples (Fig. 70).

At the north-west corner, where, as we have already stated, the palace is broken off, although it did not end there originally, a hole is cut from the north low down into the massive brickwork, which contained a pottery coffin of very unusual size. After it had been inserted the hole was once more bricked up with Nebuchadnezzar's bricks. As the outer fortification wall, which runs parallel and completely concealed the opening, also dates from the time of Nebuchadnezzar, it is obvious that the burial must be of his time. The dead man must have been the object of deepest reverence, and with this his funerary outfit is in entire agreement. The place had been opened and plundered before we came, but in the rubbish concealed by the immense sarcophagus we found gold beads, and also a large number of small gold plates, with a hole by which they had been sewn on to some material, forming a sumptuous decoration.   Most of them are circular, but with them are some rectangular plates somewhat larger, which bear moulded representations; a bearded man offering before the symbol of Marduk, or the gateway of a fortress

FIG. 70.—Statuette of Papsukal in Nabopolassar Palace.

with towers and battlements (see Fig. 20). When we consider that only a very small portion of the outfit has escaped the tomb robbers, we realise that the body was provided with rich gold ornaments, and arrayed in garments richly spangled with gold, and that this personage during his lifetime must have occupied a very conspicuous and important position at the court of Babylon, our thoughts turn to Nabopolassar, and we almost wonder whether he himself had not been laid within his palace wall by his son.

Of the remaining buildings on this side, we have nothing of importance to communicate owing to the unfinished state of the excavations, nor is there much to report with regard to the buildings to the south of the Western Court : only a part of the Great Hall is excavated. We recognise the additional building, with its wall pushed towards the north. It is built with the two-ridged bricks of Nebuchadnezzar, and the peculiar effect of this method of building can here be seen clearly (Fig. 71). Behind the hall we again find a series of three chambers, all apparently

FIG. 71.—Wall of two-ridged bricks in Southern Citadel.

similar to each other, such as we find behind the great halls of the Principal and Central Courts. In the chambers next court 40 are two circular walled-in wells, and in each case the foundation of the chamber that contains them is also filled in with rubble brickwork.

XVII

THE FORTIFICATION WALLS TO THE NORTH AND SOUTH OF THE PALACE OF NABOPOLASSAR.

In the fortification wall south of Nabopolassar's palace,

FIG. 72.—Door in south wall of Southern Citadel.

which has been excavated to a considerable depth, Nebuchadnezzar's bricks occur even in the lower courses, while close by on the east the bricks are unstamped. There is an opening here in the wall to form an exit for the drain which runs from the Principal Citadel through the long passage. The three arched openings (Fig. 72) are very remarkable. They resemble doorways, but they have no rabbets, such as are usually found in this kind of archway. The bricks are laid in asphalt and reeds.

FIG. 73.—South wall of the Nabopolassar Palace, from the west.

At about 7 metres above zero, near this old wall another wall begins, which is also constructed with Nebuchadnezzar's bricks. It rests on a projecting smooth foundation, and its towers do not correspond with those of the lower wall. In order to form a base for this projecting foundation the space between the palace and the old wall was filled up with brickwork (Fig. 68), divided into separate blocks, each of which overlaps its neighbour in stepped fashion. This in a sense forms the exact contrary of the expansion joint, and the builders must have calculated that in this case the unequal sinking occurred so completely and satisfactorily during the course of the building that the whole of the upper portions might safely be bonded together in one solid mass.

Outside a strengthening kisu is added, which permits of the opening of the doors, but which cuts off the outlet for the drain (Fig. 73). Where the later building is joined on, a grid of wooden beams laid at right angles to each other is inserted. The later building can be easily recognised on the whole of the southern side, but here it is especially clear.

On the north, in order to support the later fortification wall, a thick foundation has been laid immediately in front of the palace. The base of this foundation is arranged on the same principle as on the southern side, with separate projecting stepped blocks (Fig. 74). Above this foundation the wall, with its closely set projecting courses,

FIG. 74.—Foundation of the fortification wall north of the Southern Citadel.

gradually extended so close to the palace wall that it actually touched it (see Fig. 69), and farther up, where they have now perished, the two must have formed one combined wall. From this point the proper towered fortification wall, which still stretches from here eastwards, may have continued on the same line. We do not know, however, in which form it originally extended westward beyond the ancient palace, for here the foundations, as well as the palace itself, were completely destroyed to make room for the junction with the western extension.

Along the north front of the palace there is a walled-in drain which collected the water of the palace and of the top of the fortification walls, and carried it off to the west (Fig. 75). The level of the intermediate space between the

palace and the mud wall was originally very deep, but in
the course of successive alterations it was gradually raised
in about the same degree as the palace pavement.   Fig. 75

FIG. 75.—Drains between wall of Southern Citadel and the
mud wall.

shows the peculiar construction of these drains.   Above
the low side walls are placed either plain bricks or moulded
bricks of half-moon shape, set edgeways.   Larger drains,
such as that of the Principal Court or those in the
Principal Citadel, are roofed over with corbelled courses, but

in these small drains vaulting is obviously avoided. Yet smaller drains were constructed of two flat brick courses placed together at the lower edge and closed in with bricks laid flat, thus forming a triangular section, such as occurs in the north-west corner of Sachn. The top of the fortification walls is regularly drained by means of vertical gutters inserted in the towers; if the towers were built of burnt brick, these gutters are simply carried down inside the towers at a distance of one brick from the front. This kind of gutter is found in the towers on the south side of Nabopolassar's palace, and in the east part of the north wall. In walls of mud brick, however, it was of course necessary to construct the gutters of burnt brick, and thus the gutter forms a vertical shaft inserted in the mud brick building which surrounds it on three sides (see Fig. 95), while the fourth side lies flush with the outer wall. We shall meet with this remarkable construction, which often attains very considerable proportions, both in the inner and outer town walls, as well as in some of the temples.

XVIII

THE WESTERN EXTENSION

To the west of the palace of Nabopolassar there is an additional building 40 metres in breadth, the lower courses of which, judging by the stamps on the bricks, date from the time of Nebuchadnezzar, and the upper courses from that of Neriglissar. It is the last addition actually made to the Southern Citadel which concerns it alone. The later buildings are connected with the Principal Citadel, and include with it the Southern Citadel, which points to an extension of the whole towards the north and west (Fig. 76).

From the first it was intended that this building should be on the same level as the eastern portion. The foundations, however, are different. The walls stand on a broadly widened base, and all the chambers are filled in to the

FIG. 76.—Western part of the Southern Citadel.

intended pavement level with brickwork. Small deep spaces
are frequently left in this filling near the corners of the
chambers, and perhaps were used in some way in marking
out the lines of the building. Elaborate precautions are
taken to guard the west wall against damp. A high bank
was piled up against it which reached almost to the " moat
wall of Imgur-Bel," and on the north and south was
supported by low walls of brick rubble. In order to
insulate the wall it was washed over with asphalt, and
overlaid with plaited matting, on which bricks were set
edgeways. Thus the wall carries, so to speak, a course
of upright bricks in addition to the usual jointing material.
The supporting walls connect with the corners of the palace
by grooved expansion joints.

Of the arrangement of the chambers there is little to
report, as here also the excavations are not far advanced.
The northern of the two gateways is protected by a
projecting tower, which had one large doorway in front
and two small ones at the sides, an unusual arrangement,
not found elsewhere in Babylon.

On the south-west corner, in the rubbish, was found the
lower part of a large inscribed 8-sided prism.

XIX

THE PERSIAN BUILDING

THE space between the palace and the " moat wall of
Imgur-Bel " divides into two parts, of which the more
southern is filled in with a packing of broken brick in mud.
A peculiarity of this packing is that the horizontal joints
of the courses are almost as deep as the bricks themselves,
and this again indicates Persian work, so far as we have
learnt to know it in Susa. The northern portion, on the
other hand, was filled in with sand, supporting a building
which for the greater part has perished, but of which
sufficient remains still exist to enable us to assign it
unhesitatingly to the time of the Persian kings.

The foundation trenches still exist, containing some scanty remains of good brickwork, which permit us to recognise a ground-plan of the type of an apadana, as it appears in the well-known palaces of Persepolis (Fig. 77),

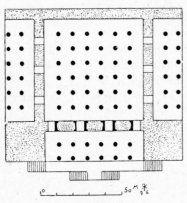

FIG. 77.—Apadana of Xerxes in Persepolis.

a pillared hall with a pillared fore-hall, flanked, in front, by two towers. It is remarkable that the distinctive character of this beautiful type of building should always have been mistaken in a most unaccountable manner. The reconstructions which have been so widely circulated even in the most recent handbooks show only the pillars, while the whole of the surrounding walls and the fronting towers are omitted. When confronted with such a representation the scholar receives much the same impression that a naturalist would experience if a boned turkey were offered him for serious study.

The pavements in the chambers as well as on the square to the north of the building consist of a flooring of lime mortar and pebbles in three layers : a coarse thick bottom layer—the festucatio of Vitruvius,—a fine shallow layer, and lastly a thin overlay of a fine red colour. This is entirely Greek, and it is a pleasure to meet with this fine coating we know so well in Athens, in Babylon of the fifth century. There are remains of a pavement made in exactly the same fashion in the ruins of Babil, where, according to the parallel inscription to the great *Steinplatten* inscription (*K.B.* iii. 2, p. 31), Nebuchadnezzar also built an *appa danna*.

Among the scanty but varied remains of this building, fragments of a plinth of black limestone found on the ruins show sufficient cuneiform signs to enable us to recognise without difficulty the remains of the name of King Darius (Fig. 78), and bases of columns of the same material reproduce precisely the forms of the bases of

Persepolis (Fig. 79).   Bricks, which like those of Persepolis are not made of clay, but of an artificial mass of lime mixed

FIG. 78.—Inscription from the Persian building.

with sand, bear representations in coloured enamels (Fig. 80).   Here, as in the enamelled bricks of the Ishtar Gate, the fields are separated by lines of black glaze.   There are ornaments and figures both flat and in relief, the figures with rich garments decorated with the woven patterns of the Persian guard of Persepolis.   A woman's face in white enamel is the only piece of the sort that we possess up to the present time.

FIG. 79.—Base of column from Persian building.

We can here recall what Diodorus, whose description was derived from Ctesias, the body surgeon of King Artaxerxes Mnemon, reports of the polychrome decorations of the royal castle of Babylon.   To begin with, he quotes (ii. 8) that there were two castles, one on the eastern bank of the Euphrates, on the modern mound " Babil," and the other on the western bank, the modern " Kasr."   He continues :

τοῦ μὲν γὰρ [εἰς τὸ] πρὸς ἑσπέραν κειμένου μέρους ἐποίησε τὸν πρῶτον περίβολον ἑξήκοντα σταδίων, ὑψηλοῖς καὶ πολυτελέσι

K

τείχεσιν ᾠχυρωμένον, ἐξ ὀπτῆς πλίνθου· ἕτερον δ᾽ ἐντὸς τούτου
κυκλοτερῆ κατεσκεύασε, καθ᾽ ὃν ἐν ὠμαῖς ἔτι ταῖς πλίνθοις
διετετύπωτο θηρία παντοδαπὰ τῇ τῶν χρωμάτων φιλοτεχνίᾳ τὴν ἀλήθειαν ἀπομιμούμενα. οὗτος δ᾽ ὁ περίβολος
ἦν τὸ μὲν μῆκος σταδίων τετταράκοντα, τὸ δὲ πλάτος ἐπὶ τριακοσίας πλίνθους, τὸ δ᾽ ὕψος, ὡς Κτησίας φησίν, ὀργυιῶν πεντή-
κοντα· τῶν δὲ πύργων ὑπῆρχε τὸ ὕψος ὀργυιῶν ἑβδομήκοντα.
κατεσκεύασε δὲ καὶ τρίτον ἐνδοτέρω περίβολον, ὃς περιεῖχεν
ἀκρόπολιν, ἧς ἡ μὲν περίμετρος ἦν σταδίων εἴκοσι, τὸ δὲ μῆκος
καὶ πλάτος τῆς οἰκοδομίας ὑπεραῖρον τοῦ μέσου τείχους τὴν
κατασκευήν. ἐνῆσαν δ᾽ ἔν τε τοῖς πύργοις καὶ τείχεσι ζῷα
παντοδαπὰ φιλοτέχνως τοῖς τε χρώμασι καὶ τοῖς τῶν
τύπων ἀπομιμήμασι κατεσκευασμένα. τὸ δ᾽ ὅλον ἐπεποίητο κυνήγιον παντοίων θηρίων ὑπάρχον πλῆρες, ὧν
ἦσαν τὰ μεγέθη πλέον ἢ πηχῶν τεττάρων. κατεσκεύαστο
δ᾽ ἐν αὐτοῖς καὶ ἡ Σεμίραμις ἀφ᾽ ἵππου πάρδαλιν ἀκοντίζουσα, καὶ πλησίον αὐτῆς ὁ ἀνὴρ Νίνος παίων ἐκ χειρὸς
λέοντα λόγχῃ.

The length of the walls are exaggerated about fourfold,
and the other measurements yet more, but the three periboli
are easily recognisable, as we shall see later. The middle
one was laid out κυκλοτερῆ, which may certainly be rendered
"annular, enclosed in itself, not open on one side, like the
outer peribolos." In any case it must not be translated
"circular," for a circular peribolos is found nowhere in
Babylon. In the central peribolos there were representations of wild animals in naturalistic colours, which were
applied to the bricks while they were still moist. These
are obviously the lions, bulls, and dragons of the Procession
Street and the Ishtar Gate. The central peribolos of
Diodorus enclosed both the Southern and the Principal
Citadel. On the walls and towers in the third peribolos,
which can be no other than the Southern Citadel, there
were also representations, coloured to life, of a chase of
wild beasts, in which Ninus and Semiramis themselves took
an active part. On no other site have we found human
figures on the brick enamels, and had there been any, they
could hardly have escaped us. We can scarcely doubt,
therefore, that Diodorus was describing the enamels of the

FIG. 80.—ENAMELLED ARTIFICIAL BLOCK FROM
PERSIAN BUILDING.

Persian building, and that the white face of a woman is the same that Ctesias recognised as a portrait of Semiramis. Whether Diodorus included among the wild animals those on the sides of the gateways of the other courts of the third peribolos—or, as we now call it, the Southern Citadel —may remain uncertain ; it is a matter of no consequence. It is, however, a most unusual incident in the history of art, that we should have been able to recover by excavation at the present day such works of art described by a celebrated historian of antiquity, and in the very place where he beheld them.

XX

THE WALLS OF THE FORTIFICATIONS AND QUAYS TO THE WEST AND NORTH OF THE SOUTHERN CITADEL.

WE must now turn to the consideration of the fortifications that are connected both directly and indirectly with the Southern Citadel. It is not always easy to gain a clear idea of these structures. In course of time the walls are displaced, the area enlarged, ancient walls are demolished, and the whole appearance of the place altered. All this occurred to a marked extent during the 43 years of Nebuchadnezzar's reign. Of the period previous to that we have only the Arachtu wall of Nabopolassar, and the supporting wall of the Assyrian Sargon north-west of the palace of Nabopolassar, which are marked A and S on the plan (Fig. 81). We will first examine those various walls in order to learn their purport and their extent, and then attempt to realise this somewhat complicated system of fortifications in its entire aspect and gradual formation.

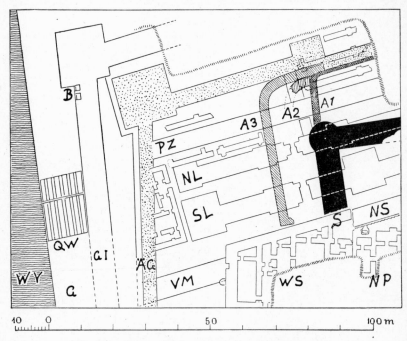

FIG. 81.—The north-west corner of the Southern Citadel.

A1 Arachtu wall of Nabopolassar,
    1st period.
A2 Arachtu wall, 2nd period.
A3 Arachtu wall, 3rd period.
AG Older moat wall.
B Wells.
G Graves.
GI Moat wall of Imgur-Bel.
NL Northern mud wall.
NP Palace of Nabopolassar.

NS Northern wall of Southern Citadel.
PZ Parallel intermediate wall.
QW Cross wall with outlets for water.
S Sargon wall.
SL Southern wall of mud brick.
VM Connecting wall.
WS Western part of the Southern Citadel.
WV Western outworks of the Southern
    Citadel.

XXI

THE MOAT WALL OF IMGUR-BEL

WE began our investigation of the western portion of the Southern Citadel, so far as we have carried it at present, by cutting a long and wide trench (Figs. 84, 85), which, in its western part, laid bare the walls of the western outworks, which in places are remarkably thick.

Not far from the Southern Citadel the trench brought to light two walls, of which the thicker one on the west

Fig. 82.—The moat wall of Imgur-Bel, west of the Southern Citadel.

replaced the older and narrower one (ÄG) (Fig. 81); they cannot therefore both have been standing at the same time. In the upper courses of the thicker wall (GI, cf. fig. 82) there is a large number of bricks placed closely together, all of which bear the following inscription (Fig. 83): " Nebuchad-nezzar, King of Babylon, the exalted prince, the nourisher of Esagila and Ezida, son of Nabopolassar, King of Babylon, am I. Since Nabopolassar, my father, my begetter, made

FIG. 83.—Inscribed brick from the moat wall of Imgur-Bel.

Imgur - Bel the great Dûr of Babylon, I, the fervent suppliant, worshipper of the Lord of lords, dug its fosses

FIG. 84.—Trench on the west of the Southern Citadel, during excavation.

and raised its banks of asphalt and baked bricks mountain high. Marduk, great Lord, behold with contentment the costly work of my hands, mayest thou be my helper, my standbye ! Length of days send as a gift " (trans. by Delitzsch). Here then we have the slope, the escarpment of the most celebrated and earliest fortification of

Babylon that bore the name of Imgur-Bel, "grace of Bel."
Nebuchadnezzar explicitly refers to an Imgur-Bel that was
built by Nabopolassar.   This Imgur-Bel of Nabopolassar
no longer exists, with the exception possibly of some

FIG. 85.—Trench on the west of the Southern Citadel, completely excavated.

fragmentary remains, but we have a foundation record of
Nabopolassar that concerns it.   The cylinder, which is
small and in excellent condition, was found in the Southern
Citadel (*u* 22) close to the Citadel wall, in rubbish south of
the Vaulted Building, and therefore not *in situ*.   The text
on it runs : " Nabopolassar, King of Babylon, the chosen

of Nabu and Marduk, am I. Imgur-Bel, the great Dûr of Babylon, which before me had become weak and fallen, I founded in the primeval abyss. I built it anew with the help of the hosts, the levies of my land. I caused Babylon to be enclosed by it towards the four winds of heaven. I set up its top as in the former time. Dûr, speak to Marduk my Lord on my behalf" (trans. by Delitzsch). From this it appears that the Imgur-Bel of Nabopolassar formed a quadrilateral, closed on all sides, and that it was constructed of burnt brick, as the deep foundations would be neither necessary nor possible for crude brick. The old part of the eastern city wall may thus have formed a portion of the Imgur-Bel of Nabopolassar. The wall of the moat unites on the south with the Citadel wall by a grooved expansion joint, but the groove is cut in the moat wall, which originally extended farther to the south and is older than the Citadel wall at this point. In the north it turns in an easterly direction, and the corner is marked by an immense bastion. On the outer side in the angle of the bastion there are two well shafts hewn out of the brickwork, the openings closed with a grating of pierced stone slabs.

Farther to the north the wall is still buried under the rubbish as far as its eastern termination, where it starts again from another great outstanding bastion to the north of the Ishtar Gate, and there rests against the exactly similarly constructed bastion of the older moat wall.

This older moat wall runs on almost the same lines as the later one, but somewhat within it. Like the latter it is laid with asphalt and reeds, but has smaller unstamped bricks, measuring 32×32 centimetres. In the trench near the Persian building we found it at a great depth, and excavated the northern portion of it with the corner bastion, in the angle of which is a well, this time a walled one. A tablet that referred to the construction of this well was found close by. The wall rests on a broad foundation banquette, and stretches in an easterly direction, ending with a substantial tower at the Arachtu wall of Nabopolassar, and reappearing at the Ishtar Gate with the above-mentioned outstanding bastion. Here we can recognise a later addition, a raising of the wall, for the strengthening of which powerful beams are jointed in. The lower part has a slight batter, and was later washed over with asphalt, like the walls of Nabopolassar's palace, which we have already described.

In the well-built but not deeply-founded cross wall, between the bastion and the Ishtar Gate, a broad doorway with a flight of steps led down westward from the level of the earlier Procession Street.

It is possible that the bastions were symmetrically repeated on the other side of the street, but the site has not yet been excavated.

XXII

THE ARACHTU WALL OF NABOPOLASSAR AND THE WALL OF SARGON THE ASSYRIAN.

NORTH-WEST of the palace of Nabopolassar, and deep below the three fortification walls which here lie in front of the Southern Citadel, there are the remains of four ancient walls, the discovery of which has been of great importance for the topography of Babylon. All four are the rounded-off corners—if we may call them so—of quay walls which slope sharply on their north and west fronts. All four are built with a lavish number of stamped and inscribed bricks, so that no doubt whatever can exist as to their use and name.

Each of these quay walls represents a rebuilding of the one behind it, and indicates a thrusting forward of the quay front to the north and west. They consist of good burnt brick, and are for the most part laid in pure asphalt (section on Fig. 87).

The wall of Sargon is the thickest, but with its crown it only attains a height of .27 metres below zero, where it is covered over with a thick layer of asphalt. Above this burnt brick has never been laid, crude brick may have been, but there is nothing to show it. Where the wall abuts on the line of the Southern Citadel it is cut away to make room for the new building. The corner is formed of a circular projecting bastion. In one special course of the front of the bastion, as well as of the straight extent of the wall, in one continuous row, there are inscribed bricks (Fig. 86) with the following legend: "To Marduk! the great Lord, the divine creator who inhabits Esagila, the Lord of Babil, his lord; Sargon the mighty king, King of the land of Assur, King of all, Governor of Babil, King of Sumer and Akkad, the nourisher of Esagila

FIG. 86.—Inscribed brick from the Sargon wall.

and Ezida. To build Imgur-Bel was his desire: he caused burnt brick of pure kirû to be struck, built a kâr with tar and asphalt on the side of the Ishtar Gate to the bank of the Euphrates in the depth of the water (?), and founded Imgur-Bel and Nimitti-Bel mountain high, firm upon it. This work may Marduk, the great lord, graciously behold and grant Sargon, the prince who cherishes him, life! Like the foundation stone of the sacred city may the years of his reign endure" (trans. by Delitzsch).

The two great fortifications of Imgur-Bel and Nimitti-Bel, so far as Sargon marks them out as his work, are no longer to be recognised. They must have been destroyed by the buildings of Nabopolassar and Nebuchadnezzar on the Southern Citadel. These cannot, however, have stood exactly over our wall, which is only 8 metres broad. Two ordinary fortification walls, such as the two mud walls which stand here above the walls of Sargon, with their

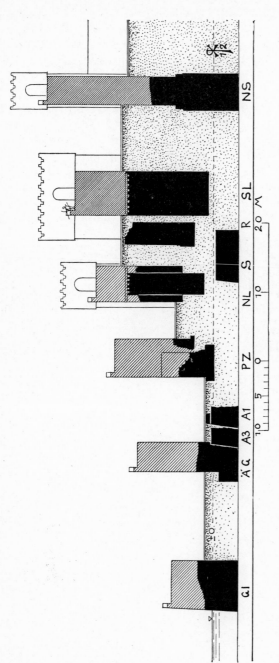

FIG. 87.—Section through fortification walls north of the Southern Citadel.

AI Arachtu wall of Nabopolassar, 1st period.   NS Northern wall of the Southern Citadel.
A3 Arachtu wall of Nabopolassar, 3rd period.   PZ Parallel intermediate wall.
AG Older moat wall.   R Ruins of an older mud-brick wall.
GI Moat wall of Imgur-Bel.   S Sargon wall.
NL Northern mud wall.   SL Southern mud-brick wall.

intermediate space of one metre filled in with rubbish, occupy with the outer spring of their towers a breadth of 23 metres. Thus they must have lain behind, and Sargon's wall must have served practically to protect the bank, exactly as we have already observed in the moat wall of Imgur-Bel.

It is an important point that Sargon mentions the position of his wall : on the side of the Ishtar Gate to the bank of the Euphrates. This shows that in Sargon's time the Euphrates flowed here.

The Nabopolassar inscriptions on the bricks of his wall that directly adjoins the Sargon wall are, some of

FIG. 88.—Stamped brick of Nabopolassar's Arachtu wall.

them stamped, some chiselled, and some written. They are, however, placed without any sort of method, mixed together in close proximity in all three periods of the wall. In the stamped legend (Fig. 88) the king states that he had bright burnt bricks struck, and with them made the wall of the Arachtu. Thus in the time of Nabopolassar the Arachtu must have flowed here, and indeed at exactly the same place where, according to the Sargon bricks, the Euphrates flowed. The difficulties raised by this circumstance, as well as by a number of statements in the Babylonian literature, may be overcome in two different ways. Either Arachtu is only another term for Euphrates, or we must arrive at the somewhat involved conclusion that in course of time the Euphrates frequently changed its bed and had interchanged with that of the Arachtu. In this case the ancient Euphrates must be supposed to have described a curve or bow towards the west, the chord of which was the Arachtu in its straight southward course, thus forming an island of half-moon shape. This would have been the position of affairs which Sennacherib happened upon when he cast the zikurrat Etemenanki into the Arachtu.

In Sargon's time, on the contrary, the western bed of the Euphrates would have been sanded up, and its waters would have flowed directly in the bed of the earlier Arachtu, and thus past our Sargon wall. Nabopolassar, on the other hand, would have restored the Arachtu, for by his time the Euphrates must have once more resumed its earlier western channel, while Nebuchadnezzar would have destroyed the Arachtu, and extended his citadel actually to the Euphrates.

FIG. 89.—Inscribed brick of Nabopolassar's Arachtu wall.

As already said, this is a very perplexing theory, but it is the only one that remains for those who reject the complete identity of the Euphrates and the Arachtu.

The building of the Southern Citadel destroyed the Arachtu wall at this point, but immediately to the south of the Southern Citadel the excavations have once more laid it bare and followed it up nearly to the Amran mound. Here also there are numerous Arachtu bricks of Nabopolassar in the brick masonry.

On the inscribed bricks (Fig. 89) it is stated that "Nabopolassar, etc., the restorer of Esagila and Babylon, made the wall of the Arachtu for Marduk, his lord." In this the explicit placing together of Babylon and Esagila as two parallel names of equal importance is very striking. It entirely agrees, however, with what has been already said of the original and actual Babylon, in its narrowest meaning, that in the earliest period Esagila was independent of it (cf. p. 87 et seq.).

The inscriptions chiselled on the burnt brick (Fig. 90) state that " Nabopolassar, etc., surrounded the Dûr of Babylon with a wall of burnt brick for protection." Of this we have found only four examples, and they are all in the walls to the north of the Southern Citadel.

The beginning of the oldest Nabopolassar wall rests on the round tower of the Sargon wall. Its bricks, which are laid in pure asphalt, are very irregular in size. Their length varies between 30, 31, 32, 33, and 34 centimetres ; the last have the chiselled inscriptions. The wall outside has a decided batter and inside is markedly stepped. It reaches only to 20 centimetres below zero, and on it

FIG. 90.—Chiselled brick of Nabopolassar's Arachtu wall.

was placed, at the part that runs from north to south, a wall of brick rubble.

At the rounded-off corner a wall, of which a small portion only now remains, stretches out to the west, and belongs to a second building period (Fig. 91).

Immediately in front lies the building of the third period, which towards the east only extends a very short way beyond the corner, but of which the north to south portion adds to the earliest building a strip of land about 16 metres broad. It rises higher, and is as much as one metre above zero ; in the west it is formed of broken brick, in the north of crude brick. This wall passes under the two mud walls, and within the Southern Citadel it breaks off with a set-back. This latter must certainly have formed part of an outlet of which the corresponding half must have been destroyed by the building of the Southern Citadel. In this place a bonding of the wall front is employed, which rarely occurs elsewhere.

FIG. 91.—View of north-west corner of the Southern Citadel.

It is formed throughout of one whole brick with a half
one behind it, followed by a half brick with a whole one
behind it.　In the course above there is the same arrangement shifted by a half brick placed sideways.　This same
method of bonding occurs with Nebuchadnezzar's bricks at
the stairway which leads up to the north-east corner of
the Kasr.

It is now evident that the older moat wall is also no
other than an Arachtu wall, which for the greater part of
its northern length lay in front of its predecessor, with no
intervening space, while its western portion added once
more a strip of land to the old enclosure.

XXIII

THE WESTERN OUTWORKS

To the west of the Southern Citadel, and therefore at
the place where originally the Euphrates flowed, there
is a remarkable building that strikes one by the immense
thickness of its walls, 20 to 25 metres in width.　It is not
yet completely excavated.　The upper part has been
removed at no very distant period by modern brick robbers,
and the many holes and mounds in the neighbourhood still
bear witness to their nefarious handiwork.　The wall
throughout is of solid compact brickwork, built with excellent Nebuchadnezzar bricks laid in asphalt.

Between this building and the moat wall of Imgur-
Bel a narrow ditch is left ; at its north and south ends only
connecting pieces are jointed in, pierced by several holes
to allow the water to pass.　The western limits are not
yet clearly definable.　The somewhat long quadrilateral of
the ground-plan was divided by cross walls into a number
of separate divisions, of which the southernmost remained
open, while the others were occupied by a number of
dwelling-like chambers.　A great stairway or ascending
ramp is recognisable in the north-east corner of the southern

open space. During the building the ground plan was subjected in various places to slight alterations.

The Nabonidus wall, which stretches from the south, joins on to the south-west corner of the building with a tower, and the canal that flows from the east passes through this tower.

It is evident that this building is the place referred to in Nebuchadnezzar's Sippar cylinder (*K.B.* iii. 2, p. 49, col. 2 l. 19): "In order that no harm (?) should happen to the strong-hold of Esagila and Babylon, I caused a great fortification to be built in the river (ha-al-zi ra-bi-tim i-na nâri) of bitumen and bricks. I raised its foundation on the depths of the water, its top I exalted like the wooded mountains" (trans. by Winckler).

XXIV

THE THREE GREAT FORTIFICATION WALLS NORTH OF THE SOUTHERN CITADEL

We now turn our attention to the three fortification walls, that follow the direction of the ancient Arachtu walls, but which overlap them and stretch farther to the west.

The northernmost consists of brick rubble, and extends from the cross wall near the Ishtar Gate right over the ancient fosse wall, apparently to the moat wall of Imgur-Bel. In front of it lay a building of which several parallel lines of wall still remain. In these are cavities, due to the insertion of upright bricks, where the beams of an upper storey rested; the lower storey, of which the flooring still exists, has the very moderate height of about 1.5 metres. Corresponding cavities for beams are hewn out in the wall of brick rubble, as well as some isolated niches, which may well have served to afford more space in these narrow chambers. The two mud-brick walls are of course later than the Nabopolassar walls that lie below them, but older

L

than Nebuchadnezzar's Ishtar Gate. Where the southern thicker wall abuts on the wing of the gate, there was a space one metre wide, enclosed on the north side only by a slight mud wall. Here also it is obvious that the mud wall was cut off for the purpose of building the Ishtar Gate. At the time when the latter was built the two walls were repaired and raised, and the narrower wall was turned slightly northward in order to secure a flush fitting to the wing of the gate erected there. The southern wall, which is 6 metres thick and has a scarcely perceptible batter, has a curtain length of 15.3 metres, with large towers placed across it and smaller ones placed lengthways in regular alternation (see Fig. 81). At the west it ends with a specially large tower. In the second mesopyrgion from the west there is a door, of which the earliest embrasure consists of unstamped burnt bricks measuring from 32 × 32 to 31 × 31 centimetres. The pavement is only 2 metres above zero. At a later period the jamb also was faced with burnt brick with Nebuchadnezzar's stamps, and the pavement was raised to 2.65 metres, and later again to 4.5 above zero. At this later period the part of the Southern Citadel which is opposite our door did not yet exist, and the threshold rested on a sharply sloped supporting wall which lies immediately in front of the Southern Citadel. It is built of mud brick, and on the inside every second course was laid with broken brick. It is possible that this supporting wall was made in order to safeguard the path while these portions of the Citadel were built. At a later period the embrasure was strengthened and the pavement was raised to 5.5 metres above zero. It is a double layer, the lower one of broken brick and the upper one of Nebuchadnezzar's paving tiles, 51 centimetres square, and completely covered the interval to the Southern Citadel. In the pavement and in holes made for the purpose in the mud walls there were interments in brick coffins, with gable-shaped covers formed of bricks placed edgeways, which are very characteristic of the culture of Greece and its allies. It is the latest important style of pavement lying here, and we can scarcely err if we assign it to the Babylonian kingdom on account of its great similarity with the pavement of the Southern

Citadel. On this floor rests also a reinforcement of a section of the mud wall accompanying it on the south side.

All these pavements lead upwards from west to east, and under each is the drain belonging to it that carried off the water towards the west.

On the 5th tower from the west, at a height of 13 metres above zero, there can be seen the cavities of a thick grid work laid lengthways. It apparently carried the baulks of a cross grid which no longer exists, and both were intended to serve as a new footing for a heightening of the wall. The corners of the towers are secured in places by wooden braces inlaid at the corners one over another.

In the space between the walls we again find several pavements laid one above another. Among them, in the eastern part, are the great paving tiles of Nebuchadnezzar, 13 to 14 metres above zero. Less substantial mud walls have been patched in the central part and extend over the northern wall, which must therefore have been ruined at that time. On the other hand, near the 3rd tower from the east, there is part of an older thick mud wall, which was cut through at the building of the double wall. It is over 3 metres thick, with a marked batter on the north side, and descends as deep as 3 metres above zero. Its direction differs somewhat from that of the double wall, and is roughly that of the Sargon wall. It is not probable, however, that it dates back to the time of Sargon; we have dug especially deep at this point, as much as one metre below zero (Fig. 92), and can therefore state with certainty that there is no foundation here such as that of the Sargon wall. Remains of a flooring of bricks measuring 29 × 29 centimetres lie 20 centimetres below zero.

Originally the northern wall consisted entirely of mud bricks, but at the time of the building of the Ishtar Gate it was faced on both sides with broken brick laid in asphalt and mud. On the east these descend as deep as 4.5 metres above zero, and on the west, where the whole enclosure lay lower, 2.2 metres. This refacing formed only part of the alterations (see Fig. 87). At the level where the old mud wall ended a massive wall of burnt brick began, of the thickness of the mud wall, including its two facings. At the western part this was placed at a height of 13 metres, where, as in the southern wall, the thick wooden grid still remains in its cavities. At the west end the burnt-brick wall begins at 3.5 metres, and still stands in place on the mud wall. Thus the wall appears as one of burnt brick, containing an older core of mud brick in the lower part.

That the refacing was not part of the original plan is shown by the fact that in some of the mud-brick towers the cavities of walled-up gutters still remain, such as we find in the city walls and the temples. The brick casings of the gutters were taken away, and in their place the brickwork of the facing was jointed in. With the exception of being widened the wall was little altered by the new building. The towers correspond in no way with those of the principal wall, at any rate it is only in the eastern portion that the same principle has been adopted, and a tower placed crossways is always succeeded by a smaller one placed lengthways. Here too, however, the western end consists of an especially large tower exactly in a straight line with that of the principal wall.

The gateway in the west forms, in its position, its facings, and alterations a fairly exact counterpart of that in the principal wall. But, besides this, the mud wall had also four other gateways, of which only the one in the 5th mesopyrgion was retained in the rebuilding. A drain with two inlet shafts carried off the surface water from here with a sharp fall to the south, probably to the main conduit behind the principal wall.

In front of the two wall heads at the west lay a building with the usual arrangement of a court and surrounding chambers. It was built over the ancient fosse wall, which by that time was destroyed, and might well represent the dwelling of the commandant of the walls.

There were also two wall lengths of mud brick of a similar kind on the east of the Ishtar Gate. They are not long. The thicker one breaks off in the 2nd mesopyrgion, and is there supported by a later sloping embankment wall, which turns off in a south-easterly direction, where we have already followed it for 25 metres. The northern wall length is still

FIG. 92.—Space between the two mud walls.

shorter. The excavations, which at this point were carried considerably below the base of the mud wall, yielded mud and river sediment that apparently came from the Euphrates, which during the Persian period washed the eastern side of the Acropolis. In Nebuchadnezzar's time these walls certainly extended farther east, and united themselves in some way, which is not yet entirely explained, with the inner city wall, which according to the inscriptions found there is to be recognised as the Nimitti-Bel of Sardanapalus. This is the more certain because the Ishtar Gate is also named in inscriptions as belonging to Imgur-Bel and Nimitti-Bel. Thus it is imperative that we should make a slight digression of 1000 metres to the east in order to observe this fortification. After that we will return to the Kasr.

XXV

THE INNER CITY WALL

A LOW embankment (Fig. 93), which passes Homera closely on the east, and runs approximately from north to south through the plain for a length of 1700 metres, conceals the ruins of the inner town wall (see Fig. 249). This is a double wall with an intermediate space of 7.2 metres. The western wall, which is 6.5 metres thick, has large towers placed crossways alternating with smaller ones placed lengthways, with a frontage varying from 9.4 to 9.7 metres, at regular intervals of 18.1 metres. The larger towers have a depth of 11.4 metres, the smaller ones of 8.06 metres (Fig. 94). The mud bricks measure 32 centimetres square. In the west side of the smaller towers gutters are constructed of burnt brick from 30 to 32 centimetres square. They open below with triangular mouths.

The eastern wall, which is only 3.72 metres thick, has towers at regular intervals of 20.5 metres with a frontage of 5.1 metres and depth of 5.8. The crude bricks measure 33 centimetres square. Here also there were gutters to carry off the water, but they were inserted in the curtains (Fig. 95). The base of the thick wall reaches a depth of 67 centimetres and that of the narrower wall of 19 centimetres below zero. The thick wall alone shows traces of an earlier building on which it stands, and was later repaired by short lengths of supporting walls built with 33-centimetre bricks in front of it.

In the intermediate space, close to the narrower wall,

FIG. 93.—Northern end of the inner city wall, from the south-east.

but in the rubbish of the fallen walls, and not *in situ*, several foundation cylinders of Sardanapalus were found (Fig. 96), with the following text : " To Marduk, the King of all the Iggigi and Anunnaki, the creator of heaven and of earth, the predestinator of the final aim (?) who inhabits Esagila, the lord of Babil, the great lord. I Sardanapalus, the great king, the mighty king, the king of all, king of the land of Assur, king of the 4 quarters of the world, son of Esarhaddon, the great king, the mighty king, the king of all, king of the land of Assur, the ruler of Babil, king of

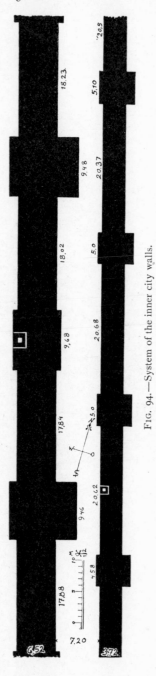

FIG. 94.—System of the inner city walls.

Sumer and Akkad, the repopulator of Babil, builder of Esagila, renewer of the temples of all cities, who appointed the rites in them, and established their regular offerings which had come to an end, and restored the statutes and ordinances as of old, grandson of Sennacherib, the great king, the mighty king, the king of all, king of the land of Assur, am I.— Under my government the great lord Marduk held his entry into Babil with rejoicing and entered upon his dwelling in Esagila for ever. The regular offerings of Esagila and of the gods of Babylon I established, the protectorship of Babil I retained. In order that the strong should not injure the weak I appointed Shamash-shumukin, my twin (?) brother to reign as king over Babil. Also I filled Esagila with silver and gold and precious stones, and made Ekua shining as the constellations in the sky.—At that time Imgur-Bel the dûr of Babil and Nimitti-Bel its šalḫû, which had become old and fallen, had sunk to the ground. In order to make the fortress of Esagila and the temple of Babil strong, with the might of my troops with all haste (?) I caused Nimitti-Bel its šalḫû with the art of the brick god to be made new and raised its city gateways. Door leaves I caused to be made and placed them in its doorways. —Future prince, under whose rule this same work may come to ruins, consult wise artists. Imgur-Bel the dûr, Nimitti-Bel the šalḫû make according to their ancient excellence. Behold the records of my name, and anoint them with oil and offer a sacrificial lamb, lay them near the records of thy name, so will Marduk hear thy petition. Whoever shall destroy the records of my name or of the name of my twin (?) brother with most evil deed, and will not lay the records of my name near the records of his name, him may Marduk the King of all behold with wrath and destroy his name and his seed in the land" (trans. by Delitzsch).

Thus the inscription refers expressly to the building of Nimitti-Bel alone, and it is important to discover from

FIG. 95.—Drain in the inner city wall.

which of the two walls it came; that, however, cannot be ascertained at present. It is true that the cylinders lay close to the narrow outer wall, but the fact must be taken into consideration that at the foot of the broader wall there is a much larger bank of its own fallen rubbish than there is at the base of the narrow one, and that any object such as the cylinders which came from it would roll down the bank much nearer the narrow wall than that from which it fell. If the cylinder belonged to the thick wall, Nimitti-Bel must have been a double wall; if it belonged to the narrow wall, the thick one may be Imgur-Bel; certainty can only be obtained by further excavation, which must level the greater part of the thicker wall, in order to bring to light the records which are probably hidden somewhere inside it. Such levelling would so greatly disfigure the ruins that hitherto I have avoided entering on the work, but it must be done before the conclusion of the excavations. The difficulties connected with the mud walls on the Kasr are very similar, though with some slight differences. Here also the simplest solution would be to identify the thick wall with Imgur-Bel and the narrow one with Nimitti-Bel. Many difficulties, however, arise against doing so. The moat wall of Imgur-Bel lies to the west of the Southern Citadel, where these mud walls actually do not survive. According to the above-quoted cylinder, Nebuchadnezzar surrounded Babylon

FIG. 96.—Nimitti-Bel foundation cylinder of Sardanapalus.

on all four sides with the wall Imgur-Bel, while the two mud walls enclosed an area which undoubtedly was open towards the west. Here also complete and decisive understanding of the problem must await further excavations.

At the site of the 14th tower from the north in the thick wall there is below a piece of wall the breadth of the tower, which consists of Nebuchadnezzar's burnt bricks laid in asphalt. A small drain roofed with high-pitched slanting bricks pierces this block of brickwork and continues for 19 metres farther to the east. This block of brickwork, which is 4.2 metres broad and contains the channel, gives the impression of being a roadway, and therefore one would expect to find a gateway at this place in the city wall (Fig. 97). Both walls, however, are so ruined here that nothing of the kind can now be recognised. The brickwork of the drain is strengthened with small pilasters at the sides,

which grip into the ground like teeth, and would clearly
prevent any slipping of the walls which slope towards the
east. The drain itself
also continues west-
ward.

FIG. 97.—Drain through inner city wall.

Apart from this,
on the entire length
of 1½ kilometres of
the city wall, there is
no indication of any
gateway. A short
distance from the
southern end there is
a small mound with
walls of burnt brick
laid in asphalt, which
may perhaps be the
remains of a gateway,
but which is not yet
excavated.

Upon the ruins of
the wall and near it
there are numerous
clay coffins, often as
many as 30 between
one tower and the next. They are widened with a bulge
on one side, and many are anthropoid, and may belong to
the Persian or latest Babylonian period.

The exploration of the inner city wall cannot be
regarded as complete. We will now turn back to the Kasr
to study the northern extension, which abuts on the
Southern Citadel.

THE PRINCIPAL CITADEL

THAT part of the Kasr that is enclosed on the south by the two mud walls, and on the north by the deep valley in square 7 of the Kasr plan (Fig. 13), we call the Principal Citadel. It was enclosed by a fortification wall, which in the east ran by the side of the Procession Street and in the north turned westward in the great valley just mentioned, where it must have reached the Euphrates of that period. The Principal Citadel in this quarter is, however, only the outcome of a second scheme of Nebuchadnezzar, and the one that was actually carried out. The first scheme, which does not appear to have been carried out, only enclosed one half of the area which was later built upon. Of this we have found the remains of a thick wall in the centre of the Principal Citadel which was intended to form the northern end. It (*k* 13) ran from west to east, and where it reaches the Procession Street it turned in a southerly direction to join the bastion of the fosse wall at the Ishtar Gate. The wall of burnt brick laid in pure asphalt is 17 metres thick, and is therefore one of the strongest and most massive fortification walls we possess. At the part already excavated there is a doorway which leads through the wall and looks like a long passage. On the north side there are outstanding towers ; the extension to the west and eventually to the south we have not yet made out. It is only built to a height of 6.8 metres above zero, and at 4.25 it rests on a foundation banquette.

Of the second completed scheme a terrace of brick rubble was constructed over the entire area, of which the upper level lies at 8 metres above zero. On this terrace stand the foundation walls of the palace, which even now rise as high in parts as 15.5 metres. At about this height the ancient pavement must have been laid. The space between the foundation walls was built up with brick rubble. Thus, in comparison with the Southern Citadel,

FIG. 98.—Blocks of brickwork in the Principal Citadel.

immense care has been bestowed on the regularity of the foundations. The area lies immediately north of the Arachtu wall, which points to the conclusion that the Principal Citadel was constructed in the bed of the original water-course, and this explains the unusual form of foundations both here and in the western part of the Southern Citadel, which also overlapped the ancient Arachtu wall.

In the great courts round which the palace buildings are grouped, as in the Southern Citadel, the filling of brickwork is not arranged in a solid mass but in the form of long blocks about 2 metres in breadth and height. One course of these runs from east to west, the next above from north to south, as is clearly seen in *m* 12, and again in the south-east corner.

The bright yellow bricks in the upper parts are some of the hardest and best of those struck by Nebuchadnezzar; 7- or 3-lined stamps are used almost exclusively. In the narrow, often scarcely measurable joints there is fine white lime-mortar as hard as stone, and here and there matting or reeds, which, however, do no damage to the hardness of the brickwork. In the lower parts the bricks are redder and softer and the mortar is grey, less solid, and reddish at the edges. For this reason the brick robbers have here preferred to work underground in search of the lower bricks, which are more easily removed. Thus the high walls have been largely robbed of their supports, and they are now sunk and split, as though they had been flung together by an earthquake (Fig. 98).

During the progress of the building the details of the plan were frequently altered. Walls were thrown down and doors were displaced, so that at every 10th or 12th course a new plan was adopted. The royal builder must have insisted very specially and with great energy on his own wishes being carried out, for no architect would of his own free will alter plans so frequently during the course of building.

The decorations were still more splendid than those of the southern palace. Remains have been found of large reliefs consisting of a beautiful blue paste, similar to lapis lazuli. The figures were made up of separate pieces, each

of which only contained a small part, such as a lock of hair.
On the back of these separate pieces there was a prismatic
addition, by which they were affixed to some background
of which we know nothing.

Paving stones of white and mottled sandstone, limestone, and black basalt were used for the pavements, at
any rate in the courts. They measure 66 centimetres
square, and bear on their edges the name of Nebuchadnezzar,
and in one case that of Evil-Merodach (Fig. 99). Here

FIG. 99.—Inscribed paving slabs—above of Evil-Merodach,
below of Nebuchadnezzar.

also the ceilings were not vaulted, but according to the
inscription quoted later on, they consisted of cedar, cypress,
and other wood. In the entrances stood gigantic basalt
lions similar to those of Assyrian palaces ; of these we have
found immense paws and other portions in the north-east
corner.

All these facts we have gained as the result of the
comparatively trifling excavations hitherto undertaken.
These are limited to the central portion with the thick
wall mentioned above, a cutting against the east front, and
a similar one against the north front and on the north-east
corner, but they have occupied a great deal of time owing
to the amount of rubbish, as much as 8 to 12 metres deep
or more, which has had to be cut through. Limited as the

work has been, it has already yielded abundant proofs of
the treasures of art and learning that Nebuchadnezzar
and his successors heaped up in this portion of the palace
for the "amazement of mankind," as the king states in his
inscription. It must always be remembered in this connection that the Kasr has been burrowed over, not once or
twice, but repeatedly by brick robbers, for it is not without
reason that the mound bears in addition to the name Kasr
that of Mudshallibeh, which means "the overturned."
Here in the Principal Citadel this is more apparent than in
the Southern Citadel, for here not only the foundation walls
but also the spaces between them, which in the Southern
Citadel consisted chiefly of earth, have yielded a supply of
the greedily-sought brick materials.

At the north-east corner (Fig. 100), in q 8 of the plan,
before our excavations began there was a great basalt figure
of a lion trampling on a man who lay beneath him with
his right hand on the flank of the animal, and the left
on his muzzle. This latter has been chopped away by
superstitious hands, and he is marked all over by the
stones and flint balls that have been, and are still, flung at
him ; for he is regarded as the much-feared "Djin." On
one side the Arabs have dug out a deep hole in his flanks,
which is now filled in with cement. The reason of this is
as follows. A European once came here, and inquired
about the lion, which he had probably read of in the books
of earlier travellers. The Arabs showed it to him, and after
looking at it attentively, he chose from among the small
holes in the basalt the right one, into which he thrust a key
and turned it, whereupon his hand was immediately filled
with gold pieces. Having accomplished his practical joke
the traveller went his way, unable as he was to speak
Arabic. The worthy Arabs, however, in order to render the
treasure available, hammered this hole in the lion, which
must have caused them immense labour, for the stone is
extremely hard. The figure is not completely carved, and
is still little more than blocked out. It therefore looks more
ancient than it really is, for it can scarcely be earlier than
the time of Nebuchadnezzar (Fig. 101). People are divided
as to its meaning. Some see in it Daniel in the lions'

Fig. 100.—North-east corner of Principal Citadel, from the north.

M

den, and others Babylonia above defeated Egypt. But a concrete past is throughout this period never represented otherwise than in reliefs, and, on the other hand, it is foreign to Babylonian art to take as a basis the representation of an abstract idea.

Close to the lion but deeper down was found a fine large stela of white limestone, which the "governor of the lands of Sukhi and of the lands of Maër" caused to be

FIG. 101.—The basalt lion in the Principal Citadel.

made in his honour (Fig. 102). His name was Shamash-resh-ussur, and his lands lay in the neighbourhood of the Khabur, on the Euphrates. He caused himself to be represented in the midst of the gods worshipped by him, and the name of each figure is inscribed close to it. In his left hand he holds the club with the rounded stone head, the same that is in use here to-day and called "Hattre." When the club has the same shaped head in asphalt instead of stone it is called "Mugwar." His right hand, which is clenched in votive fashion, is raised to the statue of Adad the weather god, who stands before him, with a long beard and long hair, and with shafts of lightning in his hand, and a feather crown on his head. His girdle is wound twice round his body, and then tucked in slanting, exactly as the town Arabs of to-day wear their girdles.

Fig. 102.—The Shamash-resh-ussur stela.

Next to Adad stands the somewhat smaller statue of Ishtar. She is raising the right hand in greeting, and is leaning on the bow with her left, upon which her star Venus is resting. The arrangement of her hair differs from that of a man, as one lock hangs long in front of the ear. The third statue is largely broken away. The three great shields worn by the figures in front of the lower part of the body are remarkable, but they are found on representations of other divinities. They hang one above another, and are held in place from behind by ornamented bands. We must suppose them to be gold plates, and they do not occur on the dress of human beings. The statues stand on pedestals, which are decorated with a pattern representing mountains, rows of semicircular peaks which form the same scheme of decoration that the cotton-printer in Persia to-day uses to express mountains on his so-called " Perde " hangings. Other divinities beside these three are introduced by means of their emblems : Marduk by the shafted triangle on a pedestal, Nabu by his writing-stick, Shamash by the winged disc of the sun, which, however, is half broken away, and Sin by the new moon. The relief is worked in the flat level manner characteristic of the Assyrian provincial style of the seventh century B.C.

On the stone face surrounding this sunk relief there is a Neo-Babylonian inscription of many columns, which is thus epitomised by Weissbach : " It begins with a sudden invasion of neighbouring foes (the Tu'mânu people) who were some of them killed, and some overthrown (col. 2, 17-26). Restoration of the fallen canal of Suhi and inauguration of the same by a trial voyage (2, 27-37). The planting of date-palms and setting up of his throne in Ribaniš (2, 38-44). Founding and laying out of the town Gabbari- KAK. Malediction (col. 3). With this the inscription originally ended. The governor, however, continued his works of peace, the planting of palms and introducing of bees (?), and described these further in the 4th and 5th columns." The stela was inserted in a plinth with the aid of a tenon at the base, as was always done with stelae. This one does not appear to have arrived in Babylon by peaceful methods. As a rule a prince would not have allowed any addition to be made to his inscription.

The ancient Hittite stela which was found to the east of the lion (Figs. 103, 104) must also be regarded as booty. On the front of the somewhat coarse-grained block of dolerite there stands the weather god (Teshup ?), with the rays of lightning in his left hand, the axe in his right hand, and a sword in his girdle. He wears a short-sleeved

garment, peaked shoes, and a remarkable cap with a knob
at the top and horns or double rims at the sides, as well
as bracelets and an anklet on the right foot.   The lips are
shaven, and a long lock of hair falls down on his shoulder.
The rounded back of the stela contains a long, well-preserved

FIGS. 103, 104.—The Hittite stela.
Obverse.   Reverse.

inscription of Hittite hieroglyphs,—a script which is still
undeciphered.   There is a similar representation on the
east side of the outer citadel gateway of Sendjirli, and no
doubt our stela comes from the same region of Northern
Syria.   The style of its relief is between that of the
citadel gateway and of the town gate of Sendjirli, and it
may therefore be ascribed to the tenth century B.C. (see
F. v. Luschan, *Ausgrabungen von Sendschirli*, iii.).

The same prolific site yielded also a basalt paving
stone with an inscription that showed it to belong to the
palace of Adad-nirari (ii.), the son of Asurdan, son of
Tiglathpileser (Fig. 105). Whether this palace of Adad-
nirari (911 ?–891) stood here or in Assyria cannot be
proved. At any rate this paving stone appears to have
been set in the
Principal Citadel
of Nebuchadnezzar
as an object of
interest.

Fifteen frag-
ments of dolerite
with inscriptions
belong to stelae
of the same kind
as one that was
found by brick
robbers shortly be-
fore the beginning
of our excavations,
in the north-east
corner of the Prin-
cipal Citadel. It

FIG. 105.—Pavement slab of Adad-nirari.

is an upright semi-
cylindrical block inscribed on both sides, on which
Nabonidus reports in detail on his endowment of temples
in Babylon and other places (see Scheil, "Inscription de
Nabonide," in the *Recueil de travaux rel. à la philologie*, etc.,
xviii. p. 15). A block of dolerite which formed part of a
thick large stela was found in *r* 9 of the Kasr plan. It
contains in Neo-Babylonian writing a duplicate of the famous
inscription which Darius Hystaspes (521–485) engraved on
the rocks of Bagistana in Persian, Susian, and Babylonian.

The numerous fragments of building cylinders which
have been found on the Kasr, naturally refer principally to
the building of the palace, the Ishtar Gate, and the fortification walls. The greater number are Nebuchadnezzar's, but
there are a few of Sardanapalus, Nabopolassar, Nabonidus,
and Neriglissar.

A number that were found actually in the Principal Citadel are of buildings outside the Kasr, such as Etemenanki, and of buildings outside Babylon. Thus we have an inscription of Nabonidus of E-ḫul-ḫul in Haran, one of E-bar-ra in Sippara, and one of Nebuchadnezzar from E-ul-la in Sippara, and also an E-an-na of Sardanapalus and others. It appears therefore that such documents were systematically collected and preserved in the Principal Citadel.

Any one who compares the comparatively small area that is excavated with the extent of that which is yet untouched, and realises how much has already been found, will see how much yet remains to be done and acquired in the Principal Citadel, apart from the gain to science that would ensue from laying open the palace buildings.

The palace did not extend quite as far as the fortification wall on the north. The foundations of the front consist of excellent brickwork laid in asphalt and reeds, while in the foundations behind broken brick laid in lime mortar is employed throughout.

Between the palace and the fortification walls there was an open strip in which a wide canal, originally 13 metres broad, which led from the Euphrates, flowed from here almost to the eastern wall. Smaller conduits, 1.2 metres wide, roofed over with tilted bricks, branched off from it through the massive foundations of the Principal Citadel to supply it with water. They were connected with the palace level by quadrangular well-shafts. The embankment of the canal in front of the palace and of the northern fortification wall, projecting from their foundations, formed a rampart 2 metres broad, and at this level we have fixed our zero, which serves as the starting-point for the level of the entire city and its buildings. The water-level of Nebuchadnezzar's time was at about this height, for here the projecting courses of the coverings of the smaller conduits begin, and the pavement in the door of the northern wall is only some 1.5 metres higher than our zero.

It is obvious that the great canal was open above. It was later replaced by a smaller one only 1.8 metres wide, which runs beside its southern bank wall and was certainly

covered in.   At this later period a broad road 9.5 metres
wide led between the palace and the north wall, which consisted of three brick courses laid in asphalt.   Upon it were
Parthian houses and brick graves.   We cut into them with
our trench at the mound "Atele" (*n* 8).   On this hill,
which rises to 18 metres above zero, stood in Oppert's
time a nebek tree; the Arabs believed that this had
grown out of a tent stake that Ali had driven in here.
From a shoot of this tree the solitary nebek sprang that
still flourishes in the long low region of the Northern
Citadel.

For a time I held the opinion that this canal was the
Libil-ḫigalla, because bricks with the Aramaic stamp
"Libilḫi" were found here.   Later on, however, similar
bricks were found on other parts of the Kasr, which
rendered my earlier reasons fallacious.

The following passage in the great *Steinplatten*
inscription, 8, 31-9, 28 (*K.B.* iii. 2, p. 27), refers principally
to the palace of the Principal Citadel, but includes also
the fortification walls of the Northern Citadel, to which
we shall return later : " Because my heart did not wish
the dwelling-place of my Majesty to be in another place,
because I did not build a royal dwelling in any other place,
and because I did not consign the kingly property to all
lands, my dwelling-place in Babylon grew insufficient for
the dignity of my Majesty.   Because the fear of Marduk
my lord dwelt in my heart, I did not change his street
in order to widen my fortress, the seat of my royalty in
Babylon.   I did his sanctuary no damage, nor did I
dam up his canal, but I sought at a distance room
for myself.   That no assault of battle may approach
Imgur-Bel the dûr of Babil, on the other side of
Nimitti-Bel the šalḫû of Babil, for 490 ells of land I made
for a protection two mighty walls of asphalt and burnt
bricks as dûr like mountains, and built between them a
building of burnt brick (bitik agurri), and made upon it a
lofty seat for my royal dwelling of asphalt and burnt brick,
and joined it to the palace of my father.   In a not un-
favourable month, on a propitious day, I grounded its
foundations firmly on the bosom of the underworld, and

raised its summit high like the mountains. Within 15 days I finished the building and made the seat of government illustrious. I caused mighty cedars, the product of high mountains, thick asûḫu-trees, and selected fine cypresses to be laid lengthways for its roofing. Door leaves of mismakanna, cedar, cypress, and usû-wood and ivory inlaid with silver and gold and adorned with copper ; bronze hinges and thresholds I fitted into its doorways, and caused its summits to be encompassed with a blue cornice (? kilîli). A mighty dûr of asphalt and burnt brick I caused to surround it mountains high" (trans. by Delitzsch).

By the blue cornice is meant either the frieze of lions on a blue ground or the above-mentioned reliefs in lapis-lazuli paste. That asphalt alone is mentioned as mortar, and not the lime that was so freely used in the Principal Citadel, need cause no wonder in face of the usual inaccuracy in regard to details. The statement that the palace was built and completed in 15 days is, however, truly marvellous and scarcely credible, and something must lie behind these words that has not yet been correctly understood. It was believed, however, in the ancient world without reservation. Berosus (Josephus, *Antiq. Jud.* x. 11) apparently derived his information from the same inscription when he says that the second palace which joined on to the ancestral palace was finished in 15 days, notwithstanding its magnificence and size.

XXVII

THE FORTIFICATION WALLS OF THE PRINCIPAL CITADEL

The Principal Citadel, which adjoins the Arachtu wall on the south, was protected on the east and north by two strong walls, while the western front probably lay open until Nabonidus built his Euphrates wall here.

The southern portion of the 7-metres-thick west wall

was placed on the old wall of Nebuchadnezzar's first
projected building, which we lighted on in the centre of
the Principal Citadel. In it the main entrance to the
palace undoubtedly lay, but the wall is not yet completely
excavated. Small mud houses backed against the wall
and were placed on the upper Nebuchadnezzar pavement,
but they were buried below the later pavement that
laid the Street horizontal.

On the other side of the Procession Street there ran
a parallel wall also 7 metres thick. The part that connects
it with the Ishtar Gate corresponds with the cross wall on
the other side, and like it has shallow foundations. Later
a strengthening piece was added to it. It contains two
doors close to each other, and a third door lies at a short
distance from the northern end. The footing of the
wall at the east was concealed by a bank of earth piled
up against it, which with its walk on the top reached
almost to the height of the Procession Street. At the
edge of this walk there is an additional slender wall which
may have been built in Persian times, and which appears
to have surrounded the whole of the northern Kasr,
and to have cut through several of the older walls that
stretched eastwards. At the north both walls end in a
powerful bastion. These marked the corners at which one
turned westward, the other eastward from the Procession
Street at an obtuse angle. Transversely across the Procession Street between the bastions there are two mud
walls, each with a door in the centre, forming a gateway
court, which in conjunction with the bastions bore the
appearance of an actual fortified gateway. This gateway
was destroyed when the whole length of the Street was
laid horizontal with the latest pavement of broken brick.

The wall that turned westward protected the palace
of the Principal Citadel on the north. Not far from the
corner there is a gateway (Fig. 106), which was roofed over
at the very moderate height of 1.5 metres with beams
of palm wood. Bricks placed upright formed the cavities
for inserting the beams, and in them the print of the wood
in the asphalt can still be seen ; in the middle of the
pavement, which is strongly laid in asphalt, a well-shaft led

down to the small conduit.   This roofed-in space appears
to have been only a sort of underground chamber that
gave access to the well-shaft; the actual door must have
been higher at about the level of the palace.   In the

Fig. 106.—Doorway with drain, in the north wall of the Principal Citadel.

outside angle near the bastion Neriglissar constructed
a quadrangular well-shaft with his stamped bricks.   We
have not yet followed up the wall to its western end.

We have, on the contrary, followed the wall that turns
to the east up to the end (Fig. 107).   It has a length of
about 250 metres, guarded by towers placed closely

together, and a door in each mesopyrgion. It represents
therefore a site admirably adapted for sorties. The
gateway embrasures lie exclusively on the north. At

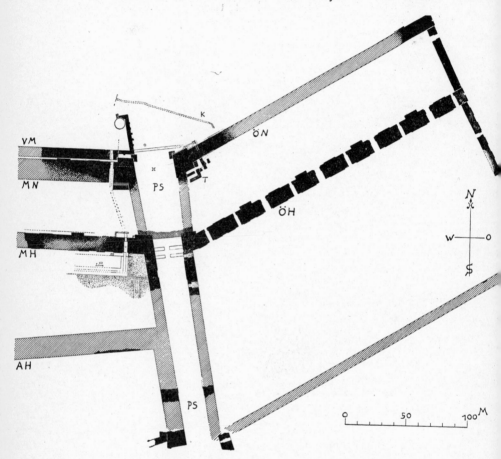

FIG. 107.—Plan of the northern bastions, north-east of the Kasr.

AH Ancient wall of the Principal
    Citadel.
K Canal.
MH Wall of the Principal Citadel in
    the north.
MN Wall of the Northern Citadel.

ÖH Eastern wing of wall of Principal
    Citadel.
ÖN Eastern wing of wall of Northern
    Citadel.
PS Procession Street.
T Ascent by steps or ramps.

the east the wall turns to the south and joins with one
leading from the Procession Street that has not yet been

examined in detail. All these eastern walls have been
destroyed from the point where they were cut through
by the Persian advanced wall down to a great depth,
so that it is only with difficulty that a few brick courses
could be found above water-level. Above the ruins there
lies silt which was evidently formed by water passing
over it at some time. On this and immediately below
the present level there are remains of later houses either
of mud brick or of burnt brick. A little above the ruins,
in the line of the northern wall, there was an anthropoid
clay coffin (see Fig. 200), the face represented with an
Egyptian beard. I believe that the Euphrates, as in
Persian times it worked its channel eastwards, thus placing
the Kasr on the right bank, first ruined these eastern
walls and then formed a muddy peninsula with their ruins,
while the actual river flowed still farther east. This is,
however, not yet proved.

The position of the double walls that flanked the
Procession Street is described in the inscription on a great
cylinder that we found on the eastern slope of the Amran
hill. It had been used there for some technical purpose,
and is much worn. The part that refers to our site runs
thus : "At that time I bethought myself to strengthen
the stronghold of Babylon. 360 ells of the land the sides
(*or* of the sides) of Nimitti-Bel, the šalḫû of Babylon, I
built as a protection from the banks of the Euphrates to
the left threshold of the Ištar Gate two mighty walls of
asphalt and burnt brick for a dûru like a mountain. Between
them I erected a terrace of burnt brick, and upon it a great
castle (?) as a dwelling-place of my kingdom. Of asphalt
and burnt brick I built high, joined (it) with the palace,
which (lay) within the city, and caused the dwelling of my
lordship to be glorious. Besides, from the right threshold
of the Ištar Gate to the lower turru of Nimitti-Bel in
the east 360 ells broadside, (measured) from Nimitti-Bel,
for protection, a mighty dûru of asphalt and burnt brick
I built mountain-high. The stronghold I strengthened
with skill. The city of Babylon I protected" (trans. by
Weissbach).

As we have seen, the Ishtar Gate had a central door

and two side ones. These last are evidently intended for
the left- and right-hand thresholds of the Ishtar Gate.
The distance from the wall at the threshold to the north
side of the bastion on the eastern wall is 192 metres, and
on the western wall 196 metres. This gives as measure
for Nebuchadnezzar's ells .533 or .544 metres. These
measurements must, however, be taken again more accurately on the completion of the excavations. The length
of 490 ells, which is quoted for the same area in the
great *Steinplatten* inscription, includes the northern
extension of the wall, to which we shall soon turn.

XXVIII

THE NORTHERN CITADEL

THE Northern Citadel, as we call the part of the Kasr
north of the square 6, is still in process of excavation.
Various results have already been gained from it which
admit of description, though with some reservations. The
work has been on the eastern part, the prolongation of the
Procession Street and its termination at the north.

The site, so far as it has been opened up, is on the
whole a repetition of what we have seen in the previous
chapter. Both the measurements and directions of the
walls are entirely analogous with those of the earlier ones.
Here again are the two walls flanking the Procession
Street, ending in bastions, and then turning off east
and west.

Here also we have followed the eastern wall to the
end, where it turns southwards until it joins the corner
of the earlier wall. There is some indication that the
architect intended at least a continuation of this plan
towards the east, and in fact at the east end of the inner
and older wall there was a groove in the brickwork that
points to such an intention. We, however, have not
found the slightest trace of any such wall, although we
have carefully searched for it both close to the angle

Fig. 108.—Ascent to the Acropolis.   Homera in the background.

of the wall, and also farther east. Nothing has been found in the trenches made for this purpose except the ruins of later houses above and mud with a complete absence of buildings below. Thus from ancient days

FIG. 109.—Stone wall of the Northern Citadel, from west looking east.

till its downfall this site remained without any prolongation to the east.

At the angle of the bastions near the Street smaller towers were added, which strengthened the fortifications that guarded this main entrance to the Acropolis, while the later Persian outer wall appears to have narrowed and thus strengthened the entrance.

An ascent is added at the inner corner of the eastern bastion (Fig. 108) which united the low-lying area between the two parallel walls with the Procession Street, and actually with the crown of the wall and the plateau of the bastion. It was a winding path, which ran round a

FIG. 110.—Stone wall of Northern Citadel with inscription.

newel wall, but whether or not it had steps we do not know. In front of the gate that faced eastward there was another defensive building with two exits.

We have excavated the western wall at its junction with the bastion. Its farther course is marked in a deep valley which extends almost as far as the Euphrates on the west (Fig. 109). In the north, immediately in front of the bastion, without any intermediate space, there is a stone wall formed of immense blocks of limestone bound together with dove-tailed wooden clamps laid in asphalt. Four courses of this have so far been laid open above

N

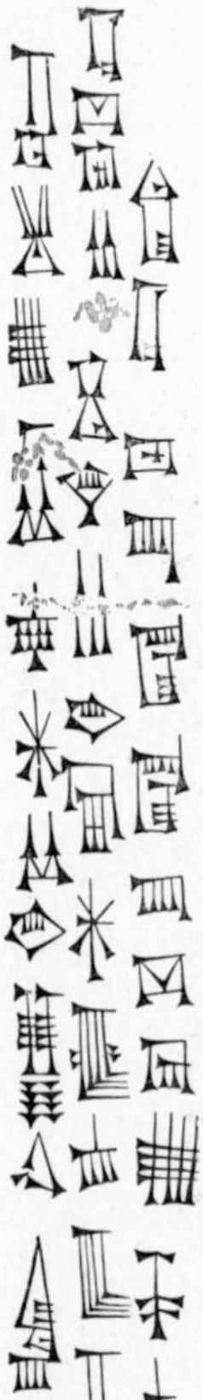

Fig. 111.—Inscription on the stone wall of the Northern Citadel.

water-level (Fig. 110). In the upper courses a wall of burnt brick overlaps the stone masonry. In the third course of masonry from the top each block has an inscription chiselled out in large Old-Babylonian characters (Fig. 111): "Nebuchadnezzar, etc., am I. The dûru of the palace of Babylon I have made with stones of the mountain (followed by a prayer)." With this statement we will compare that part of the great *Steinplatten* inscription (9, 22) where it says, "Beyond the dûr of burnt brick I built a great dûr of mighty stones, the production of the great mountains, and raised its summit high as a mountain." Thus it is clear that the previous mention of the Principal Citadel included the Northern Citadel, and in consequence the length there assigned to the wall of 490 ells covers the entire stretch from the Ishtar Gate to the north front of the northern bastion. According to our provisional measurement, this length consisted of 251 metres, which would make an ell of .512 metres. If this result does not agree exactly with that quoted above (p. 174) the reason is probably that we do not know accurately the points to which Nebuchadnezzar measured.

Close to the bastion a gateway led through the western wall, which is exactly similar both in plan and construction to the gateway in the wall of the Principal Citadel. The canal that passes through the gateway must certainly have been connected with the canal in the wall of the Principal Citadel. The construction is very plain here; so far as it lies in the burnt brick wall it is covered in with corbelled tiles, and in the stone masonry with large blocks of limestone laid flat (Fig. 112).

In front of the wall to the north there was water, the moat of the fortress, a part of the Euphrates or of the Arachtu. A sudden assault on the fortress by water might easily be accomplished by means of these canals,

Fig. 112.—Doorway with canal in the stone wall.

and to guard against this huge gratings formed of stone blocks were placed across the channel below the water, thus closing the passage. Every part of the defences, wherever they are intersected by a water-channel, is carefully guarded by gratings either of stone or of burnt brick, to safeguard them against invaders.

An assault by means of the water-channel must
therefore have been feared by the ancient architects, even
if the account of the sacking of Babylon in this manner
by the Persians is legendary.

The wall like that of the Principal Citadel was guarded
by alternate narrow and wide projecting towers. The
principal wall in the
north is clad by a later
strengthening wall.

The moat, which
lay in front of this wall,
and which we have also
to surmise in front of
the eastern wall, was
bridged over by a dam
which led up to the
gentle ascent to the
Procession Street.
This dam was flanked
with sloping walls, of
which we have ex-
cavated the western
one. It bites into the
earth with short pro-
jecting buttresses. At
the northern end a
circular cistern was in-
serted later.

Fig. 113.—Canal in front of the Northern Citadel,
on the north.

Thus the dam led
over the defensive
moat, and afforded access to the main entrance to the
Acropolis. A narrow roofed-in canal led through the
dam (K in Fig. 107) and conducted the water from west
to east. The roof is laid sloping with bricks placed edgeways (Fig. 113), and like the rubble walls of Nebuchadnezzar it is laid in mud. The technique is the same as
that of the canal on the south of the Kasr. Close to the
place where the canal turned off from the principal one a
brick with the Arachtu stamp of Nabopolassar has been
inserted. The canal itself can scarcely be recognised as

Arachtu, but we may perhaps conclude from the reverential reuse of the ancient brick that the channel from which this canal branched off bore the name.

If these descriptions will enable the reader to picture to himself the accumulation of masses of towered defensive walls that guarded the entrance to the Citadel, he will realise that it could hardly have been possible to construct a more imposing approach to this ancient gateway than this one, with its gradual ascent between the walls of the Procession Street, decorated with the long multi-coloured rows of lions, up to the Ishtar Gate and through that to the actual Bab-ilani.

XXIX

RETROSPECT OF THE KASR

THE gradual raising of the buildings on the Kasr and their development into the Acropolis of Babylon may be classified in their principal features under the following periods :

1. The wall of the river bank built by Sargon. Imgur-Bel and Nimitti-Bel, the walls connected with it, no longer exist.

2. Nabopolassar's palace of mud brick on a foundation of burnt brick, surrounded by an enclosing wall which included the *irsit Babil* and to which the arched door belongs. Building of the Arachtu walls in three successive periods.

3. Nebuchadnezzar replaced the mud brick of his father by walls of burnt brick, restored the enclosing wall, built the older moat wall, and renewed the Ninmach temple of Sardanapalus.

4. Building of the two mud walls, which may prove to be Imgur-Bel and Nimitti-Bel, and in which stood the ancient Ishtar Gate, which no longer exists.

5. Building of the east part of the Southern Citadel. Raising of the enclosing wall, of the Ninmach temple, and of the Procession Street.

6. Rebuilding of the Ishtar Gate with the brick reliefs, and heightening of the two mud-brick walls.

7. Construction of the moat wall of Imgur-Bel. Raising of the Nabopolassar palace.

8. Extension of the palace to the west. The whole Southern Citadel now lay on the higher level. Completion of the southern water arm (Libil-higalla?), which also encircled the Southern Citadel in the east.

9. Project for an advanced building in the north, of which the 17-metres-thick wall in the Principal Citadel is part.

10. Building of the Principal Citadel, with the two parallel walls that flank the Procession Street and the two wall lengths that turn east and west. Raising of the Procession Street and stone pavement, of the Ishtar Gate with the enamel reliefs, and of the Ninmach temple.

11. Lengthening of the parallel walls to the north. Building of the flanking walls and the stone wall.

12. Neriglissar's and Nabonidus' restorations, of which there are scanty traces.

13. Uniting of the entire Kasr by means of the Persian advanced wall of the Acropolis, after the Euphrates had removed its channel to the east side. Building of a palace on the western Southern Citadel by Artaxerxes Mnemon.

14. In the Parthian period the downfall and demolition began. Houses of burnt brick and brick graves among the ruins. The Euphrates returned to its ancient bed.

15. A large necropolis of late Parthian or Sassanide times in the principal court of the Southern Citadel.

It must be admitted that these epochs cannot be always clearly differentiated. They form only an approximate sketch of the development so far as it has hitherto been possible to recognise it, and for some time to come will require emendation and amplification.

xxx

THE PERIBOLOS OF ETEMENANKI

THE route from the south-west corner of the Kasr to Amran leads first to a small mound which we have named the south-west building. It consists largely of mud-brick masonry that belongs to the later Parthian (?) period. So far we have done little excavation here. We next pass the long low-lying stretch that now represents a water-channel that once lay here. We then ascend a range of mounds that also extends from east to west. A cross-cut has shown that it consists of the ruins of Babylonian houses of crude brick, lying one above another, as we shall find them later in Merkes. This was the town site of the common people.

On the other side of this range of mounds a some-what considerable plain of remarkable uniformity stretches away to the hill of Amran Ibn Ali, cut through diagon-ally by the road that leads from our village of Kweiresh to Hilleh. It is called Sachn, literally "the pan," a term which in modern days is applied to the open space enclosed by arcades that surrounds the great pilgrimage mosques, such as those of Kerbela or Nedjef. Our Sachn, however, is no other than the modern representation of the ancient sacred precinct in which stood the zikurrat Etemenanki, "the foundation stone of heaven and earth," the tower of Babylon, surrounded by an enclosing wall against which lay all manner of buildings connected with the cult (Fig. 114).

This enclosing wall forms almost a square, divided by cross walls into separate parts, three of which we have already recognised. All the buildings consisted largely of crude brick, and only, as an exception, the very consider-able crude-brick core of the tower in the south-west corner was enclosed in a thick wall of burnt brick, which has been removed deep down by brick robbers. Now only their deep and broad trenches are to be seen, but these enable us to recognise the site of a great open stairway

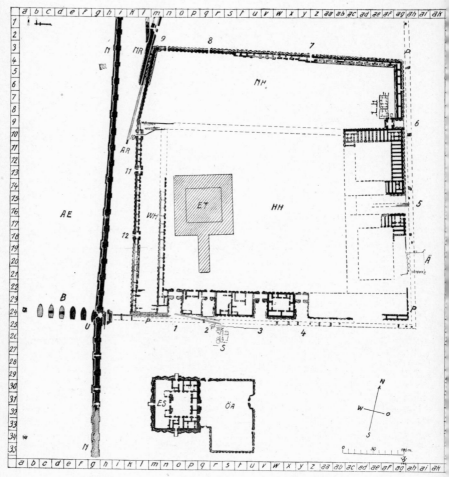

FIG. 114.—Plan of Esagila and Etemenanki.

AE	Ancient bed of Euphrates.	NR	Nebuchadnezzar wall.
AR	Arachtu wall.	ÖA	Eastern annex.
Ä	Earlier building.	P	Procession Street of Marduk.
ıB	Bridge over the Euphrates.	S	Later Parthian (?) buildings.
ES	E-Sagila, the temple of Marduk.	U	Urash (?) Gate.
ET	E-Temenanki, the tower of Babylon.	WH	Western court.
HH	Principal Citadel.	1-12.	The doorways in the peribolos of
N	Nabonidus wall.		Etemenanki.
NH	Northern court.		

which led up to the tower from the south. The ruin is
not yet excavated.

Many additions and restorations were carried out in

Fig. 115.—East side of the peribolos of Etemenanki.

connection with these buildings, and they can clearly be
distinguished, especially in the enclosing wall itself.   The

east end of the northern front is very instructive in this respect. We can distinguish the original building and a strengthening wall, the kisu, in front of it. Here it is of crude brick, but on the west front, like the kisu of Emach, it is of burnt brick. On the original building three periods lie superposed, as also on the kisu. Of each of these building periods slightly projecting towers are placed on the walls close together, and differently distributed, which considerably aids us in distinguishing the periods, as the mud - brick courses are frequently placed immediately over each other (Fig. 115). Inside the lowest

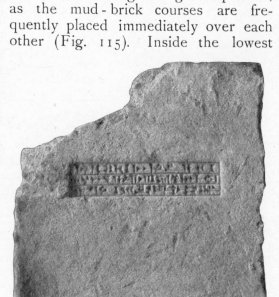

FIG. 116. — Esarhaddon's Etemenanki inscription.

FIG. 117. —Sardanapalus' Etemenanki inscription.

kisu, somewhat farther to the west, there is a vertical gutter of the kind we have already observed in the inner city walls. In this were inscribed bricks of Esarhaddon (Fig. 116), with the statement that he built the zikurrat of Etemenanki. The two upper portions of the kisu must therefore belong to a later period, and the

lower part of the main building to an earlier period, than
that of Esarhaddon. The other excavations have produced
in addition 12 stamped bricks of Sardanapalus (Fig. 117)
and 4 inscribed bricks of
Nebuchadnezzar (Fig. 118),
all of which refer to the building of Etemenanki. Even if
these bricks were not intended
for the peribolos, but for the
tower itself, their occasional
use for the former is in no way
surprising. All that we have
been able to excavate so far
is connected with the original
building, of which the later
repairing and rebuilding carefully follow the ancient line of
wall. We need not therefore
lay too much stress on the
various periods.

The surrounding wall is
for the greater part a double
wall, in which uniform broad
chambers are constructed by
means of cross walls. The
ornamental towers on the
inner walls are always placed
between two doors of these
chambers, while on the outside, where the two ornamental
grooves that used to decorate
both the towers and the intermediate spaces still exist in
places, both towers and spaces
are of the same breadth.

FIG. 118.—Nebuchadnezzar's
Etemenanki inscription.

There are buildings at other points of the encircling
walls always joined to the outer wall. Large as they are,
they have none of the characteristics of temples. Two
large buildings lay on the east side, each with a large
court surrounded by deep chambers uniform in size. In

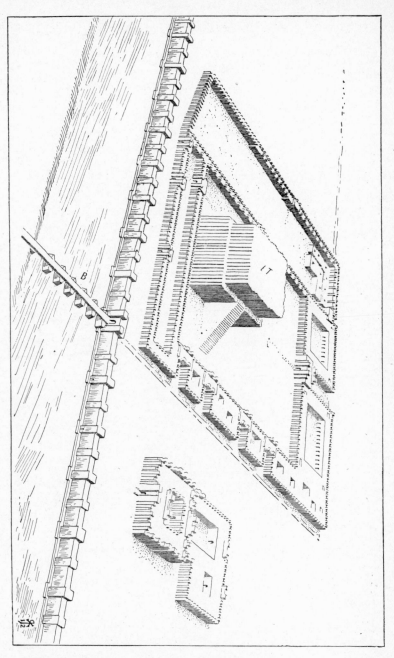

Fig. 119.—Reconstruction of the peribolos, with the tower of Babylon, the temple Esagila, the quay wall of Nabonidus, and the Euphrates bridge. The tower is shown incomplete. (B) Bridge. (ET) Etemenanki.

the corner there is a dwelling grouped round a courtyard, and on the south side there are four similar ones, which, although smaller, are very large and dignified mansions. At the east of the northern part the usual small private houses form an independent line of street.

Two doors in the north and ten elaborate gateways with an inner court and towered façade afforded access to the interior. The two eastern of these and the four at the south are placed at the end of deep recesses formed by the outer wall being carried back, thus forming roomy forecourts. The four southern gateways have the typical towered façade also on the side that faces inwards. The southern gate on the east side, which was the largest, is destroyed, but we can reconstruct it without difficulty.

Very little remains of the south-east corner. Near the south-west corner a chambered wall projects to the north, and with the outer wall forms a long narrow court in which there were no other chambers than those formed in the wall. Apparently this narrow court extended as far as the northern gateway in the western wall, and here apparently it joined at right angles another wall which extended here in the same line as the northern front of the great building on the east side; of this wall, however, only the western end now exists. It skirted a northern area, in which the above-mentioned private houses lay.

We have thus three divisions inside the peribolos: the northern court (NH on Fig. 114) with the small houses, the long narrow western court (WH), and the principal court (HH), which contained the zikurrat of Etemenanki (ET) and all the other monumental buildings (Fig. 119).

Low down on the north, close to the zikurrat, there were ancient buildings orientated in an entirely different direction, and on the east front, also at a great depth, there lay a large ancient building (Ä), over which the main building of the peribolos was carried. Neither of these had anything to do with the sanctuary as such.

We can only hazard a guess as to the purpose of all those buildings. The wall chambers are adapted by their simplicity to house a number of pilgrims, who could dwell there and have direct access to the great courts. The buildings in the south I take to have been priests' dwellings. Under no circumstances can they have been temples, as all the necessary features are absent, such as the towered façade and the postament niche. The priests of Etemenanki must have occupied very distinguished positions as representatives of the god who bestowed the kingship of Babylon, and the immense private houses to the south of our peribolos agree very well with the supposition in regard to this Vatican of Babylon, that the

FIG. 120.—Duck weight with inscription.

principal administrative apparatus would be housed there. The numerous chambers of the two great buildings in the east will be recognised by all as store-rooms where the property of the sanctuary and the things needed for processions, etc., could be stored. In one of these chambers, which for the most part are not yet cleared, we found a great stone weight in the form of a duck (Fig. 120), the usual form of such weights. It weighs 29.68 kilogrammes and, according to the chiselled inscription on it, was called a "correct talent." All the buildings are much ruined, often as low down as beneath the ancient pavement. In the north-east corner of the peribolos a stela with emblems of the gods was found (Fig. 121).

The main approach lay between the two store-houses just mentioned, where from the existence of a specially deep and wide recess we can surmise a specially large gateway, which, though it exists no longer, admits of easy reconstruction. The turminabanda pavement of the Procession Street reaches as far as this, and continues in

FIG. 121.—Upper part of a stela with divine emblems.

the recess where the paving-blocks still lie that bear the inscription of Nebuchadnezzar on their edge. Some of these have the name and title of Sennacherib on the under side (cf. Fig. 36).

In the Ripley-cylinder of Neriglissar (*K.B.* iii. 2, p. 79) the peribolos is called "lânu ma-ḥir-tim." According to Muss-Arnolt's dictionary the words mean "enclosure" and "store-house." With the exception of these two words I give Bezold's translation, which otherwise only requires correction in slight details : " The peribolos of the store-houses of Esagila to the north, wherein the consecrated temple treasury of Esagila rests (trans. by Delitzsch, 'wherein the priests of Esagila dwell') whose foundations an earlier king laid but did not build its summit, (this building) had sunk in its foundations, its walls were fallen down, its joints were loosened, and its base had become weak. Then my lord the great Marduk inspired me to raise up the building, entrusted me (?) with the splendour (?) and the regulation of the temple tribute. In order to incur no Shiddim and no offences, I dug up the ancient foundation stone and read it (its records). On its ancient foundation stone I based it (the building), its summit I raised like a mountain, I made firm its threshold and fixed the doors in its doorway. The firm Kisu I built of asphalt and burnt brick (?)" According to this the Kisu of burnt brick which was found in the excavations on the west side was of Neriglissar.

The original of the second Babylonian text that refers to the enclosure has disappeared. We possess only an epitome of it given by Smith[1] (Hommel, *Geographie*

---

[1] Smith's Etemenanki Inscription :—

I have discovered a Babylonian text, giving a remarkable account of the temple of Belus at Babylon, and as my approaching departure for Nineveh does not allow me time to make a full translation of the document, I have prepared a short account for your readers, giving the principal points in the arrangement and dimensions of the building. . . .

First, I must remark on the Babylonian measures used, that they are principally the cubit, equal to about one foot eight inches English, and the gar or sa, equal to 12 cubits, or 20 feet English ; but there is another series of numbers used in measuring, consisting apparently of numbers of barleycorns arranged in sixties, thus the first number is a length of 11 . 33 . 20, which consists of $11 \times 3600 + 33 \times 60 + 20$ barleycorns, or 1155 feet 7 inches. The barleycorn was the standard unit of measure among the Babylonians, and for this reason was used sometimes in measures of length without the other terms.

First in the tablet we have the measure of the outer court, called the " grand Court," which is given at 11 . 33 . 20 in length (that is about 1156 feet) and 9 in breadth (that is, 900 feet). There is a calculation as to the area of this court, which I pass over, and come to the next court called the " Court of Ishtar and Zamama." This space is reckoned as 10 . 33 . 20 in length (1056 feet) and 430 (450 feet) in breadth. There is again here a calculation of the area which I omit.

Round the court were 6 gates admitting to the temples. These were : 1, the grand gate ; 2, the gate of the rising sun (east) ; 3, the great gate ; 4, the gate of the Colossi ; 5, the gate of the Canal ; and 6, the gate of the tower-view.

The next division is the space or platform apparently walled, and called a ki-galli, sur, or birut. It is uncertain if this was paved, and its extent is also uncertain. It is stated as a square, 3 ku in length, and 3 ku in breadth, but the value of the ku is un-

Vorderasiens und Nordostafrikas, p. 315, and Thureau-Dangin, *Journal asiatique*, janvier 1909). But the statements can only be reconciled with the existing remains with great difficulty, and then only in general. The

---

certain. The 4 walls faced the cardinal points, in this agreeing with the other parts, all the buildings having their sides east, west, north, and south.

There were 4 gates, one in the centre of each side of this division : 1, the gate of the rising sun (east) ; 2, the southern gate ; 3, the gate of the setting sun (west) ; 4, the northern gate.

Inside stood some building or enclosure, the name of which is damaged. It was 10 gar long and 10 gar broad (200 feet by 200), connected with the great Ziggurat or tower, which was the inner and crowning edifice of the group. Round the base of the Ziggurat or tower were ranged the chapels or temples of the principal gods, on its 4 sides and facing the cardinal points.

On the eastern side stood a sanctuary or temple 70 or 80 cubits long and 40 cubits broad (117 or 133 feet by 67), with 16 shrines, the principal being the shrines devoted to the god Nebo and Urmit, or Tasmit his Wife. Nebo was considered the eldest son of Bel, the great deity of the temple.

On the northern side stood 2 temples, one devoted to the god Hea, the other to Nusku. The temple of Hea was 85 cubits long and 30 broad (142 feet by 50 feet), and that of Nusku was a square, 35 cubits each way (58 feet by 58 feet).

On the southern side stood a single temple dedicated to the two great gods Anu and Bel. This was 70 cubits long and 30 cubits broad (117 feet by 50 feet).

On the western side were the principal buildings, consisting of a double house, with a court between the two wings. On the one side the wing was 100 cubits long and 65 cubits broad (166 feet by 108 feet), and the space between them was 35 cubits wide (58 feet). The building at the back was 125 cubits long and 30 cubits broad (208 feet by 50 feet). I do not properly comprehend the disposition of the buildings of this side, and my description of the position of the western temples must be taken as conjectural. In these western chambers stood the couch of the god, and the throne of gold mentioned by Herodotus, besides other furniture of great value. The couch is stated to have been 9 cubits long and 4 cubits broad (15 feet by 6 feet 8 inches).

In the centre of these groups of temples stood the grandest portion of the whole pile, the great Ziggurat, or temple tower, built in stages, its sides facing the cardinal points.

The bottom or first stage was a square in plan 15 gar in length and breadth, and 5½ gar in height (300 feet square, 110 feet high). This stage appears to have been indented or ornamented with buttresses.

The next or second stage of the tower was also square, being 13 gar in length and breadth, and 3 gar in height (260 feet square, 60 feet high). The epithet applied to this stage is obscure ; it had probably sloping sides.

The third stage differs widely from the lower ones, and commences a regular progressive series of stages, all of equal height. It was 10 gar in length and breadth, and 1 gar in height (200 feet square, 20 feet high).

The fourth stage was 8½ gar in length and breadth, and 1 gar in height (170 feet square, 20 feet high).

The fifth stage was 7 gar in length and breadth, and 1 gar in height (140 feet square, 20 feet high).

Probably by accident, the dimensions of the sixth stage of the tower are omitted in the inscription, but they can be easily restored in accordance with the others. This stage must have been 5½ gar in length and breadth, and 1 gar in height (110 feet square, 20 feet high).

On this was raised the seventh stage, which was the upper temple or sanctuary of the god Bel. This building had a length of 4 gar, a breadth of 3½ gar, and a height of 2½ gar (80 feet long, 70 feet broad, and 50 feet high).

Thus the whole height of this tower above its foundation was 15 gar or 300 feet, exactly equal to the breadth of the base ; and, as the foundation was most probably raised above the level of the ground, it would give a height of over 300 feet above the plain for this grandest of Babylonian temples . . . (see App. p. 327).

O

measurements given for the three courts should agree with the ruins, at least as regards the relations of length to breadth, but this is not so whether we take the measurement of the walls outside or of the open space within the courts. The only possible solution appears to me to be that we take the measures given as those of the "great court" to be meant for the south-east portion, including the buildings surrounding it, that we take the "court of Ishtar and Zamana" to mean what we call the north court, and the third to mean the inner open space of our great court. But even so there are difficulties. Under these circumstances we need not attach any great importance to the measurements given for the alleged 7 stages of the tower. Those uncertainties are caused by the fact that the original inscription is not at hand, we do not know the object for which these statements were made (see App. p. 327).

Herodotus (i. 181) names the group of buildings "the brazen-doored sanctuary of Zeus Belus." The zikurrat inside the sanctuary he describes as a massive tower on which stood a second, third, up to an eighth tower, above which was a "great temple." This is the sole ground for our conception of the "terraced towers" of Mesopotamia. In Khorsabad there was the ruin of a tower, where the excavators suspected similar retreating stages to have existed, but Place clearly formed his conclusion under the long-accepted suggestion drawn from the description given by Herodotus, and the ruins themselves no longer exist. In the words of Herodotus himself, however, there is nothing whatever about stepped terraces. He speaks of 8 towers standing one above another, but he does not say that each was smaller than the one below it. I myself desired to accept the general conception of stepped towers, but I know of no safe ground for such a conception. The only remedy I can see for this difficulty is to excavate the best-preserved zikurrat we possess, that of Borsippa.

From the ruins as they now exist before excavation, we must assume that a colossal stairway led up from the south to the top of the immense mass of building. Steps in antiquity were always extremely steep, as we have found them here, and the height and breadth were usually the same, so according to the measurements of the length of the foundations of the steps we may take their height to have been 50 metres.

We do not know the complete height of the tower. Nabopolassar, however, lays great stress on it (M'Gee, *Zur Topographie Babylons*, A. i.), and so does Nebuchadnezzar (M'Gee, B. vi.) in his cylinder-inscription of Etemenanki. Nabopolassar says: "At this time Marduk commanded me . . .; the tower of Babylon, which in the time before me had become weak, and had been brought to ruin, to lay its foundation firm on the bosom of the underworld, while its top should stretch heavenwards" (trans. by Delitzsch). Nebuchadnezzar says: "To raise up the top of Etemenanki that it may rival heaven, I laid to my hand." In both inscriptions mud brick, burnt brick, asphalt, mud, and mighty cedars of Lebanon are mentioned as the materials employed. The latter could scarcely have been employed otherwise than to roof in the temple on the top of the tower.

In distinction to this upper temple Herodotus calls Esagila lying before it to the south the κάτω νηός, the lower temple. In the upper temple, according to Herodotus, there was only a golden table and a κλίνη, and according to Ctesias three gold figures of Zeus, Hera, and Rhea. My opinion is that the designation of the zikurrat as bearing a temple is confirmed by this. The Babylonian term only expresses height, and nothing that can suggest stages. It is obvious that the roof of so lofty a temple would be welcomed by the Babylonian astronomers as a platform for their observations. It would be necessary for them to be raised above the thick atmosphere of the plain. Owing to excessive dryness, the air is almost opaque at a distance, and the horizon up to a height of 10 or 20 grades is a dusky circle of dust, through which the sun and moon often assume torn and distorted forms, if their setting can be seen at all.

It is true that during the summer we have no clouds, with the exception of the *Bachura*, a type of weather that occurs at the beginning of August, but we have sandstorms, through which the sun appears like a blood-red disc. The greatly-renowned clearness of the Babylonian sky is largely a fiction of European travellers, who are rarely accustomed to observe the night sky of Europe without the intervention of city lights.

The original complete height of the tower of Babylon we do not know. The east side of the peribolos, which is almost similar to the north side, measures 409 metres in round numbers. · For the entire sacred enclosure Herodotus gives a measure of 2 square stadia, and 1 stadion as the side length of the area of the zikurrat; the ruins themselves show 90 metres.

But what is all this written information in comparison with the clearness of the evidence we gain from the buildings themselves, ruined though they are. The colossal mass of the tower, which the Jews of the Old Testament regarded as the essence of human presumption, amidst the proud palaces of the priests, the spacious treasuries, the innumerable lodgings for strangers—white walls, bronze doors, mighty fortification walls set round with lofty portals and a forest of 1000 towers,—the whole must have conveyed an overwhelming sense of greatness, power, and wealth, such as could rarely have been found elsewhere in the great Babylonian kingdom.

I once beheld the great silver standing statue of the Virgin, over life-size, laden with votive offerings, rings, precious stones, gold and silver, borne on a litter by forty men, appear in the portal of the dome of Syracuse, high above the heads of the assembled crowds, to. be brought out in festival procession with inspiring music and among the fervent prayers of the people into the garden of the Latomia. After the same fashion I picture to myself a procession of the god Marduk as he issued forth from Esagila, perhaps through the peribolos, to proceed on his triumphant way through the Procession Street of Babylon.

Herodotus must have seen the enclosure in a comparatively good state of preservation. Under Alexander it needed repairs, and 600,000 days' wages were spent on clearing out the precincts and removing the rubbish (Strabo, xvi. 1). During the eleven years of our work we have expended about 800,000 daily wages for the great clearance of Babylon.

Before we pass to the temple of Esagila, which was so closely connected with Etemenanki (p. 204), we will inspect the walls that lie to the west of the enclosure, and the Euphrates bridge.

XXXI

THE EUPHRATES BRIDGE

THE Procession Street which, with its strongly-asphalted brick pavement, runs close to the southern side of the peribolos, ended in the west at the land pier of a bridge of burnt brick and asphalt. Seven river piers have been excavated. The western one differs somewhat in plan, and may have been the end pier on the bank at that side (Fig. 122), but this is not yet certain. The complete length of this bridge, as far as we have made it out, amounted to 123 metres, and the pier lengths of 21 metres may have exceeded the breadth of the roadway very considerably. The piers are 9 metres wide and are placed 9 metres apart. They are built with a very marked batter. Their bricks are of the small size 31 × 31 centimetres and are unstamped, from which we may conclude that the building dates from Nebuchadnezzar's first period or from Nabopolassar. There are rectangular cavities in the piers in which, as far as we can judge, strengthening baulks of wood once lay 50 centimetres apart. Above this, at a distance of 2 metres, there was a second similar course of wood. The sides of the piers are convex and meet in a point in front facing the current on the north. The back is also slightly curved. Thus the ground-plan of the pier follows the water-line of a ship.

Herodotus (i. 186), Diodorus (ii. 8, after Ctesias), and others speak of this bridge. They report that stone blocks were used for it, and it is very probable that the brick piers were roofed over with stone, on which the rafters for the roadway were laid. We have seen in the north wall of the Kasr that Nebuchadnezzar bound his blocks together with dove-tail clamps, and this is also reported of the bridge. Diodorus calls special attention to the peculiar shape of the

FIG. 122.—The western pier of the bridge over the Euphrates.

piers, which is specially adapted to the requirements of the current. The measurements here also do not agree on all points. The length is given as 5 stadia, the breadth 30 feet, and the distance between the piers 12 feet. But it appears to me rash to argue from this lack of agreement the existence of a second stone bridge. This is the most

ancient stone bridge of which we have any record, and its
well-deserved fame is evident from the fact that it was the
only one remarked on in the scanty reports of the ancient
historians.

The ancient bed of the river is clearly marked just in
the vicinity where a long depression between the mounds
of ruins extends to the village of Kweiresh.   In the south-
west, close to the bridge head, one of these mounds of
ruins rises to a considerable height.   Its western side is
worn away by the modern Euphrates into a vertical steep
declivity, and the mud walls of the houses that stand out
between the usual rubbish in the mound are here laid bare
and clearly visible.   They extend down below the usual
level of the water.

Among the Babylonian texts that refer to the bridge, it
is described by Nebuchadnezzar as the work of Nabopolassar in the E-ulla cylinder (M'Gee, B. ii. col. 1, 8):
" The embankment wall of Arachtu . . . from the Ishtar
Gate to the Urash Gate, my father, my begetter, had built
with asphalt and brick, had erected piers of burnt brick for
the crossing over of the Euphrates" (see *K.B.* iii. 2, p. 21,
l. 7, and p. 41, l. 38).   The meaning of the words *ma-ka-at
a-bar-ti Puráti* as " bridge over the Euphrates" was kindly
given me as early as the year 1904 by Lehmann-Haupt.

XXXII

THE BRIDGE GATEWAY

BETWEEN the land pier of the bridge, and the first river
pier, a gateway was inserted that lay in the line of a long
fortification wall that stretches to the north with stamped
bricks in it of Nabonidus.   As usual with city gateways, it
had an inner court and two massive fronting towers.   The
bricks, so far as we can see, have Nebuchadnezzar's stamp,
and, like the wall itself, are laid in asphalt.   In the entrance
lies a brick pavement of many courses, and also the great

southern door socket of the west door.   In the middle of
the east doorway there is a brick set upright, which projects slightly above the pavement and served as a stop for
the leaves of the door.   The pavement is 3.10 metres
above zero, rather higher than that of the Procession Street,
and above it 12 metres of the rubbish of the Amran hill is
still piled.   The gateway was inserted partly in the land
and partly in the river pier, and both are cut away to some
extent to accommodate the later building.

As we have followed the Arachtu wall from the
Southern Citadel up to the peribolos, and as this is the first
great gateway in this vicinity after the Ishtar Gate, this
building must, I think, according to the inscription just
referred to, be the Urash Gate.   It is, therefore, a matter
of indifference whether our building is the same that
existed in Nebuchadnezzar's time, or whether it is later and
dates from Nabonidus, for in the latter case a gateway that
bore the name of the Urash Gate existed previously and in
much the same place if not on exactly the same spot.   It
is possible that the massive brickwork that lies immediately
to the west of the land pier belonged to this earlier gateway.   This consists of two projections, between which there
is a stepped wall.

The excavations here are still incomplete.

XXXIII

THE WALL OF NABONIDUS

We have not yet followed the fortification wall connected with the gateway just described far to the south.
The ruins here lie deep under the rubbish of the Amran
mound, and are difficult to get at.   On the north the
excavations have laid open this wall as far as the village
of Kweiresh.

The wall, which is 7.67 metres thick, with its cavalier
towers stands on the river bank upon a massive projecting

banquette like the older moat wall, the Arachtu wall, and
the north wall of the Principal Citadel. This arrangement
can thus be clearly recognised as a peculiarity of walls
that lie on a water-channel. Towers, alternately broad and
narrow, are placed at a distance of about 19 metres from
each other. The broad ones are 7.3, the narrow ones 6.3
metres wide. In some of these towers there are fittings for
double doors, from which a somewhat steep ramp leads
down to the river. The walls are in very bad condition,
and it is impossible to say whether there were similar
doors in every tower, or, if not, at what length of interval.
The pavement is .47 above zero. In the north, a short
distance in front of the Southern Citadel, the wall for two
mesopyrgia bends somewhat towards the west to unite
by a tower with the Western Outworks (p. 144). In this
tower was the outflow of the eastern canal that flowed
past the Southern Citadel. The bend is obviously contrived in order to include the Western Outworks of the
Southern Citadel in the city area.

Not far from the north-western corner of the peribolos
we made a cross-cut through the high mounds that cover
the wall, and here we found also the Arachtu wall of
Nabopolassar and Nebuchadnezzar. The cut has been
continued for some length to the north on the other side
of the depression caused by the river-bed, and there it
yielded walls of burnt-brick buildings of considerable thickness, but the river wall that corresponds with that on the
left bank we have not yet uncovered. This excavation
is very far from complete. The wall is apparently the
same that was called by Herodotus (i. 180) αἱμασιή, which
joined on to the wings of the outer city wall, and which
Ctesias (Diodorus, ii. 3) called κρηπίς.

THE ARACHTU WALLS AT THE PERIBOLOS OF ETEMENANKI

IMMEDIATELY in front of the northern portion of the west front of the peribolos there lies the Arachtu wall of Nabopolassar, of which we saw the commencement in the north at the Southern Citadel. As soon as we began the cross-cut mentioned above, we came on a length of wall in which was an inscribed brick that explained its purpose. Later on in the farther reaches of the wall we found numerous bricks of the same kind *in situ*. The text is identical with that already quoted on page 138 *et seq.* The wall lies lower than the burnt-brick kisu of the peribolos wall at this point. The Arachtu wall, which stands in water, reaches up only to .33 metres below zero with its ruins, while the kisu of the peribolos extends down to 2.24 metres above zero. The upper level of the river banquette lies without any intermediate space in front of the Nebuchadnezzar wall, which is 6 metres thick, and is exactly at zero level. The Nabopolassar wall consists of unstamped 31-centimetre bricks, the facing wall of 33-centimetre bricks, with the Nebuchadnezzar stamp. The smooth front of both walls faces west, the back is left rough as it was built up against the bank behind.

Both walls extend as far as the northern corner of the peribolos. From there the Nabopolassar wall runs in a straight line northwards to a distance of about 20 metres from the Southern Citadel, where it breaks off in ruins. Its line runs approximately on the western boundary of the additional building, and must therefore originally have made a curve in order to join at its commencement with the Sargon wall. From the Nebuchadnezzar wall a branch turns off at a very sharp angle at the above-mentioned place, and runs exactly in the direction of the ancient moat wall. Another branch joins on here with a doubly-grooved expansion joint, and runs in the direction

of the northern part of the Nabonidus wall. Thus there
are parts of four walls close together here, all of which
belong to four consecutive changes in direction. At the
same place a culvert passes through each of the walls,
which must have carried off the surface water that collected
to the north of the peribolos. Somewhat farther to the
north we came upon two descending stairways in the
Nabopolassar wall, which were walled up in a second
building period. They are similar to those in the gateways in the Nabonidus wall.

The three walls are so near together, and follow so
closely in the same direction, that if we prefer to consider
the Arachtu to be a canal of the Euphrates, it here lies
so close to the Euphrates that its existence is very
problematic. The Euphrates wall of Nabonidus has
here obviously replaced the Arachtu wall of Nabopolassar,
which further argues for the identity of the Euphrates and
the Arachtu (see p. 140). That the Nabonidus wall and
the stone bridge are buildings on the Euphrates, no
systematic investigator can doubt. Otherwise we must
assume that besides the two buildings found by us there
existed yet a second embankment wall of Nabonidus which
lay on the Euphrates, and a second stone bridge that
led over the Euphrates. Without wishing to anticipate
further research, I am inclined to assume the Arachtu to
be, not a canal nor an arm of the Euphrates, but a semicircular widening of the river (see Hommel, *op. cit.* p. 283,
note 1, Arach) (moon, fem. Arachtu?), which possessed a
special name, and for which the name Arachtu could be
used as well as that of Euphrates, as in the case of the
Binger Lock on the Rhine. Possibly it was the haven of
Babylon.

Nebuchadnezzar mentions his own wall among others
in the Eharsagila cylinder (*K.B.* iii. 2, p. 41, l. 41): "I
. . . built the embankment walls of the Arachtu of asphalt
and burnt brick, and strengthened it by means of the
embankment walls that my father had made."

ESAGILA, THE TEMPLE OF MARDUK

(A. The Principal Building)

The ancient celebrated temple, Esagila, according to Jastrow "the lofty house" (*Religion of Babylonia*, p. 639), the temple of Marduk, lies beneath the hill of Amran Ibn Ali (Fig. 123) buried to a depth of 21 metres below the upper level of the hill. We have already excavated some part of it, and by means of deep shafts and galleries we have established the ground-plan and the different divisions. There are two buildings adjacent to each other; the principal one on the east is very regularly and magnificently planned, of the Western Annex we have only recovered the outer circuit. We will first survey the principal building.

The temple is almost square, with its northern front of 79.3 metres and its western front of 85.8 metres long. Inside it is a court 31.3 metres broad and 37.6 metres long. On the west of this court, as we learn from the mighty-towered façade, there was the principal cella, that of Marduk. The chambers are not yet excavated. On the south side towards the east there is a smaller cella, which can be recognised as such by the niche in the wall. The cella lies on the east side of a square, which on the west side has a door leading to a small chamber which may also be the remains of a cella.

A third cella has been excavated on the north side of the court. It is apparently the sanctuary of the god Ea, who in Greek times was identified with Serapis (see *Tempel von Babylon*, p. 43). It was here that the generals of Alexander sought counsel of the god with regard to his illness, whether the king should permit himself to be transported hither in search of healing. Doors lead north to two chambers behind the cella, an arrangement that is not found in any other cella. If my expressed opinion is

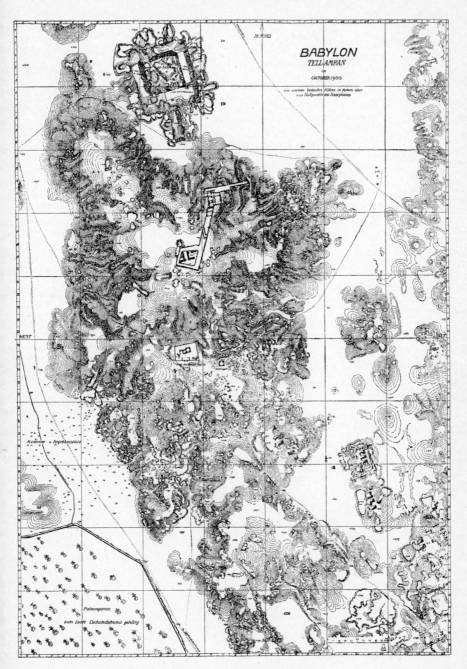

FIG. 123.—Plan of the mound Amran.

correct these chambers may have been the dormitories in which oracular dreams could be secured. In the cella, which also had a side chamber at the east end, the

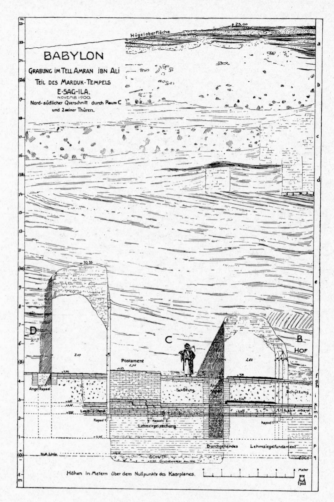

FIG. 124.—Section through Esagila.

postament for the statue still stands in front of the niche. Imprinted on the asphalt covering of its flat top we found traces of a wooden throne, which, during the conflagration, had become charred and broken up. Of the richly carved

work some fragments could still be recognised, the figures
that supported the throne, holding the water vase with
which Ea, god of the abyss of waters, was usually represented, a fine head of a dragon, a fish, and so forth.

The paved floor with its wash of asphalt is slightly
dominated by the postament, which has in front of it a
shallow step flanked by two small balustrades.

The pavement was repeatedly raised, and with it the

FIG. 125.—Esagila brick of Sardanapalus.

mighty door sockets and the postament (Fig. 124). Of the
six pavements the two upper ones are Nebuchadnezzar's,
and the two middle ones are of Sardanapalus, who states
on the stamps of his brick, 33 × 33 centimetres (Fig. 125),
that he made the " bricks of Esagila and Etemenanki." In
this pavement there was one, 40 × 40 centimetres, brick of
Esarhaddon, which, according to the stamp, belonged to
"the pavement of Esagila" (Fig. 126). The name of the
temple is therefore fully established by inscription as
Esagila. On bricks found by us in the vicinity, Esagila

is often mentioned in conjunction with Etemenanki or with
Babylon (Fig. 127). The two lower pavements have no
stamps. The walls of the court at this lower and more
ancient level are adorned with mouldings, while the walls
above are plain.

At the doors, and in front of the wall piers, we again
found the brick caskets; in one of these lay a clay figure

FIG. 126.—Esagila brick of
Esarhaddon.

of a bearded man with bull's feet, and holding a palm or
something of the kind (Fig. 128).

The upper pavement lies on an average 4.5 metres
above zero. The enclosing walls, which, including the 2-
metres-thick kisu, are 6 metres thick, consist, like the entire
building, of mud brick, and the kisu of 32 × 32-centimetre
unstamped burnt brick; it must therefore be older than
the time of Nebuchadnezzar, who does not appear to have
carried out any vigorous restoration here.

The treatment of the walls is similar to that of Emach
in an intensified form. Here every tower is placed
between two flanking towers, thus forming a unit of three

towers. This also occurs in the great temple of Nebo in Borsippa. Exactly in the middle of each side there is a great gateway elaborated with massive projecting towers. Paved ramps, with side balustrades, lead up to the three gateways on the north, west, and south. All is on a larger scale than in other temples. The symmetrical planning which in other temples leaves much to be desired, is here

FIG. 127.—Esagila and Babylon brick of Esarhaddon

remarkably accurate, and here alone is an entrance to be found on each side.

Although from the outside these gateways all appear to be alike, the east gate must have been the principal entrance, as it has a passage through a magnificent vestibule that leads direct to the court, while the entrance through the north and south doors leads first into a small vestibule and then through a corridor that runs by the side of it. On the walls of the court also doorways and towers are symmetrically alternated.

P

A considerable similarity exists between our temple and the description of the "temples" that lay near the zikurrat given in Smith's summary of an inscription (see p. 192 *et seq.*). Smith was not then aware of the difference between Esagila and the Bel sanctuary of Herodotus. His "temples" have measurements and

proportions which, on account of their disproportionate length, are entirely impossible as such. For enclosed chambers they are far too widely spanned. They can therefore only be measurements of the area of separate parts of the temples, including the adjacent walls. If all of these are added together we find that they amount almost exactly to the occupied area of Esagila. Furthermore, these areas can with ease be arranged so as to fill in the ground plan of Esagila with very few discrepancies.

Then again the principal cellae are here, that of Marduk and of Zarpanit in the west, and that of Ea in the north, while that of Anu and Bel may at least find its counterpart in the double cella in the south of Esagila. Thus the measurements of Smith's "temples" must have been taken either directly from Esagila or perhaps from the temple on the top of the zikurrat, which must then have had much the same dimensions and arrangements as Esagila. It is to be expected that the further excavations of Esagila will throw light on these most interesting questions.

FIG. 128. — Terra - cotta figure from brick casket at Esagila.

Allusions to Esagila, and information regarding its rebuilding and endowment, are, of course, very frequent in Babylonian inscriptions, especially in those of Nebuchadnezzar, who calls himself the "fosterer of Esagila" on every one of his millions of bricks. In the *Steinplatten* inscription he says (col. 2, 30, *K.B.* iii. 2, p. 15): "Silver, gold, costly precious stones, bronze, mismakannu—and cedar wood, all conceivable valuables, great (?) superabundance, the product of the mountains, the wealth of

the sea, a heavy burden, a sumptuous gift, I brought to
my city of Babil before him, and deposited in Esagila, the
palace of his lordship, a gigantic abundance. Ekua, the
chamber of Marduk, lord of the gods, I made to gleam
like the sun.   Its walls I clothed with solid (?) gold
instead of clay (?) or chalk (?), with lapis and alabaster the
temple area.   Kaḫilisir, or the ' door of state,' as also the
Ezida gate of Esagila, I caused to be made bright as the
sun—Du-azag, the place of the naming of destiny, that is
Ub-šu-ukkenna, the chamber of destiny, in which at
Zakmuk or the New Year, on the 8th and 11th day, the
' King of the gods of heaven and of earth ' the lord of the
gods takes up his abode, while the gods of heaven and
of earth, reverentially awaiting him, bow before him, at
the place where he allotteth the destiny of eternal duration
as the lot of my life :—the same chamber, the chamber of
majesty, the chamber of the lordship of the wise one
among the gods, the exalted Marduk, that an earlier king
had furnished with silver, I clothed with shining gold, a
magnificent adornment.   The outfit of the temple of
Esagila I beautified with solid (?) gold, the Kua-ship with
sarîr and stones like unto the stars of heaven.—The
temples of Babil I caused to be re-established and I
took care of them.   I covered the top of Etemenanki with
blue glazed burnt brick.—My heart impels me to build
Esagila, I keep it perpetually before mine eyes.   The
best of my cedars, that I brought from Lebanon, the noble
forest, I sought out for the roofing over of Ekua, the
chamber of his lordship, with deliberate care, the mightiest
cedars I covered with gleaming gold for the roofing of
Ekua.   The šibi below the roofing cedars I decorated
with gold and precious stones.   For the restoration of
Esagila I make supplication every morning to the king of
gods, the lord of lords " (trans. by Delitzsch).

The four doors of Esagila are mentioned by Neriglissar
in his cylinder inscription (*K.B.* iii. 2, p. 73) : " Esagila
and Ezida I beautified.   The temples I placed in order,
noble worship (?) I adhered to (?) perpetually.   The
bronze serpents . . . (?) on the face of the walls (i-na ki-si-i)
of the doorways of Esagila which . . . are placed standing

at the 'door of the Rising Sun,' at the 'door of the Setting
Sun,' at the 'door of Abundance,' at the 'door of . . .'
(which) no earlier king had erected, I the humble, the
submissive, who am learned in the worship of the gods,
have erected. Eight serpents standing upright (sirruš)
. . . (?) which hiss deadly poison against the nefarious and
the foe, I have clothed with a covering of shining silver ;
and at the door of the Rising Sun, at the door of the
Setting Sun, at the door of Abundance, and at the door of
. . . on the walls of these self-same doors according to
ancient custom . . . silver . . . in accordance with its
exalted destiny, set up in . . ." (trans. by Bezold). The
eight sirrush were undoubtedly on the balustrades of the
entrance ramps, two at each gate.

Herodotus calls the temple the κάτω νηός, in which,
according to him, there was a great seated statue of Zeus,
that like the throne, the footstool, and table was formed
of gold of the weight of 800 talents.

Small objects found on the pavement show that this
must have remained open as late as the Seleucid period.
Thus the building existed long unroofed, and crumbled
into an accumulation of rubbish amounting to 4 or 5 metres
high. Then the mud walls fell down flat, and in this
position we found them (Fig. 129), and over them rubbish
of all sorts was accumulated for a long period, which,
during our excavations, appeared in most unpleasant guise
as a horrible, black, powdery mass. At a height of 14
metres above zero mud-brick houses begin once more,
which become poorer in the higher parts of the midden,
until at last they almost entirely disappear. The upper
layer certainly contains traces of habitation, and among
them many Arabic glazed sherds, but scarcely walls, and
the Babylon of that period, whose inhabited area was
confined to this mound, must have presented a somewhat
miserable aspect. As Hilleh was founded in the eleventh
century A.D., we may assume that Babylon ceased to be
inhabited at that time. The sacred tomb of Amran Ibn
Ali (Fig. 130), somewhat to the south of the temple,
consists of two cupolas inside the walls of a court, against
which various halls and secondary buildings are placed.

FIG. 129.—The excavation of Esagila.

It is the latest building on the town site of Babylon, for the Euphrates flowed previously where the village of Kweiresh now lies.

FIG. 130.—Tomb of Amran Ibn Ali.

XXXVI

THE EASTERN ANNEX (B) OF ESAGILA

ON the east front of Esagila there lies an annex, of which so far we have only excavated the external ground-plan by means of underground galleries. The quadrangle projects at the south beyond the line of the principal temple. Like it, it consists of mud brick with a kisu of burnt brick. The north front measures 89.4, the east front 116 metres. In addition to several doors there are four gateways that lead into the interior, two close to the principal building on the north and on the south, and two at the east, of which the northern one, placed in a shallow recess of the enclosing wall, may be regarded as the main entrance. They all have the usual towered façade, and the walls have the closely placed grooved towers.

The method of excavation was as follows. We dug

out narrow galleries following the wall lines deep down, and rendered them accessible from the hill level by means of narrow shafts. On one side of these shafts stepped recesses were constructed, of a man's height, each of which afforded standing room for a workman. As many as twelve men could stand in these recesses one above another, who could reach the baskets of earth and pass them on to the next man in succession without changing their place. Above-ground the earth was carried off in trucks and thrown somewhat to the side, thus preventing the accumulation of heaps near the opening of the shaft.

Our first digging, by which we ascertained the existence of Esagila at this place, was an open excavation. We cut a trench half-way up the hill from the north, thus making a road for our tramway. At the end of this trench, which lay at about the centre of the hill, we marked out a square space about 40 metres each way, which we contracted slightly as we descended deeper. After much toil and difficulty, and notwithstanding incessant reiterated assertions both from Europeans and Arabs that we were working in an entirely wrong direction, the pavement of Esagila was at length reached, and on the 23rd November 1900 the inscribed bricks of Sardanapalus and Esarhaddon were found. To accomplish this eight months' work was necessary, and the removal of about 30,000 cubic metres of earth.

XXXVII

THE LATER BUILDINGS ON THE NORTHERN EDGE OF AMRAN

IMMEDIATELY at the entrance to the hill Amran, the above-mentioned tramway trench cut through some buildings of later—apparently Parthian—times, which would be well worthy of being completely excavated. We have hitherto only been able, however, to widen the trench slightly to east and west. A pillared hall can be seen, a peristyle

with several chambers, the walls of crude brick still standing
to a considerable height in the mass of the hill (Fig. 131).
The pillars consist of brick rubble laid in mud and plastered
over with gypsum, a method of building which is characteristic of the later Grecian and Parthian periods. By the
walls there were peculiar small mud constructions thickly
covered with gypsum ; flat shallow pans supported by tiny
columns sharply contracted half way up their height.
What they were intended for I do not know.

Somewhat farther to the north there lies a Stoa built in
the same way, of coupled semi-columns, of which we have
excavated 23 transoms without arriving at the end. A
similar series is near the Bridge Gateway. Several pillars
of the peristyle of a house also came to light on the east
side of the Eastern Annex. All these remains lie at about
the same height of 10 metres above zero, which is about
6 metres higher than the Nebuchadnezzar pavement of
Esagila. At Amran it is hardly possible to dig at this
level without coming upon such pillars. A similar unmistakable introduction of Greek pillared architecture can
be observed in all ruined sites which flourished at the time
of the Neo-Babylonian kings, as at Nippur, where the
great palace belongs to this period, but which Fisher has
strangely ascribed to the Mycenaean period (*Journal of the
Archaeological Institute of America*, vol. viii. 1904, No. 4,
p. 403). Meanwhile it appears that the Babylonian house
grouped round a courtyard was also at this period still in
use by the autochthonous population, while the Greek
insisted on having his pillars even in this land, the climate
of which was so unpropitious to columnar art.

Near the railway trench to the westward of the first-
mentioned house there was a large number of Graeco-
Parthian burials. Pottery sarcophagi and wooden coffins,
surrounded by brickwork, lie here as low as 80 centimetres
above zero. Some of them are rich in small plastic
deposits. There are alabaster statuettes of women with
finely worked wigs of black asphalt and inlaid eyes (Fig.
132). One type is lying on the hip, and another is standing,
and both occur also in hollow terra-cotta. They vary
between the older fine and animated style and the later

Fig. 131.—Later buildings on northern slope of Amran.

dry lifeless treatment. The ancient Babylonian forms, such, for instance, as those of the Ninmach terra-cottas (p. 277), have entirely disappeared by this time, and are superseded by Greek models. Simultaneously with these decidedly graceful pieces there occurs, sometimes in the same coffin, another style of modelling, which strikes one as rather barbaric. They are small nude female figures made from cylindrical bones flattened on one side and carved on the face. There were seven of these pieces in one grave, which differ greatly from one another in style. All alike have a

FIG. 132.—Alabaster figure with asphalt perruque.

coarsely formed body with disproportionately broad hips, while the head is frequently very finely worked.

Some of the alabaster and clay figures certainly wore genuine tiny garments, as is shown by the movable jointed arms. The corpse itself frequently wears a naturalistic wreath of leaves or a narrow diadem of very thin gold fastened by a band that was inserted in two holes. The face was often wrapped in pieces of thin gold-leaf.

In addition to the plain wooden coffins, others are found, though not *in situ*, very richly decorated. The remains of one of these lay in the western cross-cut at the peribolos, rich with the gilded bases of small pillars, the channellings of which were overlaid with glass fillets, gilded cupids, and the like, all made of gypsum and specially adapted for fitting on to wood. The sarcophagus in which the wooden coffin was placed was built of bricks, with a gable roof formed of bricks placed edgeways, and tilted up over the opening, the whole bedded in a liberal supply of gypsum mortar.

Besides this class of burial we find still in use at this time the usual Babylonian trough coffins of terra-cotta, either with a separate cover, or tilted up over the body. The slipper sarcophagus is also naturalised in Babylon (Fig. 133), which, like many of the trough sarcophagi, has a beautiful blue glaze, which, however, easily flakes off. The necropolis in the principal court of the Southern

FIG. 133.—A slipper sarcophagus.

Citadel was full of them. The shape of the slipper sarcophagus, in which the head of the corpse lay below an opening which was closed by a separate cover, appears to date back in Nippur to a very early period. It is evident that a great variety of types of burial were in use in Babylonia. The long trough sarcophagi which here in Babylon were first used in Neo-Babylonian times, and later, with the double-urn coffin and the short high pan coffin, were already common in Fara (Shuruppak), in the prehistoric period, only deeper in shape ; while the double-urn coffin first appeared there with the beginning of writing (3000 B.C.). In prehistoric Surgul the body was burnt with the help of high inverted coffins. Interments in underground vaults, which are numerous in Assur, occur very rarely in Babylon, and only under Assyrian domination (?) The methods of burial and their sequence differ in every town where research has been carried on.

If it appears amazing that burial by burning should have been practised in Surgul, it must be remembered that up to the present time, with the exception of the lowest levels of Fara, it is the only prehistoric site that has been explored in that part of the world. While the ethnologist and the student of western prehistoric and early culture possesses a wealth of material to illustrate the development of a few centuries, in Babylonia the prehistoric period embraces many thousands of years, and its material is confined to that derived from Surgul and Fara. From Bismaya, where, according to Banks the excavator, burnt interments were found, little has yet been gained, and nothing is known of Telloh in this connection. It also happens that the difference in time between the periods of these culture strata is very great. At Fara the upper layer belongs to the period of the beginning of writing in the fourth or fifth millennium, while the lowest strata 8 or 10 metres lower down belong perhaps to the tenth. This we can only surmise, we cannot prove it. Surgul after its time of prosperity apparently lay deserted for countless centuries, before its occupation in the time of Gudea of which the scanty remains now lie upon the surface. The interval between Nebuchadnezzar and Entemena, which is generally regarded as very long, is, in fact, remarkably short when compared with the duration of the prehistoric period in Babylonia, the length of which it is at present impossible for us to estimate. And what do we know of it? Only a few disconnected strophes from among the great, lengthy, and doubtless highly didactic epic of the development of Babylonian culture. It is therefore no wonder that there is a marked, and at present an incomprehensible difference between the various data. But it is urgently to be desired that these ancient ruins should be more widely and actively studied in order to gain the fullest possible elucidation regarding the long dawn of the development of Babylonian culture, for what I was able to gain by the excavations at these two sites was nothing but the result of a mere preliminary reconnoitre.

In the mud-brick houses under the previously

mentioned Parthian building, a bead manufacturer appears to have deposited his raw material. It lay there in two baskets, of which the structure could be easily recognised, and included ancient valuables of onyx, lapis lazuli, agates, rock-crystal, and other stones. We need not here describe them in detail, some of them are of interest as samples of the temple treasure of Esagila as it once existed. A strip of lapis lazuli bored through its length like a gigantic bead,

shows the figure of the god Adad with the feather crown, brandishing the lightning in his right hand (Fig. 134). With the left he is holding the reins of some fabulous creature which cowers before him, and another thunderbolt. Three shields adorned with stars hang one below another suspended by belts from his girdle. On

FIG. 134. — Esarhaddon's Adad kunukku from Esagila.

FIG. 135.—Marduk-nâdin-shum's Marduk kunukku.

the piece there is an Assyrian votive inscription of Esarhaddon, and a Neo-Babylonian supplementary inscription on which the object is called "treasure of the god Marduk" and "Kunukku of the god Adad of Esagila."

Even if this were not so named there are other objects that might be recognised as having formed part of the treasure of Esagila. There is a similar bar of lapis lazuli dedicated to the god Marduk by an inscription of the King Marduk-nâdin-shum (*circa* 850 B.C.). The figure of Marduk is very finely carved on it (Fig. 135), with a ring and a kunukku in his left hand, and a boomerang (?) in his right. Before him lies the sirrush, the dragon of Babylon, already known to us from the reliefs on the

Ishtar Gate, and which here shows both horns. On this god also three decorative shields are hanging, the lowest adorned with oxen. The garment on the upper part of the body is beset with stars and the plinth is marked with the rippled lines of water. Thus Marduk is here represented as supreme god of the heavens, the earth (sirrush), and of the water. We may picture to ourselves the golden cultus statue of Marduk, which, according to Herodotus, was enthroned in Esagila, as similar to this, but seated.

If the principal statues were of gold others consisted of a combination of stones of many colours, which we discovered in separate pieces in our find. The hair was made of separate fragments of lapis lazuli which formed curls and locks and fitted into each other. The white of the eyes was represented by the core of a shell, the iris by a conical piece of stone, which was surrounded by a thin cornet-shaped piece of lapis lazuli forming a narrow blue line round the iris. For decorating the garment and the feather crown, the numerous button-shaped discs of onyx were employed, which are frequently inscribed with dedicatory texts. They are usually fixed on to the underlay by means of an invisible hole bored in the top. Numbers of them can easily be recognised on the crown of Marduk in our illustration. We do not yet know what formed the main part of such a statue. According to his Bavian inscription, Sennacherib battered the statues to pieces, and it is quite possible that such broken-up statues may yet be found in the lowest levels of Esagila.

From a throne, and apparently from the projecting end of the chair back, comes a thick piece of rock-crystal the size of a hand, bored through with irregularly disposed holes, to which at some time other separate ornaments were attached.

All this when considered as a whole may give some idea of the exceptional splendour of such statues of the divinities.

XXXVIII

THE OTHER PARTS OF THE HILL OF AMRAN IBN ALI

CLOSE to the sacred tomb of Amran, where there is also the cupola of a private burial, lies the modern Arab cemetery, which stretches out as far as the western plain. Here a high mud wall called a *Tof* surrounds the palm gardens of the village of Djumdjumma. Towards the south the hill gradually falls away in irregular lines. We have not yet dug there, but isolated walls of mud brick, which project out of the ground, show that here also there are ruins of dwelling-houses. On the eastern slope some excavations undertaken by us yielded dated business tablets of the time of the Persian kings. Here also the great Nimitti-Bel cylinder was found which had been removed here, and of which we have already (p. 173 *et seq.*) given an account.

XXXIX

TEMPLE "Z"

OPPOSITE Amran on the east there stretch out the low "Ishin aswad" (Fig. 136), as the heaped-up city ruins are called. In the valley between them lie the ruins of a temple of which we have not yet found the name, and which we therefore distinguish as "Z."

The temple was built with great regularity (Figs. 137, 138). It is an accurate rectangle of mud brick, with a kisu of burnt brick, for, like so many others, it has been heightened. It is divided into two clearly distinguishable parts : the eastern, intended for the cult with the cella to the south, in which the postament stood in the niche in the wall ; and the western, which resembled a private

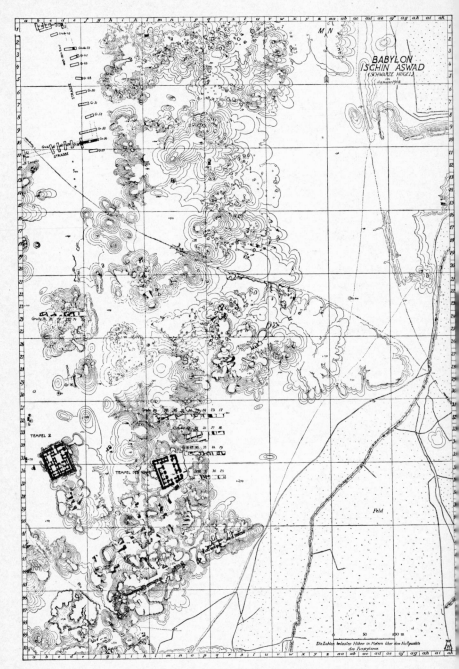

FIG. 136.—Plan of Ishin aswad.

house of two courts.   Here the priest, the temple ad-

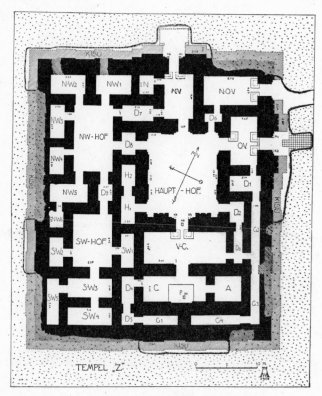

FIG. 137.—Ground-plan of temple "Z."

ministrator, may
have lived. Two
gates distinguished
by the towered
façade, led, each of
them, through a
vestibule into the
court in front of the
cella. In addition
a doorway gave
direct access to the
chamber in the

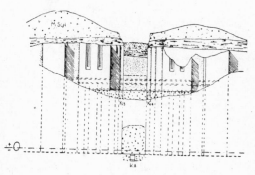

FIG. 138.—Cella façade in temple "Z."

Q

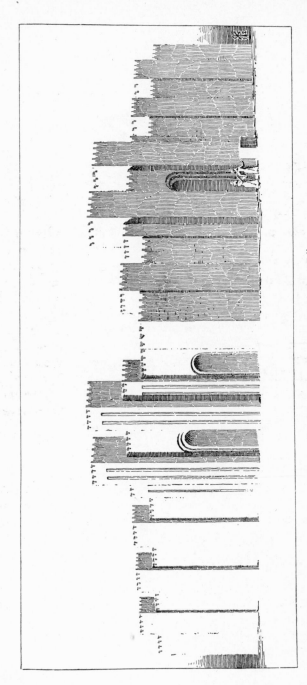

FIG. 139.—Reconstruction of temple "Z."

north-east corner, where the public could transact business with the temple officials, without being forced to enter the enclosed part of the temple. The northern gate was indicated as the main entrance by the paved site for an altar (Fig. 139). The brick casket at its eastern jamb contained a pottery dove, and a small piece of pottery with an inscription that has not been satisfactorily explained hitherto, although it is fairly clearly written.[1]

Even at the lowest pavement level of 20 centimetres below zero the temple was in use. Here stood the oldest postament, and below it, as was to be expected, was the brick casket (simâku) with the statuette of Papsukal inscribed on its shoulder-blades (Figs. 140, 141). Above this postament there lay four more pavements divided from each other by layers of earth, which represent four successive heightenings of the temple

FIG. 140.—Figure of Papsukal from temple "Z"—front view.

FIG. 141. — Figure of Papsukal from temple "Z"—back view.

level, carrying it up to 5.84 metres above zero. The slight raising of half a metre would make scarcely any change in the building, but when the level was heightened as much as 4 metres at one time, a heightening of the roof and other rebuilding was unavoidable. At the same time the former ground-plan was generally retained with

[1] *Oriental Literaturzeitung*, 1911, No. 7 :—
Ungnad translates the inscription: 1. (işu) şupur işşuri(?) li (?)-in-ti-ka (?) 2. pa-an . . -šu(?)-du abulli-šu 3. l[i]-ni'-irat-su 4. mit-gar-šu u(?) ki-bi-su(?) li-in-na(?) [. . .]. " May the claw of the bird (?) tear to pieces (?) the countenance of him, who . . . his gate, and may it hold back his breast ; him who is favourable to him and (?) . . . may he. . . ."
Peiser translates: 1. şupur işşuri lintikā 2. pān nakri šudu abullim 3. linī' iratsu 4. nuḳaršu u kibīsu linnasiḫ. " May the bird's claw press down the countenance of the foe before the door, and check his breast, may his devastating step be turned away."

such great care, that at this temple we observed nothing on the walls themselves resulting from such rebuilding, although we laid them bare to a height of 9 metres.

The outer circuit shared in this heightening to an equal extent, or, to speak more accurately, it was the continual heightening of the roads that lay around it that was the reason for raising the temple. The same arrangement can be seen to-day in Oriental cities. The newly-built houses are of course so constructed that the ground floor is on about the same level as the street. As the latter, however, serves as the depository of all sorts of rubbish it is not long before the ground floor is below the street level. In Bagdad, for example, one has always to step down on entering an old house from the street, and the older the house the deeper the step. When the building becomes ruinous and requires rebuilding, the new floor is of course made level with the street. Part of the rubbish of the destroyed house is used to raise the level of the house, the rest is thrown into the street. If the houses are built of burnt brick a large part of the building material can be re-used, but with houses of mud brick almost the whole of the material becomes rubbish, which when spread out gradually raises the whole area. It follows that in the course of hundreds or thousands of years such a town site must become very considerably higher (see Fig. 154).

It must be taken into consideration that later and more cultured periods yield higher deposits of rubbish than earlier ones, which are remains of simpler conditions of life, and of unpretentious dwelling-places. Also in the course of a long period the rubbish is much more pressed together by its own weight than in a shorter period, when the process of compression has not been so prolonged.

Thus in the 1700 years between Nebuchadnezzar and the eleventh century A.D., Amran rose 21 metres, while at Merkes, as we shall see presently, the mounds of rubbish, which are also the accumulation of 1700 years, from the time of Hammurabi 2250 B.C. to Nabonidus 550 B.C., rose only 6 metres. According to this we must reckon on a retrocessive sequence of the density of the layers, which is expressed in the figures 21 and 6. While in Amran we must reckon 80 years for every metre of depth of rubbish, in Merkes every metre represents 280 years. The application of even an approximately rapid sequence at Fara leads to a height of antiquity which at first we hesitate to accept, but to which we may have to accustom ourselves, as geology has accustomed itself to the remote periods which are now universally accepted for the genesis of certain strata.

In spite of all these heightenings which were carried on in the temples, they rarely rose to any considerable height above their surroundings, and they were always on the same level as the city, in opposition to the highly placed temples at the zikurrats.

Somewhat to the north of temple " Z " we made a transverse cut through the narrow back of the mound, and in the mud-brick houses that lay there we found a number of business and scientific tablets.

XL

EPATUTILA, THE TEMPLE OF NINIB

A short distance to the east of temple " Z," in the actual Ishin aswad, lies the temple of Ninib, of which the name Epatutila, according to Hommel (*Geographie Vorderasiens*, p. 313), means " House of the sceptre of life " (Bit-ḫaṭ-ṭu-balâṭi). Its principal part was built by Nabopolassar (Figs. 142, 143).

The somewhat oblique-angled ground-plan shows three entrances which led into the great court through vestibules, with the usual side-chambers. In front of the eastern one lay the altar, and opposite it on the other side of the court was the principal cella, with towered front and two side cellae. Each cella had its postament for the statue in front of the wall niche exactly opposite the door. On the north and on the south were wide gateways, also with towered façades, which must have been placed there to provide entrance and exit for the festival processions that passed in front of the cellae.

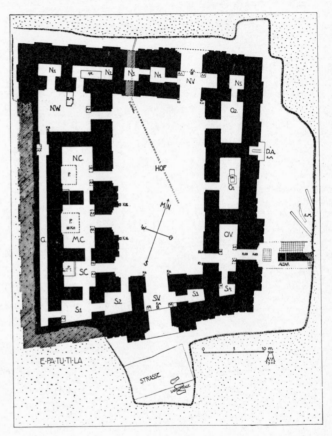

FIG. 142.—Plan of Epatutila.

From a small secondary court in the north-west corner a long narrow passage runs behind the cellae to the chamber at the south corner, from which a concealed entrance appears to have been contrived to the three cellae, which were themselves connected with each other by doors.

The main flooring, a double layer of 31 × 31-centimetre

bricks, lies 2.4 metres
above zero, while the walls
reach down to 22 centi-
metres below zero. Close
under this flooring, in the
doorways of the cellae, and
merely laid in the sand of
the filling, were the foundation cylinders of Nabopo-
lassar (Fig. 144). In the
inscriptions, which are
identical, Nabopolassar
says (l. 17): "The As-
syrian who since many
days had ruled the whole
of the peoples and had
placed the people of the
land under his heavy
yoke;—I the weak one,
the humble one, who
reveres the lord of lords,
through the mighty war
power of Nabu and Mar-
duk my lords kept back
their foot from the land
of Akkad and caused their
yoke to be thrown off. At
that time E-pa-tu-ti-la, the
temple of Ninib, which
(is) in Šú-an-na-ki, which
before me an earlier king
had caused to be built, but
had not completed his
work, upon the renewing
of this temple was my
desire (fixed), I summoned
the vassals of Enlil, Šamaš
and Marduk, caused them
to bear the allu, laid upon
them the dupšíkku. With-

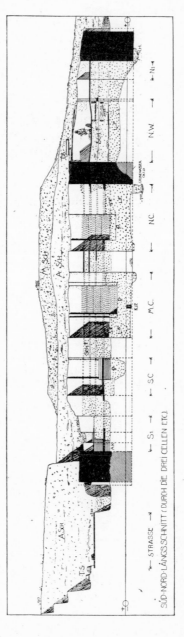

FIG. 143.—Section of Epatutila.

out ceasing I caused the work of the temple to be com-

FIG. 144.—Epatutila foundation cylinder of Nebuchadnezzar.

pleted.   Mighty beams I laid for its roof, lofty doors I placed in its gateways. This temple I caused to shine like the sun and for Ninib my lord to glow like the day" (trans. by Weissbach). There is nothing in the ruins to show how much of the lower part of the walls should be ascribed to the earlier build-ing mentioned in this inscription.

A number of brick caskets lay at each side of the main gateways and in the entrance of those at the north and south. In them, formed of some

FIG. 145.—Figure from brick casket of Epatutila, restored.

FIG. 146.—Figure of Papsukal from principal cella postament in Epatutila.

perishable material (wood?) (Fig. 145), there stood figures of which some remains have been recovered ; sword belts with a copper sword, a silver girdle, small clubs with knobs of onyx still clasped in the wooden hand, and small copper buckets (situlae). About 1 metre below the posta- ment of the principal cella stood a well-preserved figure of Papsukal, the divine messenger, now so well known to us, in his narrow brick *simâku* (Fig. 146).

After the time of Nabopolassar the floor was three times raised with Nebuchadnezzar's bricks to a height of

Fig. 147.—Ruins of Epatutila.

4.2 metres above zero. At 6 metres above zero the wall ruins end. Here in the rubbish of the ruins lie the trough sarcophagi of the Seleucid period.

The exterior (Fig. 147), as well as the court, is enriched with plain towers, while the gateway towers are grooved. At the northern door, through which the processions passed out, the projection of the towers is less than in the other two. At the south-east corner, where two gateways adjoin each other, an additional grooved tower is introduced. A large vertical gutter, built of 31 × 31 -centimetre bricks, in the east front carried off the rain-water from the roof.

Among the terra-cottas found here during the excavations, the most frequent types are : (1) a bearded figure holding a vase in both hands (see Fig. 212) and wearing a long frilled garment on the cylindrical lower part of the body ; (2) a nude female figure with arms hanging down (see Fig. 211); (3) an ape. If the two first represent Ninib and his consort Gula, the third cella is left for the ape. What part was played by these creatures

FIG. 148.—Terra-cotta apes, male and female.

in Babylon I will not attempt to discover. It must have been an important one, for the figures of these squatting apes are found not only here, but over the whole area in great numbers (Fig. 148). The workmanship varies ; some are modelled in the finest and most realistic manner, others are treated more or less as idols, and many are practically mere crude upright lumps of clay, in which the figure of an ape would be unrecognisable were it not possible to compare them with innumerable examples of somewhat better workmanship.

Beside these types we found a number of small figures of horsemen. The oldest of these, which date back to the time before Nabopolassar, and of which several have

been found in the temple, are some of them glazed (Fig.
149); the details are always roughly modelled by hand,

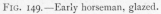

FIG. 149.—Early horseman, glazed. FIG. 150.—Later horseman, Parthian (?).

and the rider sits like a lump of clay on the neck of a
barely recognisable horse.   Later on these riders were
more carefully worked, the horse's head
was slightly modelled, while the legs
remain shapeless stumps, the rider becomes a long strip sitting across the
animal, and only the bearded head of the
rider is produced from a fairly good
mould (Fig. 150).   He wears a hood,
which in one type has the point erect,
while in another it falls on one side, as
in the figure of Darius in the mosaic of
Pompeii.

It is only in yet later examples that FIG. 151.—Woman in
the complete modelling of both horse covered litter, on horseback.
and rider first makes its appearance.
The figure of a woman, of which several examples have
been found in the temple, is entirely analogous both in
form and general workmanship.   She is carried on a horse

in a covered litter with a semicircular top (Fig. 151). A similar form of litter is in use in the neighbourhood to-day under the name of *Ketshaue*.

THE EXCAVATIONS TO THE NORTH OF THE NINIB TEMPLE

NORTH-EAST of the Ninib temple we have cut four trenches through the hill to the plain beyond. Here we found the same strata of private houses and streets that we shall meet with again in Merkes.

Here, at the depth of the water-level, were some small plano-convex clay tablets with carefully modelled reliefs of lions, fabulous creatures, etc., on the flat side, as well as some figures in the round, also worked with great minuteness. Among these there is a fine bearded head with the hair tied up in a napkin, as, beside others, it is worn by Marduk on the piece of lapis lazuli described above. They appear to be working models for a large statue.

Beside the numerous scantily ornamented pottery vases, there were some decorated in coloured glazes with concentric lines, rosettes, and plaited bands (Fig. 152—*Frontispiece*). They come from the lower levels, which apparently date back to the time of the Assyrian domination. In one place where rubbish had been thrown, there were numerous tablets containing business, literary, or scientific inscriptions. It is possible that they came from the temple and formed part of the temple library, which, as is generally supposed, every temple possessed. No systematic storing of inscriptions has yet been discovered in any temple, including those of Babylon, Khorsabad, and Assur, all of which have been completely excavated. It is true that these were buried under a proportionately shallow covering of earth, while Esagila lay protected under fully 20 metres of untouched accumulations, and is still unexcavated.

The mound itself proves to be thickly strewn through-

out with potsherds, and the mud-brick walls of the houses
lie close below the surface.   They are only thinly covered
by a uniform layer of dust.   In the plain, on the contrary,
as our trenches at the Ninib temple have shown, the
house ruins lie under a layer more or less high, of
drifted sand, and the surface contains exceedingly few
potsherds.   All this is explained if we take the trouble to
realise the antecedents of the formation of these ruins.   At
the time when the site was deserted and fell into ruins the
surrounding contours were far more marked than they are
at present.   The heights were higher and the depths were
deeper.   The mud-brick walls, which at first stood out
above the soil, crumbled away after they lost their roofs
into dusty heaps of clay, which accumulated against the

FIG. 153.—Schematic diagram of the transfer of the upper levels (A, B, left)
of a mound of debris to lower-lying region (A, B, on the right).

walls and covered the pavement higher and higher, while
the walls themselves, so far as they over-topped these
heaps, disappeared, and thus all was levelled to an irregular
undulating surface.

But the process of destruction of the city did not end
here.   Every winter, however short, with its frost and rain,
and the long summer with the torrid heat of the sun, split,
shattered, and pulverised all that still clung together and
turned it to a light powdery dust, which was easily whirled
away by the strong recurrent summer winds and deposited
in the lower-lying parts.   Thus the heights were continually denuded and lowered and the depths were gradually
raised (Fig. 153).   The heavier objects, such as pieces of
burnt brick and fragments of pots and sarcophagi, were
thus sifted as it were and left exposed on the surface, and
the higher the mound had been in which they lay scattered,
the closer they would now lie together.   Thus on the
surface of ancient mounds that were not inhabited later we

find small objects in very large numbers. Clay coffins,
which at the time of burial were laid deep in the ground,
are now on the surface, and as the process continues they
form a small heap of sherds. A specially striking example
is the appearance of the wells and sunk shafts, which consist of pottery rings placed one above another. Originally,
of course, they all ended at the level of the pavement of
the buildings to which they belonged. When these fell
to pieces and were blown away and disappeared with a
large part of the earth on which they stood, the lower part

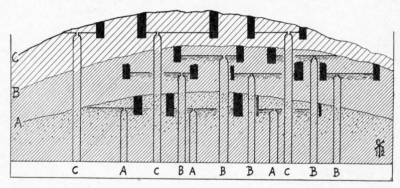

FIG. 154.—Schematic diagram of section through Babylonian house ruins, with wells.

of the well which was in the ground was covered over with
a small heap of fragments from the broken upper part,
which stood out above the surrounding ground as an
exposed drum (Fig. 154).

The longer the ruin as such had remained fallow the
more marked are the traces of this abrasion of the fallen
material and the emergence of the harder objects. In
Merkes and in Ishin aswad we can, on the whole, scarcely
count on more than one wind-swept stratum of habitations.
At Fara (Shuruppak) there were more of them, and at
Surgul and El-Hibbah there were many. Every new
inhabited stratum, so long as the mounds rose, joined on
new wells to the old ones as the latter disappeared from
sight, while on every denuded dwelling site the well
appeared on the surface together with those of the pre-
ceding layer. This is the reason why the well rings

visible on very ancient ruins, such as Surgul and El-
Hibbah, are so exceedingly numerous, a fact which is
unintelligible to those who do not understand their origin.
Many erroneous explanations have been given, among
others that they were drains intended to keep the hill dry,
whereas they had absolutely nothing to do with that
purpose.

XLII

MERKES

MERKES, which means a city as a trade centre in distinction
to a village, is the name given by the Arabs to the line of
mounds to the north of Ishin aswad (Fig. 155). Here the
houses of the citizens of Babylon are easier of access than
in the lower quarters of the town. They occupy in different levels, one above another, the entire mass of the hill,
which rises to 10 metres above zero. Our excavations cut
through the layers down to a depth of 1·2 metres below the
surface, where the water-level stopped farther progress,
although the ruins themselves continued lower. Thus the
water must now stand at a higher level than in ancient
times.

As it did not seem advisable to accumulate great masses
of rubbish in the vicinity where occupied town area was
everywhere to be expected, we worked over the site with
a system of pits 7 metres square, with gangways between
them 3 metres wide. Thus when the first pit had been
sunk completely to water-level the earth from the next
one could be thrown into it, thus avoiding any possible
damage to the ruins, for the upper layers at any rate had
to be removed in order to reach the lower ones. I need
not say that all the walls, graves, and separate finds
were recorded in the drawings and sections we made of
the site.

In the 2 to 3 upper metres lay the scanty ruins of the
Parthian period, thin house walls of mud brick or of brick

rubble, with wide spaces between them, which may be regarded as gardens or waste land.

The 4 metres below this represent the brilliant time of the city under the Neo-Babylonian kings on into the Persian and Greek periods. The houses are closely crowded together in the narrow streets. There was little open ground, and what was at first a court or the garden of a house was increasingly required for house building. It was at this time that the population was richest and most numerous. The houses have strong walls of mud brick, good brick floorings, and numerous circular wells and sunk shafts, which bear witness to the comparatively high level of the requirements demanded by the culture of that time. Greek sherds and tablets with dates of the Persian period lay at the height of 7 metres above zero, and bricks with the stamps of Nabonidus and Nebuchadnezzar at 5.5 metres.

Below, the signs of dwellings are again more scanty until the level of 2.4 above zero is reached, when there are once more thick house walls similar to those of the Neo-Babylonian level, though at wider distances apart. At this level there were tablets with the dates of Merodach-Baladan, Belnadinshum, Melishikhu, and others. Thus the stratum dates from about 1300 to 1400 B.C.

Deeper down the strata were irregular. Here they do not lie throughout in one solid uniform line. At 1 metre below zero we came once more on a uniform, clearly-marked stratum with houses lying rather closely together, in which were found tablets with dates of the time of the first Babylonian kings, the immediate successors of Hammurabi (2250 B.C.), Samsuiluna, Ammiditana, Samsu-ditana, etc. The mud-brick walls of the houses are not very thick, but all of them rest on a foundation of burnt brick. They show numerous traces of a conflagration in which they were destroyed. The tablets lay among these undisturbed ashes, so there can be no doubt that they were contemporary (see section on Fig. 237).

This is a bare outline of the find in the north of Merkes. If we dig farther in the plain, we find the Nebuchadnezzar stratum nearer the surface, and the

Fig. 155.—Plan of Merkes.

Hammurabi stratum disappears below water-level. This means undoubtedly that as far back as the latter period the town level here was rising in the form of a mound, and that at the Parthian period no substantial buildings stood in the plain.

The streets, though not entirely regular, show an obvious attempt to run them as much in straight lines as possible, so that Herodotus (i. 180) was able to describe them as straight (ἰθέαι). They show a tendency to cross at right angles, about 16 degrees west of north, and therefore as many degrees north of east. The Procession Street on the whole follows the same direction, and so do the inner city walls and all the temples, including Esagila, which may perhaps be held mainly responsible for this orientation. Only the Palace buildings on the Kasr and the mound Babil face exactly towards the astronomical north. The lower and more ancient levels also maintain this direction, in general with very slight deviations in the lines of the streets. Too little is known of the Hammurabi period at present to give any general valid rule with certainty; the house walls that have been excavated face somewhat accurately to the north, as do those of the upper levels. It was this fact, in conjunction with the usual inexact rectangular arrangement of the plots of land, and the exact rectangles of the inner chambers that gave rise to the peculiar construction of the street walls, which on their whole length were furnished with projecting corners or steps, an extraordinary characteristic of Neo-Babylonian architecture, which we have already met with at the Southern Citadel (Fig. 156).

Where there was a house door the corner is advanced so that the door might be placed in a sufficiently wide wall surface. As the corners frequently lie very close together, we may conclude that there were no windows toward the street. Also we observe no stalls for selling or other trade facilities, although this is no proof that they may not exist in other parts of the city, not yet excavated. For this reason it is much to be wished that the streets of Babylon could be laid bare to a much larger extent than has hitherto been possible, so that we might be able to study the entire plan of a very wide area. Outside Babylon it is only in Fara and Abu-Hatab that a small part of the town has been unearthed, and there the streets are noticeably more irregular and crooked than those of the metropolis. Of other Babylonian towns nothing is known of the planning of the streets.

The latest researches do not uphold the statement that is to be found in modern literature of some years back, that the Babylonian buildings were orientated with their corners

Fig. 156.—View of street in Merkes.

towards the four points of the compass. The orientation is different in every town, and in every case the circumstances determining it must be studied separately.

With the exception of the Procession Street and a few streets in other quarters, such as to the south of the Ninib temple, the streets are usually unpaved. Remains of systems of drainage, such as those to the south of the "great house" of Merkes, are rare.

The smaller temples, "Z," the Ninib temple, and the temple of Ishtar of Agade to the north of our excavations in Merkes, lay in the midst of the bustle of the houses, except that in front of the latter the street widened somewhat on its southern façade.

At the south end of the excavations in Merkes, on the street which broadens at that place, there is a quadrilateral block of mud-brick building, which in default of a better explanation might be regarded as the altar. On three sides it has broad ornamental grooves, and on the west side it has two narrow ones. Similar blocks, which perhaps were built for the same purpose, have been found in Telloh. There they consist of semicircular fillets (de Sarzec, *Fouilles de Telloh*), of which the elements, though they only project from the main building as semicircles, are in reality built completely round like pillars, for which they have been mistaken. The mouldings in the ruin called Wuswas in Warka are treated in the same way, with this difference, that there the working of one course is semicircular, and the succeeding one is round.

XLIII

THE SMALL OBJECTS, PRINCIPALLY FROM MERKES

AMONG the small objects, the tablets take the first place. Our predecessors merely turned over the upper layers, the middle and more especially the lower ones were untouched. Of the inscriptions found we shall learn more of the contents when they have been worked through by experts. The most ancient, those of the time of Hammurabi, consist, as do many of the middle and upper levels, of business documents (Fig. 157). Letters also are frequently found still in the clay cases which, by some, are regarded as the equivalents of our envelopes ; if this be right, it is extraordinary to observe how very large a percentage of these letters can never have been opened in ancient days. There were also numerous specimens of omen - literature. According to Weber (*Literatur der Babylonier und Assyrer*, p. 189), these include " all texts that had for their object the observation and meaning of

FIG. 157.—Tablets of the first dynasty.

signs, of whatever nature they might be, which were sent to men by the gods as indications of their wishes, and form perhaps the most extensive group of cuneiform texts that still exists." To the same class we must certainly ascribe some of our tablets, which bear curious groups of linear scroll-work interspersed with script (Fig. 158). A series of designs on tablets of horses and chariots, fights between wild beasts (Fig. 159), etc., and some charming reliefs are interesting from an artistic point of view.

When these tablets were found in their original position they were in jars, which appears to have been the usual

FIG. 158.—Labyrinthine lines on a tablet.

method of storing tablets that were not too large (Fig. 160).
In Fara, in a room of a house that was destroyed by fire,
there was a number of larger tablets lying together in
disorder, not on the floor-level but on a heap of rubbish,
so that their original storage-place could not be identified
with certainty. It appeared that they were lying above
the fragments of the ruined ceiling of the room, and that
they had fallen from the storey above, or from the roof, on

FIG. 159.—Drawing on a tablet.

which they may perhaps have been laid out to dry at the
time when the house was burnt down.

We found the tablets far more frequently in an early
secondary position than in the original one, a fact which
clearly proves that these documents were often thrown
away when they were of no further use. They are found
in groups, either in the street or inside the houses. The
Hammurabi tablets in room 25 *p* (cf. Fig. 155) lay immediately under the floor in the filling of the foundations, and had
been laid level with some care; that these were cancelled
documents is shown by certain examples which were
struck through across and across, and also that besides
those that were complete a very large proportion were

in fragments.   In the house in Fara just mentioned there
were a number of smaller ones in good condition embedded

FIG. 160.—Pottery urn with tablets.

in the mud mortar between the courses of mud brick.   It
seems as though a certain reverence for written documents

FIG. 161.—Bowls.

frequently led the Babylonians, the graphomaniacs of the
ancient world, to cherish the specimens of their beloved
art even after they were no longer needed and had to be put

out of the way, for a later period unforeseen by them, when after thousands of years the lucky people of to-day can gain the information conveyed by them.

The specimens of ceramics are so extremely numerous that we cannot attempt in this place to obtain even an approximate knowledge of them, and thus we can only occasionally point out the changes in form and ornamentation of the different periods. We include in the following observations some finds that occurred on other parts of the site.

The small flattish bowls are innumerable, they have no brim or only a very simple one, and small inadequate bases (Fig. 161). They have often owner's marks made of punctured rows of dots. The deeper

FIG. 162.—Aramaic incantation bowl.

round bowls have generally no base, and the walls of some of them are extremely thin. In the upper layers there lay Aramaic incantation bowls (Fig. 162) inscribed with signs resembling letters arranged in a spiral, and with rough drawings of men and of demons. When found undisturbed, the rims of two of them are placed together like a small double-urn coffin. Also birds' eggs are found with fine Aramaic writing. The beakers are cylindrical or bell-shaped, with a poorly-worked base (Fig. 163), and the pointed vases are cylindrical or of cup form (Fig. 164).

Small vases have often a white glaze, some of them a yellow or a blue one, or a blue edge. Such vases occur as early as the old Kassite times, when they are also made

FIG. 163.—Beakers.

FIG. 164.—Vases.

of a coarse frit. The outline is globular, or like a calyx, or a reversed calyx. Here also the bases are small and very poor. The larger vases of coloured enamels, which we have already referred to (cf. Fig. 152), are completely rounded in profile. Their footless base is sometimes slightly rounded, and is added to the body at an angle.

Jars for containing

Fig. 165.—Storage jars, on ring stands below.   Fig. 166.—Large storage jars.

liquids (Figs. 165, 166) are always of a specially long form, rather like the pupa of an insect. They were pointed below, and were either leant up against a wall or some other support or were placed in ring stands. Their rounded throats resembled the profile of an upright cup, or of a deep bowl turned upside down. During the Greek and later periods, amphorae, bearing the stamp of

the Greek amphora on the handle (Fig. 167), were used.
In the later Parthian period a rounded jar with a neck and

FIG. 167.—Fragments of Greek Vases.

no foot was common, made in two halves, and worked
together. The join is quite
obvious on the outside.
These jars are often washed
over, inside and outside,
with asphalt. The long
jars for storage were also
used for drain pipes by
cutting off the ends and
placing the jars one inside
another. Covers for these
jars are found in numbers,
in the form of small bowls
either bored through to
attach a handle, or with a
projecting knob, an *om-
phalos.*

Small jars or flasks for

FIG. 168.—Flasks.

storing liquids have very much the same form, with a handle, a short neck, and a plain flattened base (Fig. 168). Some are found still closed with a pottery stopper surrounded by a bit of rag. On the stopper there is an impressed sealing. As early as the time of Nebuchadnezzar the alabastron was in general use, both in pottery and also in white alabaster; they vary from very small dimensions to a considerable size. The amount of the contents is frequently marked on them in cuneiform characters. Several fragments of large alabaster vases bear Egyptian inscriptions. The handles of the alabastron are typical; they are semicircular pierced discs placed on

Fig. 169.—Flat circular vases.

a small flat surface which projects slightly, broadening from below, and looks like a rag hanging down. Flat circular vases, usually glazed, are common both in the late and early periods (Fig. 169).

The early Babylonian lamp consists of a rather high vase with a long protruding curved nozzle (Fig. 170). It is often represented in this form on the ancient *kudurru*, for it is the emblem of the god Nusku. In the later forms the vase is flatter and the nozzle shorter. In both forms the vase is made on the wheel and the nozzle is fashioned by hand. The earlier higher form is only found unglazed. Some of the later form are glazed, and some of them, with their blistered surface, resemble the ancient enamel. Contemporary with these there are always some poor examples which were entirely made by hand, as is the case with other forms of pottery. But even in the most ancient ruins, the deepest levels of Fara or Surgul, we have never penetrated to depths where the potter's wheel was unknown. Occasional instances of hand-made pottery can always be identified as direct copies of contemporary ware made on the wheel, so that it would appear that in Babylonia pottery and the potter's wheel were invented at the same time.

The older higher form of lamp which, like the bowls, has often owner's marks punctured in groups of dots, is not

FIG. 170.—Lamps.

intended to stand, and the base is always rounded while the later lower form has a small flattened base. Handles first make their appearance on the shallow glazed lamps, often in the form of a separate piece added on. On these lamps also the usual ornamentation of rows of dots and beads first appears. In this and in the development of shape, the influence of the Greek lamp that came in about this period is not to be ignored. This was a shallow pottery lamp with a short semi-cylindrical nozzle, always well glazed and of the finest clay, and combined an elegance of appearance with a high level of practical utility such as had not been approached in Babylonia during the course of thousands of years. In the later Parthian forms the nozzle became less and less distinct from the body of the lamp, which was then moulded in two separate pieces, an

upper and a lower half. They were rarely unornamented
and were invariably glazed. Green glazed polylychnae
were also produced in Greek fashion with several nozzles
on one side, or with many all round them. All of these
are apparently oil lamps.

In yet later Sassanide times a lamp was in use which
consisted of a small saucer in which the nozzle was formed
by pinching it together with the fingers into the shape of
a trefoil; this was intended to contain solid fat, and has
generally a separate foot worked on to it. It was always
glazed blue or green with a black edge. Of a period
at present undetermined, and of unknown origin, is a boat-
shaped lamp of black stone. The wick passed through
a hole in the solid prow, and in the other rounded end
there was also a solid piece left, in which a vertical hole
was bored to contain the stick that formed the handle.

All the earlier vases, which are distinguished by very
poorly-formed flattened bases, are adapted for a state of
culture in which a table was not reckoned among the
household furniture of the ordinary folk. It was Greek
civilisation that first brought the table into general use.

The great storage vessels for dry goods are of semi-
globular form with an annular roll for the foot. Inside
one of these and half-way up its height there are three
projecting brackets, on which a second jar could be placed
for special purposes. The great Pithos which played so
important a part in western culture does not appear here.

Hellenistic vases are found in abundance, but always
in fragments, and also an earlier form with black figures
and a Greek inscription (see Fig. 167). The shape
cannot always be made out, but beside plates there are
the cylix, the aryballos, the alabastron, and others. This
ware, which is always highly polished, is not found in the
graves, and we may therefore conclude that the Greeks of
that period had a special cemetery which we have not yet
found. A green glazed rhyton (Fig. 171) in the form of
a calf's head lay in the upper levels of Merkes. The
masses of pottery and glass fragments of the Sassanide
and Arab levels of Amran still await examination by
specialists.

Several transparent glass goblets profusely decorated with polished concave facets lay near the rhyton. At the

FIG. 171.—Glazed rhyton.

same Seleucid-Parthian level there were numerous fragments of transparent colourless or pale-blue glass vessels, among them finely-formed handles of oinochoae and amphorae moulded while the material was still soft (Fig. 172). The earlier glass is invariably opaque and multi-coloured. The usual form is the small alabastron either pointed or rounded at the base. The ornamentation consists of a web of multi-coloured glass lines encircling the vase, which is made of a rough gritty frit.

FIG. 172.—Glass goblet and jug.

The lines while still hot are broken first from above and then from below, thus forming lines roughly S-shaped (Fig. 173). These vases certainly date back here to the same early period as in Egypt (cf. Kisa, *Glas im Altertum*, i. p. 9, "about 1500 B.C."). We need not necessarily regard them as imports, however, for the older the civilisations the more their products resemble one another. Thus the pottery vases of Nagada resemble those of Surgul. From the time of the Sargonids onwards, the importation of Egyptian glass and other wares may first

be observed without any doubt, such as apotropaic eyes, weird scaraboids, and the like. Decorative glass beads made like the alabastrons just described, and which are general in Babylon in early times, date back as far as the fourth millennium in Fara.

A number of utensils and toys were found, especially in Merkes. Several pottery utensils of remarkable form, which must have been employed for some business purpose unknown to us, are still inexplicable. A bell of burnt clay that occurs rather frequently

FIG. 173.—Ancient glass.

is worthy of notice (Fig. 174). It looks like a pointed beaker, but it is always perforated at the base, and near the hole it has two projections, which are often fashioned like animals' heads and must have served for suspension. A string passed through the hole, with a clapper of unburnt clay attached to it. It was only when we found one of these clappers still

FIG. 174.—Earthenware bell.

bearing the print of the string inside a bell that we could distinguish the bells as such, and not as pierced beakers; it is, of course, only rarely that the clappers are found in place.

At the top of an upturned beaker a female (?) figure is often seated (Fig. 175). Behind the seat there is a hole through which the smoke of a pastille concealed within the beaker could ascend and surround the figure with mystic vapour. Three panther (?) heads on a stake, widening out in the shape of a foot, as they are often represented on *kudurru* as symbols of a god, were doubtless intended for some religious purpose, as well as the bark (Figs. 176, 177) that frequently occurs, and in which an animal is lying. This latter cannot be identified owing to the roughness of the workmanship. The vessel is of equal height both at stem and stern, which end above in two volutes that curve inwards and are often in the form of human heads. In other, later, types the stem is often armoured with a ram. The keel is always flat and is certainly intended for use on terra firma, on which the boats could be dragged by a cord passed through a hole in the stem, for certainly these terra-cotta vessels could not float. The bark played a very import-

Fig. 175.—Woman on a beaker or omphalos.

ant part in the religious ceremonies of the Babylonian, as it did in those of the Egyptian. It was in them that the gods performed their processions under Gudea as they did under Nebuchadnezzar. Among many other divinities, Marduk and Nabu had their sacred barks, to the furnishing of which Nebuchadnezzar refers in the great *Steinplatten* inscription (3, 8, and 70). "The furniture of the temple of Esagila I adorned with massive (?) gold, the Kua-bark with ṣarîr and stones like the stars of heaven. — The Ḥêtu-canal-bark, the means of conveyance of his lordship, the bark of the procession of the New Year, the feast of Babil—its wooden karê, the zarâti which are in it, I caused to be clothed with tîri šašši and stone" (trans. by Delitzsch). The animal that lies in these pottery boats must therefore undoubtedly have represented a sirrush.

Spinning whorls are of stone or burnt clay. The stone whorls are in the form of a flat double convex disc, or a

S

truncated cone, as are also the pottery whorls. Some of
the latter have two holes instead of the usual single one,

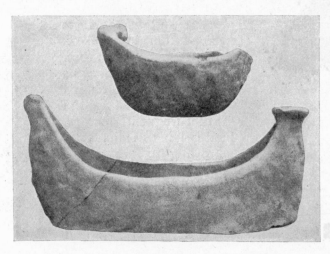

Fig. 176.—Earthenware boat.

and the spindle must, therefore, have been split below, as
the modern Arab spindle frequently is. The whorls of the

Fig. 177.—Earthenware boats with animal inside.

earlier time often have ornaments or owner's marks scratched
on them.

Of the whole range of pottery, with the exception of
the enamelled vases already described, only very few
stand out as worthy of notice owing to superior technique
or decoration that would render them fit for more ad-

vanced needs and necessities. It appears that all such demands were met by the use of more or less costly stone, as, for example, the fine white alabaster employed for the alabastron.

Storage jars of limestone were of huge dimensions. Bowls, plates, and similar forms of slate, serpentine, and finely-veined marble with delicate and graceful outlines were very numerous.

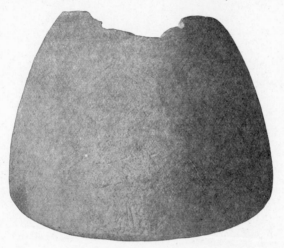

FIG. 178.—Stone vessel.

Several vases in schist (Fig. 178), with a flattened base, belong to a very ancient period, possibly prehistoric; they are decorated on the outside with incised lines in imitation of mat-work. There are numerous bowls for rubbing made in basalt, with three strong short feet (Fig. 179), and strong limestone mortars roughly hewn on the outside, but completely smoothed on the inside by use. Like the rice mortars of the present day, they must

FIG. 179.—Basalt bowl for rubbing out grain.

have been used specially for beating out grain, and required a wooden pestle. It is doubtful whether the limestone pestles found by us were used in these stone mortars.

The hand mill from the earliest period down to the latest consists of a flat lower stone, usually hollowed by use, and a rubbing stone, which was rubbed backwards and forwards on it, both of basalt (Fig. 180). Fragments of

FIG. 180.—Ancient Babylonian rubbing-mill, in use by an Arab.

FIG. 181.—Prehistoric utensils.

these rubbing-mills are found in great numbers on all the ruined sites of Babylonia, where they are mistaken by inexperienced observers for the upper parts of stelae with reliefs. Of the circular revolving mills that are found to-day in almost every Arab house, there are scarcely any remains in the upper level of Amran. Funnel-shaped mills, such as the Romans possessed, were apparently unknown. As the rubbing-stone was employed with the mill, so also the rubbing-bowls possessed small rubbers, which were held in the hand. The lower side of these show the smoothness that results from use (Fig. 181). Beside these rubbers there are many stones of much the same size that show marks of having been used for pounding; many are cubes, and have been used on all sides, others are discs, and their edges have been used. Not all of these can be assigned to the historic period.

Some stones with holes bored in them are apparently prehistoric. Some are certainly mace heads,

FIG. 182.—Prehistoric implements.

or something of the sort. Of the palaeolithic saws of obsidian and of flint, with their nuclei (Fig. 182), which are spread over the entire prehistoric world with such remarkable uniformity, various specimens are found, though naturally not so many as on more ancient sites, Fara or Surgul. In Fara some of these saws were still in their ancient setting, which consisted of an asphalt backing, in which they were set on the cutting side, often one after another, in order to lengthen the implement. In this way it was impossible to use the fine cutting edge, and in fact the polish acquired by long use appears only

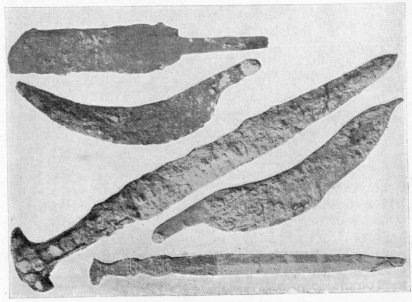

FIG. 183.—Swords, lance-head, and knives in bronze.

FIG. 184.—Bronze arrow-heads; prehistoric flint knife and saws.

on the toothed edges; but owing to the projection of the

backing the latter could never have cut into anything to a greater depth than about 1 centimetre.   Of neolithic implements only one single arrow-head has been found, and in Fara and Surgul, so far as I can remember, no neolithic implements have been found.

Babylonian weapons are comparatively rare even in the graves.   We have recovered only a few short swords, knives, and flat lance-heads in bronze (Fig. 183).   The arrow-heads alone are very numerous, and they of course occur far more frequently in the walls of the fortifications than in peaceful Merkes. They are 3-edged bolts cast in bronze, which were fixed to a shaft and are often barbed; the edges are sharply ground.   The 2-edged, leaf-shaped bolts that were inserted by a tenon into the shaft belong to a later Parthian (?) period (Fig. 184).   There are no clear traces of slings, unless we accept as evidence of them the smooth pebbles that are found in groups,

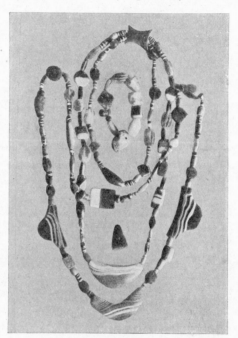

FIG. 185.—Chain of onyx beads from a grave in Merkes.

and which are certainly well adapted for such use.   In a room of a house at Senkereh large numbers of these were found placed together, and were obviously selected pebbles of the right size and shape.   Of the great stone projectiles for the later balistae, we have already spoken (p. 50).   A common weapon was the short mace with a stone knob.   It is still in general use among the Arabs to-day under the name of *hattre*, and is frequently represented on reliefs and seal cylinders.   The same club with an asphalt head is

called *mugwar* by the Arabs.   The form of the head varies,
and is sometimes globular, pear-shaped, egg-shaped, or the
like ; in some cases they bear the inscription of their
whilom owner.   Thus we have the mace head of Melishihu
with the inscription, ". . . to the great . . . ra-an, his
lord, has Melishihu, the son of Kurigalzu given (it)."
Another mace head that resembles a knot of wood bears
the inscription, "mace head (hi-in-gi) of diorite (šu-u)

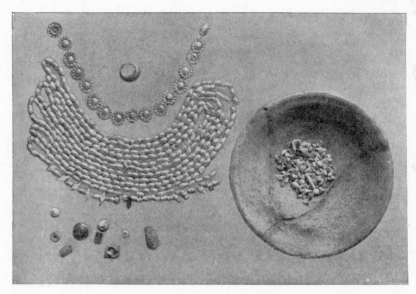

FIG. 186.—Grave deposits of gold, glass, and shell, from Merkes.

belonging to Uluburariaš, son of Burnaburariaš the king,
the king of the sea land.   Whosoever removes this name,
and inserts his name, may Anu, Bel, Ea, Marduk and
Belit remove his name!" (trans. by Weissbach).

The ornaments found (Figs. 185, 186) came mainly
from the graves, although, with some exceptions, they are
not furnished very richly.   From the early times onwards
the most usual ornaments are rows of beads, often of considerable length.   In the earliest prehistoric times which
we reached at Fara, the Babylonian appears to have been
hung round with beads, somewhat like the wildest tribes-
men of Polynesia.   Glass, or a glassy frit, was early in use

for beads, but semi-precious stones, such as agate, onyx, rock-crystal, and amethyst, were principally employed. At Fara, in the earlier times, the method of polishing them was unknown, and they were merely ground, but this art rapidly developed under the Sargonids, and specially in the Neo-Babylonian epoch, to extraordinary perfection, while the variety and beauty of form is very striking. The beads are sometimes globular, sometimes discs or slender ellipsoids; small sheets were often perforated once or several times through the flat surface, and thus formed a variety of caesurae in the threading of the separate pieces. Human heads and tiny figures, such as frogs, bulls, or tortoises, were carved with minute detail in agate and similar stones. Rings and perforated discs of oyster-shell were popular, and so were seashells, perforated for threading, ctenobranchia (cowries), dentalia, and also the siphonal cylinders

FIG. 187.—Leg-bones, each with five anklets, from Merkes.

of the siphoniatae—the latter more especially at a very early period—and others. Circlets of bronze, silver, and iron decorated wrists and ankles. In the graves we often found the lower end of the leg-bones decorated with as many as three or five pairs (Fig. 187). Ear-rings were generally of gold or silver; the usual form is either a roll drawn out in narrow wires bent together into a ring or a boss soldered on to a hook-shaped wire. Elaborate patterns are rare (Fig. 188); often on one corpse there would be not merely one or two, but many of the same form, which must surely indicate that they were deposited in the coffin with the deceased as votive offerings. The fibula (Fig. 189) for fastening the garments together consists of a semicircular or angularly bent hoop decorated

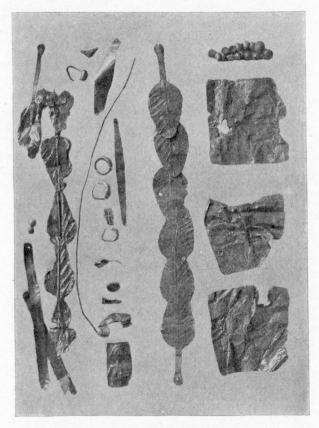

FIG. 188.—Gold ornaments.

with a regular series of transverse rings. The pin fastened at one end and made elastic by various twists, fits at the other end into a haft shaped like a hand, and often actually modelled as one. The semicircular form is represented on the clothing in sculpture, and also on the kudurru, where it forms the figure of a constellation.

Finger-rings are not so numerous in the early period, but they begin to come into common use during the Persian period, when they were used as seals, and superseded the ancient seal cylinders (Fig. 190).

The form of the seal face, which is also frequently impressed on tablets of Persian dating, is elliptical or bi - segmental. Animals are most frequently represented. Those rings, which are

FIG. 189.—Bronze fibulae.

generally cast in bronze and more rarely in silver, consist usually of a small plate, which, when not engraved as a seal, is set with precious stones, on a plain hoop.

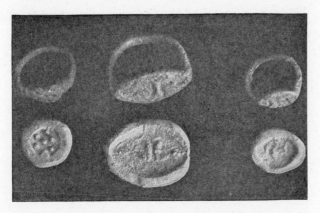

FIG. 190.—Rings and their seal impressions.

The most important form of the Babylonian seal was the cylinder (Fig. 191). In addition to these there were at all periods numerous button seals, parallelepipeda, and calottes of circular and ellipsoidal forms; also comparatively early there were scarabs and scaraboids. The materials used included agate, lapis lazuli, marble, flint, magnetite, and sea-shell, as well as glass and frit. All seals were

FIG. 191.—Cylinder seals and signet with their impressions.

bored, in order that an eyed peg might be fixed into them. If the perforation were long, as with the seal cylinders, it was worked from both ends, and a slight projection may be seen inside in the centre. The usual representations are of divinities and their emblems, heroes and animals in combat with each other, or with gods and champions. The principal gods are symbolised thus : Shamash by the sun's disc, Sin by the new moon, Ishtar by a star, and here in Babylon more especially, Marduk by a triangle on a staff, and Nebo by a rod.   Ornamentation is extremely rare. Inscriptions in cuneiform, the name of the owner and his devotion to a specified god, who is not always neces- sarily indicated in the re- presentation, are specially frequent on seal cylinders, while Aramaic inscriptions are found only on other forms of seals.   Owing to the great number of these objects we can observe the gradual development of art with delightful clearness. The ancient seal, which reaches back into prehis- toric times, notwithstand- ing the primitive tools em- ployed, often shows great vigour of execution.   These are merely engraved, but with the discovery of the wheel and drill the art

FIG. 192.—Stone amulets.

progressed with the development of the means of expres- sion, and gradually and steadily rose to its greatest per- fection at the time of the last of the Assyrian and Babylonian monarchs.   In consequence of the over- whelming use of the wheel, the art then became gradually though not uniformly so conventionalised that the repre- sentations often consist merely of dots and lines.   But even at this stage specimens of astounding artistic merit are not rare.   Glyptic art in Babylon is always in advance of the other contemporary plastic arts.   It is only moulded pottery reliefs that in any degree keep step with it.   Modelling in the round, more especially in stone, remains markedly behind the contemporary productions of the stone-cutter.   Baby- lonian plastic art in the round never attained the excellence

of the Greek masterpieces of about the fourth century B.C.
In any case it was gem-cutting that from the beginning was
the pioneer of Baby-
lonian art.

FIG. 193.—Greek coins in a jar.

Representations or
reliefs of an apotropaic
nature occur on stone
amulets, which must
have been hung on sick
persons (Fig. 192).
They are small tablets,
which bear the repre-
sentation on one side
and an inscription on
the other; at the top a
hole is bored to admit a
string.

There are no Baby-
lonian coins, although
minting commenced in
the West, in Lydia or
in Ægina, as early as 700 B.C.   The first coins we find in
Babylon, rare though they
are, are Graeco-Persian
(Darius). The coins of
the time of Alexander
are more numerous, and
specially those of his
successor Lysimachus
(Fig. 193). Parthian,
Sassanide, and Arab
coins are found occasion-
ally, especially in Amran.
There also a glazed
amphora was found,
filled with Arab coins,
and still stoppered with
a wad plugging; the contents have not yet been laid out
and examined.

FIG. 194.—Two vertebrae, a boar's tusk, and
three bone joints prepared as sword handles.

The remains that have been found of food and of

domestic animals still require to be studied by experts.
Charred grain and date stones are frequently found. The
latter occur absolutely all over the ruins, and in all the
levels of Babylon, as well as of Fara and Surgul. The
ancient Babylonians do not appear to have eaten shell-fish,
but on the contrary we often find fish bones, among them
the lower jaw of a carp, such as is still caught in the
Euphrates. Sheep, cattle, poultry, and pigeons are also
not infrequent. The knuckle bones of sheep have
survived more especially, possibly because they were used,
as they were by the Romans, for the well-known game.
They are also found cast in bronze. There is often the
boar's tusk (Fig. 194), which was bored through at one end
and carried as an amulet, perhaps on the horses' harness.
The mongoose (*Herpestes mungo*), of which the skull is often
found, appears to have been a household pet, as it is at the
present day in the neighbourhood. The fore-leg of a
pachyderm, 1.15 metres long, which is almost too large to
be that of an elephant, was found at a great depth, 1.2
metres below zero, in Merkes (25 *n*). Fragments of
ostrich eggs are found sporadically.

XLIV

THE GRAVES IN MERKES

In Babylon the dead were buried by the fortification walls,
in the streets, and in such parts of the inhabited town as
were unappropriated for dwelling-houses at the time of the
burial. They were laid from 1 to 2 metres deep in the
ground. The house ruins of an earlier period were often
encroached upon, and where the ancient walls were recognisable the pit was dug parallel with them; where they
were not recognisable the walls of the ancient house were
often cut through by the grave, while the wall of a later
building period once more turned off from the burial site.
If an ancient brick pavement was reached this also was
frequently cut through, and the sarcophagus lay partly

above and partly below it.   From such clear cases, against
which situations that cannot be made out can adduce no
conclusive evidence, it can be distinctly seen that in
Babylon, at any rate, no interments took place inside
inhabited houses.   We have already (p. 219 ff.) seen how
various were the methods of burial at different times, and
in the few ruined sites of Babylonia hitherto excavated.
We cannot here enter into all the peculiarities, and we can

FIG. 195.—Double-urn burial from Merkes.

only attempt to sketch out the classes of burial that are
clear, and easily distinguishable from each other.

The lowest levels, of the time of the first Babylonian
kings, Hammurabi and his successors, contain no sarcophagi.   The bodies either lay simply in the earth, or at
most were rolled in reed mats or were roughly surrounded
by mud bricks.   They were almost always laid out at full
length, and often in an attitude that gives an impression that
they were left in the same place and situation in which
they died.

Between zero line and about 3 metres above zero, we come almost exclusively on double - urn burials (Fig. 195). They consist of two pottery vessels with the mouths joined together, in which the body is placed in a crouching position, and generally tightly packed. These double jars, of which one is per-

FIG. 196.—Trough coffin, with lid.

forated at the foot end, lie together horizontally or slightly sloping, never upright, although both vessels are provided with a broadened end. They are either alone or in groups of 6 or 8 crowded into a small space. Generally close by there is a layer of ashes, which appears to represent some burial ceremony; in this layer there are a few brick - built subterranean chambers, with barrel - shaped vaulting, such as are often found

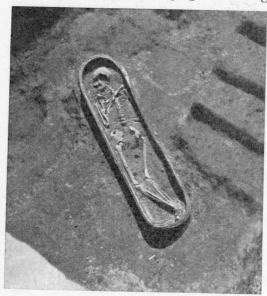

FIG. 197.—Trough coffin, opened.

T

FIG. 198.—Crouching burial.

FIG. 199.—Brick grave from Merkes.

in Asshur. Their great rarity, when compared with the masses of pottery coffins, shows them undoubtedly to be foreign to Babylonian usage.

Above the double-urn level, at 3 metres above zero, the high pottery coffins begin, which are shown by isolated finds in the Southern Citadel to belong undoubtedly to the time of Nebuchadnezzar and earlier. On the side where the head lay they are angular, the other side is rounded. The body lies crouched in them, or slightly on one side. These "crouching burials" were somewhat shallower in the upper levels, so that the body lay with the knees drawn up on one side, while the upper part of the body perhaps lay on the back; hence the sarcophagus assumes a bulging shape at the foot end. It was covered over with a flat or slightly curved clay cover.

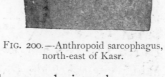

At 4 metres above zero are the shallow, somewhat short, trough-shaped coffins, in which the body lay at full length, with the knees only slightly flexed (Figs. 196, 197). The shallow vaulted covering was made of two pieces that leant against each other in the centre. Generally, however, the coffin was placed upside down over the

FIG. 200.—Anthropoid sarcophagus, north-east of Kasr.

body as it lay on the ground, thus rendering the cover unnecessary. These "crouching burials" are found as high as 7 metres above zero (Fig. 198).

It is only in the topmost levels of Merkes that the brick-built sarcophagi are found which we have already mentioned (p. 216) and assigned to the Graeco-Parthian period (Fig. 199). There is no doubt that they were usually sunk in the ground. Often, however, the roof is so carefully built with bricks tilted up cornerwise, and covered over with gypsum mortar, that we are forced to admit the possibility that this part at least may in some cases have stood above the ground. The remains of the wooden coffin that actually enclosed the body have frequently been found inside the sarcophagus.

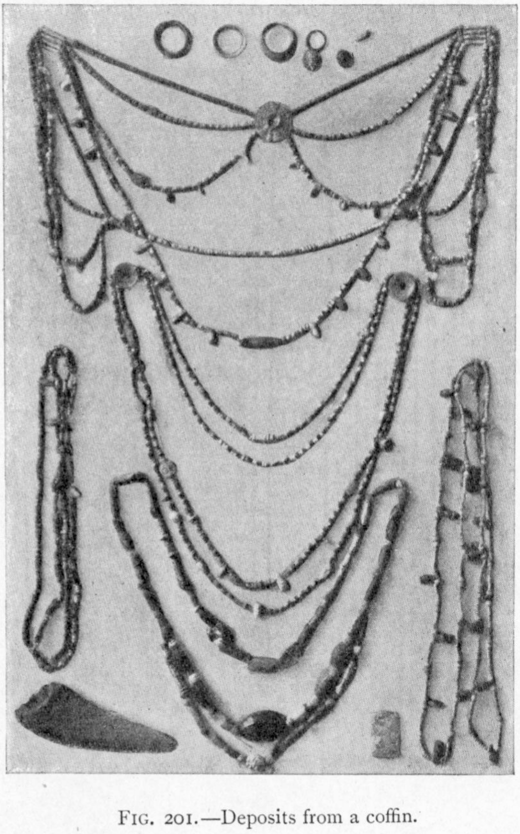

Glazed trough coffins, which were so numerous on the Kasr in the principal court of the Southern Citadel (p. 102), are almost entirely absent in Merkes, and so are the slipper and anthropoid coffins. A fine example of the latter lay on the north-east corner of the Kasr (Fig. 200). The glazed trough coffin must therefore date from a period when the main part, the wide town area of Babylon, was already completely abandoned, and only Amran, the Kasr, and Babil were inhabited.

FIG. 201.—Deposits from a coffin.

The graves on the whole were not rich in deposits. The deceased generally retained some of his wonted adornments of necklaces, rings, fibulae, bracelets, and anklets. Other ornaments, such as ear-rings, were only

occasionally added (Fig. 201).   All sorts of pottery vessels
were numerous, especially beakers and bowls.   These did
not often reach the coffin uninjured.   Even in entirely
untouched coffins there are often large fragments, or
broken vessels with some pieces missing.   Weapons are
very rarely found, but this is not surprising when we
consider the eminently peaceful character of the house-
holders of Babylon.   Seals and seal cylinders are
extremely rare in the coffins.   It is obvious that the seal
was not given to the dead man in his grave, but that it
was retained by the heir for further use.   Under these
circumstances it is impossible to draw conclusions from
the dated character of the seal impression, as to the date of
the document on which the impression is found, without
further evidence.

XLV

THE TERRA-COTTA FIGURES

THE number of terra-cottas found in Babylon is enormous.
Including very small fragments, it exceeds 6000.   Those
of the early Babylonian period are not so numerous as
those of the Middle, the Neo-Babylonian, and finally of the
Graeco-Parthian periods.   The style of the latter entirely
supersedes the Babylonian, although the types are on the
whole retained.   Any figures modelled by hand are rare.
We will here describe the main characteristics of those
that were moulded, of which all that fall within the same
group naturally display a great resemblance to each other.
The great mass of them exemplify only a few types, they
are almost all of them worked merely on one side, and the
female figures greatly exceed the male figures in number.

   1. The nude female figures with the hands folded in
each other below the breast we have already (p. 65)
observed as probably representing Ninmach (Fig. 202).
The abundant wavy hair falls on the shoulders.   She

always wears a necklace of several rows, and has numerous
anklets and bracelets. In the rounded, full-moon countenance we can recognise the Babylonian standard of beauty
which occurs in all female figures. The type goes back
to the early Babylonian period, as is seen
in Fig. 203; here the rolled-up locks,
when seen full face, appear like round
discs.

FIG. 202.—Female
figure with folded
hands (Ninmach?).

FIG. 203. — Woman
with folded hands,
old Babylonian style.

FIG. 204.—Woman
and child.

2. A nude female figure with a child at her breast
(Gula?) also occurs very frequently. The arrangement of
the hair is the same, but the figure is entirely without
ornaments (Fig. 204). This type survived into the Graeco-
Parthian period, but it is then clothed, and a fillet is added
to the hair (Figs. 205, 206).

3. A second rarer figure of a woman and child represents her with her legs crossed beneath her and sitting
on a cushion; the lower part of the body at least appears
to be clothed (Fig. 207).

4. There are numerous examples of a nude woman
with widely spread elbows, laying her hands on her breasts.

Those that are entirely early Babylonian are wearing a necklace, the Graeco-Parthian examples have in addition a diadem and ear-rings (Figs. 208-210).

FIG. 205.—Woman and child, Graeco-Parth-ian style.

FIG. 206.—Woman and child, Graeco-Parth-ian style.

FIG. 207.—Seated woman and child.

5. By far the most common type is that of a nude woman with arms hanging down, perhaps a second form of Gula (cf. p. 234). She is usually without orna-ments, her hair and figure are similar to the others (Fig. 211).

6. These five female deities are at present only counterbalanced by three male types, at least so far as moulded terra-cottas are concerned. The first is a standing bearded man clothed in a long flounced gar-ment, who holds a small vase to his breast with both hands. We have already attempted (p. 234) to identify him with Ninib. He is distinguished from Anu, who also holds a circular vessel with both hands, by the over-flowing water that is pouring out of the vessel held by the

FIG. 208.
Woman with hands supporting breasts.

FIG. 209.
Woman with hands support-ing breasts.

latter.   Of Anu we have in addition to seals a terra-cotta finely modelled by hand, with a great horned hat (Fig. 212).

7. The second male type is less common. The hands are folded on the breast like Ninmach, and the flounced garment and arrangement of the hair are exactly the same as No. 6. It is possible that we may find it surviving in a rare Parthian type (Figs. 213, 214).

FIG. 210.—Woman with hands supporting breasts, Graeco-Parthian style.

FIG. 211. — Woman with arms hanging down.

8. The only seated divinity is represented as a man with an unusually long beard, wearing a flounced garment, and holding some object in his left hand which it has not been possible to identify from the few specimens found ; the right hand rests on the right knee (Fig. 215).   The temple statue of Marduk in Esagila, according to Herodotus (i. 183), was also depicted as sitting, a resemblance with this type which can hardly be regarded as merely accidental.

9. Of the Parthian period there are numerous examples of a standing man with a flower in the right hand, which is

FIG. 212.—Male figure with
goblet (Anu ?).

FIG. 213.—Man
with folded hands.

FIG. 214. — Man
with folded hands,
Parthian style.

FIG. 215.—Bearded male
figure, seated (Marduk ?).

FIG. 216.—Man with
flower in his hand.

FIG. 217. —
Woman with
flower in her
hand.

laid on the breast; the left hand is hanging down and holds a wreath (?). He is clothed in a sleeved garment that reaches to the knees, and wears trousers; in addition he has a cloak with a hood that covers his head and chin, leaving his moustache visible; round his hips is a girdle with the ends hanging down. The cross ribbing on the sleeves and trousers is characteristic of this period (Fig. 216).

10. The female figure corresponding to this male type also holds a flower in

FIG. 218.—Woman holding palm branch (?).

FIG. 219.—Woman holding palm branch (deity?).

FIG. 220.—Woman holding palm branch, Greek style.

the right hand on the breast, and a wreath in the left hand that hangs down, but the hood leaves the round hairless face uncovered; long ringlets fall over the shoulders, and the sleeved garment is tucked up above the knees and confined below the waist with a girdle. The legs are bare (Fig. 217).

11. A rare type that belongs to the same period is the figure of a man in exactly the same clothing, but with the arms crossed on the breast.

12. A clothed figure of a woman with Babylonian

characteristics (Fig. 218) holds an upright palm branch (?)

in her left hand. Some strands of hair hang down her cheeks; the right hand is laid on the breast. The same type occurs also roughly worked as an idol (Fig. 219), as well as in good Greek workmanship (Fig. 220).

13. A head of appalling horror is either bored through at the top to be worn as an amulet or hollowed out at the throat to be fixed on to a stick. Two cross-ribbed horns stretch from the

FIG. 221.—Terra-cotta amulet.

FIG. 222.—Musician with double flute.

FIG. 223.—Lute-player.

FIG. 224.—Lute-player.

forehead over the skull; the goggle eyes are widely open;

the gaping muzzle shows all the teeth, including four powerful canines. The bristly beard
is either represented by short
locks or indicated
by rows of holes in
the smooth lower
jaw (Fig. 221).

14. Musicians
were less fre-
quently repre-
sented in the Baby-
lonian period than
in the Greek
period. They play
the double flute

FIG. 225.—Woman
with harp.

FIG. 226.—Woman with
tambourine.

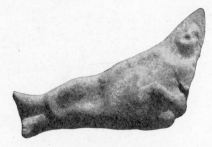

FIG. 227.—Woman reclining.

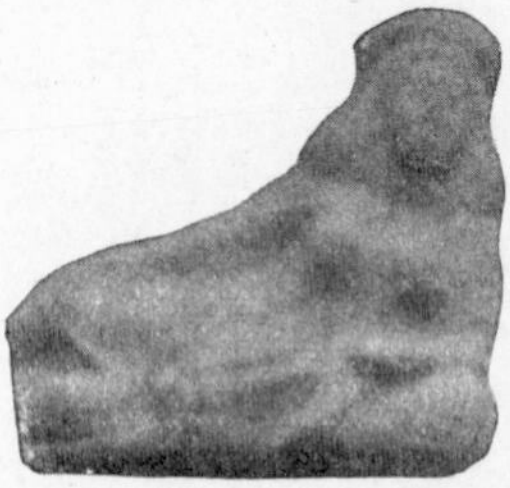

FIG. 228.—Woman reclining.

(Fig. 222) which is in use among the Arabs at the present
day and known as the *mutbak*; the
panpipe, a long lute with smaller or
wider sounding-board (Figs. 223,
224); the oriental harp (Fig. 225),
the tambourine (Fig. 226), the
cithara, and other instruments which
will afford an interesting study for
connoisseurs of musical instruments.

15. The figure seated on the
censer has already (p. 257) been
described, also

FIG. 229.—Pottery mask.

16. The ape (p. 234).

17. Female figures, clothed and lying on the left side,

belong exclusively to the Greek and Parthian periods.
With the left arm they support themselves on a cushion,
and the right arm rests on the hips.
Like similar figures in alabaster (Fig.
132), they are frequently found in the
graves (Figs. 227, 228).

18. From the later graves come
pottery masks with holes round the
edge by which they could be affixed to
a binding of some material. Many of
these masks, with wide-open mouth
and eyebrows drawn together in grief,
have the characteristics of professional
mourners (Figs. 229, 230). Satyrs,
cupids, etc., also appear as masks.

19. The number of Greek genre
figures in terra-cotta is very remarkable. In great measure they recall
those of Tanagra and Myrina. They

FIG. 230.—Pottery mask.

are mostly of
women and girls
in ample cloth-
ing, and their in-
imitable grace is
almost as re-
markable in the
slightly executed
examples as in
those of the
finest and most
careful work-
manship (Figs.
231-233). These
inexpensive and
charming fig-
ures, with the re-
spective details
of position,
drapery, and

FIG. 231.—Greek terra-
cotta.

FIG. 232.—Greek terra-cotta.

head-dress in never-ending variety, as well as the costly

and important examples, were widely distributed over
the city in inexhaustible abund-
ance. A small winged cupid was
popular as a jar handle (Fig. 234).
20. The figures of horsemen
we have already (p. 235) described.

We have thus enu-
merated some of the
principal types from
among the very large
number of small objects
already found on the
actual inhabited site of
Merkes, and this slight
review of the luxuries
and requirements and
the relative artistic feel-

FIG. 234.—
Cupid as a
jar handle.

ing of the citizens of Babylon
must suffice for the present, until
the material can be spread out and
further examined, when a more
complete description may be rendered possible.

FIG. 233.—Greek terra-cotta.

XLVI

THE GREAT HOUSE IN MERKES

In planning a Babylonian private house a square
principal chamber on the south side of a court appears
under all circumstances to have been indispensable.
Everything else might vary according to circumstances
and temporary requirements; the side chambers might
be more or less numerous, several courts with the chambers
connected with them might be added to the house, but the
court and the principal chamber are always there. Before
the introduction of Greek art there were no pillars either
in the court or in the house.

The largest house (Fig. 236) that we have yet found in Merkes possesses three courts (4, 19, 26), each with its principal chamber on the south (12, 23, 27), which corresponds in size with the court to which it is attached. The wide doorway of the house on the north is in a flat length of wall which has no toothed projections, such as all the other walls have. Through this we enter the vestibule (1), and can turn either left to the main portion with the

FIG. 235.—Reconstruction of the Great House in Merkes.

large court, or right to the private or secondary portion with two courts. The former part of the house was certainly consecrated to business and to intercourse with the general public. This is indicated by the fact that in this part only there was a second outer door on the south side, which later was walled up. This opened on a small room (13) that communicated immediately with the principal chamber, and may have served as a shop. In any case, the owner could here communicate with the outside world without being obliged to use the ceremonious northern entrance. On entering by the latter, one passed a very small room (2), the entrance chamber and porter's

lodge, the cloak- or waiting-room (3) before reaching the
court (4). To the east of this lay the servants' apartment

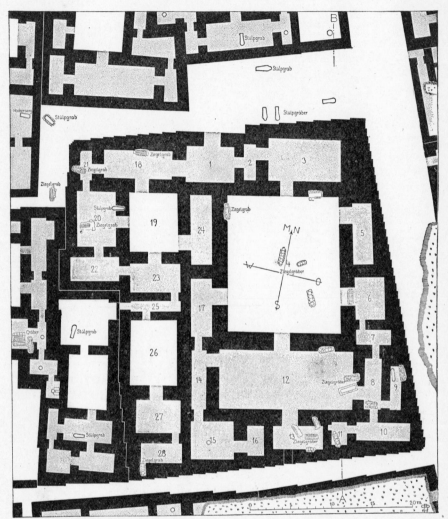

Fig. 236.—Ground-plan of the Great House in Merkes.

(5), and to the south the stately principal chamber, about
14 by 7 metres in size; with a smaller series of four
chambers to the right (17, 14, 15, 16) and a larger one of
six chambers (6-11) to the left of it. Both these series of

rooms communicated with the principal chamber by a
corridor (14, 8) and with the court
by their most northerly chamber
(17, 6), which was perhaps a mer-
chant's office. The inner rooms
(15, 16, 10, 11) must have been
perfectly dark unless they were
lighted by windows on the street,
which is very improbable. In one
of them (15) there was a well,
constructed as usual of pottery
cylinders. They may have been
store-rooms or sleeping- and living-
rooms for the people employed
there. It is scarcely necessary
to warn our readers that all these
suggestions as to the purpose of
the various rooms rest entirely on
supposition. We have no other
authority for them than the arrangement of the ground-plan appears to
afford.

The secondary group of chambers was reserved apparently for the
private life of the owner. The
rooms are grouped round two smaller
courts (19 and 26) which communicated with the principal chamber
of the northern one (23), and with
each other by means of a corridor
(25). From this corridor a door on
the west led to an adjoining house,
which had been built previously,
and of which, on the whole, the
great house represented an extension. The entrance chamber (18)
and the two principal chambers
(23, 27) are also easily recognised.
It is not necessary at present to
hazard conjectures as to the purpose of the other rooms.

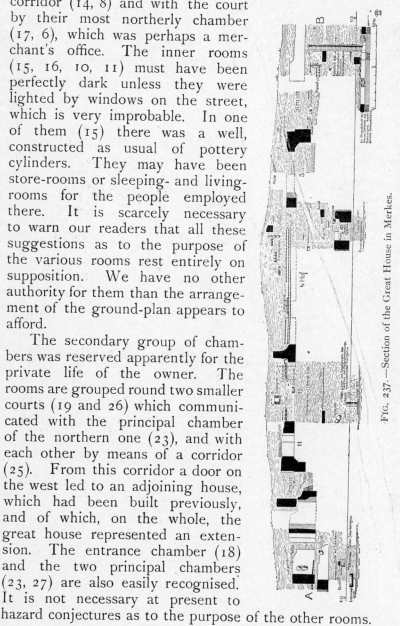

FIG. 237.—Section of the Great House in Merkes.

U

The original pavement of the house has twice under-
gone restoration (Fig. 237). Between the layers of brick,
most of which bear Nebuchadnezzar stamps, only a little
earth is laid. No one was buried in the house while it
was occupied; the 21 graves that occur on the site are
all of the period when the building lay in ruins. This is
shown by the way in which the walls and pavement were
cut through, and by the fact that the pavements were not

repaired in any way
after the burials had
taken place. The graves
are chiefly of brick, as
they are exclusively of
the Parthian period. It
is quite possible that
the house was built
during the reign of
Nebuchadnezzar; no
difficulty is involved by
the occurrence of the
bricks bearing his stamp,
as it does not force us
to infer any complete
destruction of one of
Nebuchadnezzar's build-
ings. The bricks may
very well be older
material offered for sale
by the king on the occa-
sion of one of his re-

FIG. 238.—Steps to roof in village of Kweiresh.

buildings. It is impos-
sible to say how late into Persian or Greek times the
house existed; a poorer house was built on its ruins
after the heap of rubbish had reached a height of about
2 metres.

Before the main house was built the site must long
have remained unoccupied. Under the pavement lay 4
metres of rubbish above the floor of an earlier house.
Three metres deeper again there were tablets of the time
of Kadashmanturgu, Kadashmanbel, and Kurigalzu; and

again, 2 to 3 metres deeper, were some of Samsuiluna, Ammiditana, and Samsuditana.

The mud-brick walls were plastered with mud, and over this was a wash of white gypsum mortar.

Not one of the chambers showed any traces from which we could infer the existence of a stairway to an upper

FIG. 239.—North-east corner of the Great House in Merkes.

storey.   If there were steps, which we cannot doubt, they were certainly of wood, something like the simple stairways to the roof that are used at the present time by the people of Kweiresh (Fig. 238).

When the house was built, the entire area was first surrounded by a sloping wall without any toothed projections, filled up inside with earth, this forming a substantial terrace on which the actual building stood (Fig. 239).   The top of the terrace was $1\frac{1}{2}$ metres higher than the brick pavement of the street on the north.   The terrace wall is not so thick as the outer walls of the superstructure, but it projects out on the outer side about as far as the toothed projections above it stand out, and thus forms a kind of plinth. Owing to the constant raising of the street-level this is little observable ; the plinth disappeared with the subsequent heightening of the street. The outer wall itself had more than 90 of those toothed projections, to which we have frequently referred, and is provided with a system of

FIG. 240.—Façade of house with doorway, brick grave in front, Merkes.

wooden braces, intended to strengthen the projections. A beam lies on the outside, parallel with each wall face, about the length of one projection, in the next brick course this is gripped at one end by a beam placed more or less at right angles to it. The outside must have appeared very much as it is figured in the reconstruction (Fig. 235). The frontage of another house in Merkes is given in Fig. 240.

For comparison we also give a ground-plan from Fara of about the fifth millennium (Fig. 241). It will show how few changes the internal arrangements of a Babylonian house underwent during the lapse of thousands of years.

Nothing shows more conclusively than these ground-plans the immense age of Babylonian civilisation ; for even in this remote period, which is in part prehistoric, they give clear indications of a yet earlier development from a presumably simpler and more primitive building.

The original Babylonian house, as we may assume it to have been from the present state of our knowledge, was probably a rectangular roofed-in space within a walled court. It is most desirable that we should obtain explicit evidence as to the form of the early Babylonian house in one of the prehistoric sites, but to do this is attended with difficulties. They occur generally in narrow crosscuts, or in deep trenches where the limited space renders the following up of these ancient sites very difficult. It would be necessary to open up a much wider area down to a considerable depth to afford

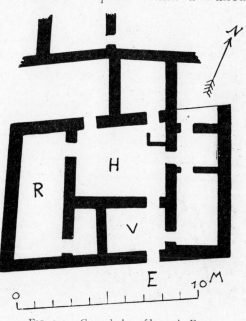

FIG. 241.—Ground-plan of house in Fara (Shuruppak).

E, Entrance.   R, Principal chamber.
H, Court.   V, Vestibule.

sufficient material for arriving at conclusions, and at Surgul and El-Hibba, as well as at Fara, there was not time to do this.

In strange contrast to these Babylonian ground-plans is the palace of Telloh. The reason why the account given of it by de Sarzec is so difficult to understand, is because it was built at three different periods, which should be clearly differentiated from each other, but which are all placed together and attributed to Gudea as the builder.

Only a small part, on the contrary, the inner part B (Fig. 242), which is not organically connected with the building as a whole, belongs to Gudea. All the rest is later, most of it very much later. In 1886 I examined and surveyed all that then survived of the palace. The dotted portion of the plan I give here was then no more to be seen ; these walls had already been carried away by brick robbers. At my second visit in 1898 the work of destruction had not

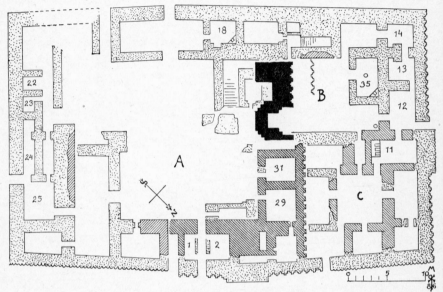

FIG. 242.—Ground-plan from Telloh.

been carried much further. The ancient portion, marked black on the plan, represents part of the facing wall of a zikurrat that lay behind it to the south-east, with a stepped and grooved façade and a large gutter for water, such as is usually found in ancient zikurrats. This portion is built of Gudea bricks laid in asphalt and mud. The grooved façade of a lower-lying wall that belongs to it, which formed part of a lower floor, a terrace, or a later kisu, is given by de Sarzec in the court (B); on the north-east various chambers abut on it, the walls of which are built with re-used Gudea bricks. The asphalt still clings in many places to the lower side of the bricks, and the drops of asphalt which naturally when the bricks were first used fell on the outer face of the bricks and left slight traces pointing downwards, in their later use point upwards.

The north-western outer front of rooms 31, 29, show simple grooved work, which disappeared behind the walls of the later building round court C, and were cut off by the surrounding wall. In our plan these portions are heavily scored. Of the third later building, lightly scored in the plan, which was also built partly of re-used Gudea bricks, and partly of unstamped bricks, laid in mud mortar, two courts can be recognised (C and B). Here we do not find the unmistakably important principal chamber, which is so remarkable a feature of genuine Babylonian buildings. In chambers 11, 35, and 18 de Sarzec reports table-shaped fireplaces, such as I have never found either in Old or Neo-Babylonian buildings, while, on the contrary, such a flat raised hearth is found in chamber XXXV of an unmistakably Parthian house in Nippur that has a peristyle (Fisher, *Journal of the Archaeological Institute of America*, vol. viii., 1904, No. 4, p. 411). In the pavement of the court adjoining it, the well-known bricks of Adadnadinakhe are said to have been found. An examination of the south-eastern quarter, which must evidently have been already much destroyed at the time of de Sarzec, furnishes the strongest evidence against his representations. Thus in front of 23, he represents a door as constructed of a thick and a very thin wall, and at 24 and 25 he reports a door embrasure actually standing opposite a door-opening. We are therefore forced to the conclusion that here also buildings of entirely different and disconnected periods have been erroneously placed together by the modern draughtsman as having formed one complete building. The peristyle that we expect to find in connection with the two courts (C and B) should be placed in A.

XLVII

THE TEMPLE OF ISHTAR OF AGADE

ACCORDING TO DELITZSCH : ê-kun (?)-da-ri

THE temple of Ishtar of Agade lies among the houses of the northern group of Merkes (Fig. 244). The entrance façade faces the south, where the street that passes it widens out into a somewhat lengthy piazza.

FIG. 243.—Figure of Papsukal, from foundation casket of Ishtar temple.

Through the principal portal, with its grooved towers, we enter the vestibule (1), from which doors to right and left lead to the side-chambers, and which opens directly on to the square court. In the cella (18) with the adyton (19) the postament that stood in the niche immediately opposite the entrance had been taken away, and only the brick casket (*k*) that contained the statuette of Papsukal (Fig. 243) was still there. Similar brick caskets lay in the court doorway that led to the buildings connected with the cella, in the middle and on the western side of the southern main entrance. The two small chambers (20 and 21) near the chamber in front of the cella are accessible from it, as well as directly from the court. The entire cella building (17-22), as in the temple of Borsippa (Fig. 246), forms a completely self-contained block, separated from the enclosing wall of the temple by a narrow passage (10). From this passage room 9 can be reached, and also the southern series of rooms. This series (11-15) consists of four rather small rooms and apparently a court (13), in which two circular storage places are built.

There is a side entrance on the east which opens into the court through a small vestibule (4) that communicates

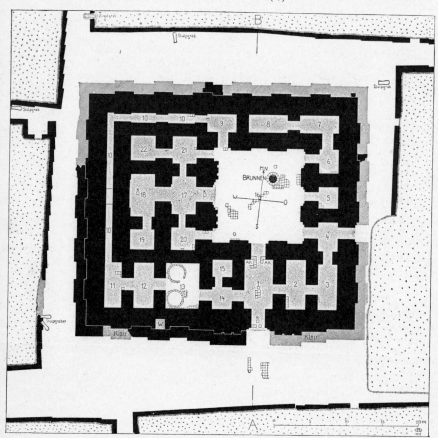

FIG. 244.—Ground-plan of temple of Ishtar of Agade, Merkes.

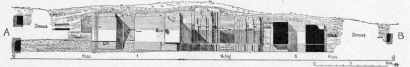

FIG. 245.—Section of temple of Ishtar of Agade, Merkes.

with the main vestibule through chambers 3 and 2. Two small rooms (5 and 6) are accessible from the court. The wall decoration is as usual composed of flat pillars on the

outside of the building and in the court. The main
entrance on the south, and the door from the court leading
to the cella (Fig. 247), are distinguished by a double framing.
The three doors on the east side of the court, the side

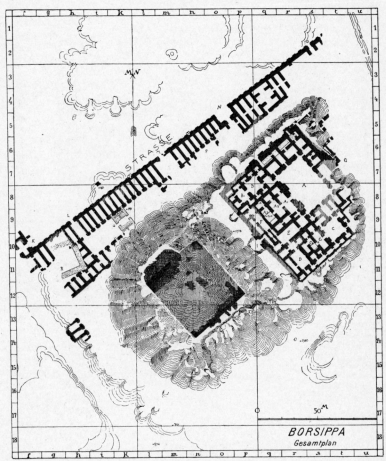

FIG. 246.—Ground-plan of Ezida, the temple of Nebo, in Borsippa.

entrance, and the actual cella door have a single frame.
The grooving on the front of the towers of the main entrance, and of the door leading from the court to the cella is
simply rectangular.   It was only during the last restoration
of the building that the simple grooves were elaborated by
stepped additions, like those of the Ninib temple.

Three building periods can be recognised here (Fig. 245). Of the earliest building only the 7 lower courses remain. The ground-plan is in the main the same as that of the later building that rests upon it, but the wall fronts everywhere deviate slightly from the lines of the latter. The pavement of the later building consists of one plain layer, that lies almost at the level at which the walls begin. The gypsum wash still adheres to the walls. At several

FIG. 247.—Temple of Ishtar of Agade in Merkes ; view of cella façade.

of the more important places, such as the main entrance to the temple, the entrance from the court to the cella, the cella door, and the postament niche, instead of a gypsum wash there is a thin wash of black asphalt, which near the edges is broken with ornamental vertical lines of white gypsum. Similar decorations, though not so well preserved and recognisable, were visible in temple " Z," and in the temples of Ninib and Ninmach. These portions stood out from the white walls with mysterious and startling effect.

The temple was raised and a new double pavement of

Nebuchadnezzar bricks was laid at a height of 4 to 4½ metres above zero. To this pavement, of course, all the brick caskets belong which lay close to the pavement of the earlier periods but above it, as, for instance, the casket in the door from the court to the cella.

An additional raising with a new brick pavement at 5 metres above zero, belongs apparently to a rebuilding undertaken by Nabonidus, according to the inscription on his foundation cylinder which was found here. The cylinder lay at about the height of the last-mentioned pavement, in the middle of the northern enclosing wall, between the first two pillars on the west, and exactly at the place where it was deposited by Nabonidus. It stood upright in a sort of basket of plaited work, of which the remains were still quite recognisable, and which had formerly shielded it from damage in the small aperture within the mud-brick wall. In the inscription the king speaks of the ruinous condition of this " Temple of Ishtar of Agade," and the work undertaken by him for its restoration.

The building was surrounded by a kisu of Nebuchadnezzar bricks which reaches down as far as 3.6 metres above zero, and which must therefore belong to one of the later rebuildings. A water conduit constructed on the south side (W in the plan), similar to that in the Ninib temple, was walled up by the kisu.

THE GREEK THEATRE

CLOSE to the inner city walls on the east there lies a group of mounds which on account of their reddish colour are called " Homera" by the Arabs (Fig. 249). Of these we have examined a northern, a central, and a southern mound, somewhat carefully, and find that from top to bottom they all are artificial heaps of broken burnt brick. Of their origin we will speak later (p. 308 *et seq.*).

The southern of these mounds has been utilised as a foundation for the auditorium of a theatre. In the débris of the building there was found the Greek dedicatory inscription on an alabaster slab (Fig. 248), according to which one " Dioscurides (built) the theatre and a stage."

The building (Fig. 253) is constructed principally of crude brick, and only in some special places, such as the pillars and the bases of the pillars, brick rubble is used, laid with gypsum mortar (Fig. 250).

For the upper part of the auditorium the artificial mound was not sufficiently high, and therefore a retaining wall of mud brick supported the upper seats, which have now disappeared. On the three broad projections of the

FIG. 248 —Inscription from Greek theatre.

retaining wall on the north stairways were apparently constructed. Of the seats only the 5 lower ranges, which must have been up to the first *diazoma*, now remain ; they consist of mud bricks on which are laid uniform courses of brick rubble. Every seat of 5 courses high has a footstool 2 courses high in front of it. Nine narrow stairs, with steps only 2 courses high, separate the *kerkides* from each other. The central stairway, with steps 3 courses high, is broader than the others, and led to a compartment which occupied an entire wedge from the orchestra to the diazoma, the *proëdreia*, intended for distinguished personages, probably the priests of Dionysos. The auditorium, the orchestra

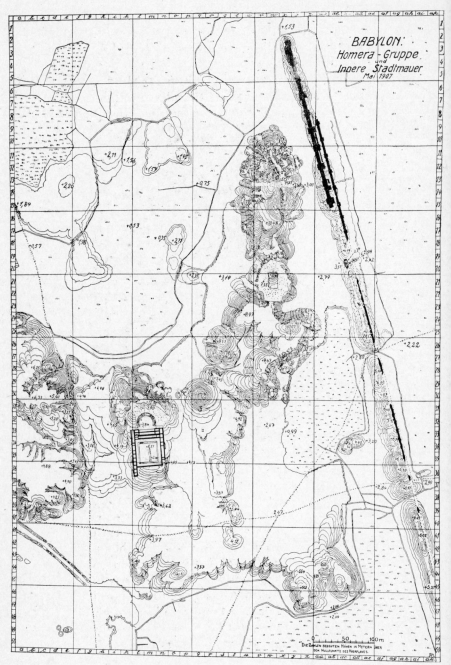

FIG. 249.—Plan of the mounds, Homera.

FIG. 250.—General view of the Greek theatre.

with its *parodoi*, and the stage at some later period, which it is not necessary to estimate as very remote from the first one, were raised by about 1 metre, which caused the rows of seats and apparently also the proscenium to intrude by about 60 to 90 centimetres into the orchestra.

At the edge of the orchestra, which was rather more than a semicircle, near the lowest row of seats, there was a

row of statues placed on brick postaments (Fig. 251), of which two at the lower level of the orchestra, with their coating of fine white plaster, are still in good condition. The statues have now disappeared, but they have left deep traces on the top of their pedestals. On the east there are remains of 8 other postaments of the same sort at the level of the second building period.

The stage exhibits between the *versurae*, in a similar external course, a row of 12 proscenium

FIG. 251.—Pedestals for statues in orchestra.

piers, small and rectangular in form, and bearing on their front face somewhat narrower semi-pillars. The intercolumnar spaces were roofed over with roughly-hewn stone blocks, one of which has fallen over and lies immediately in front of the proscenium. All these portions of the building were originally covered with two washes of fine white plaster (Fig. 252).

Similar semi-columns stand on both sides of the door leading to the orchestra. They led through two-chambered parodoi into the open air. Of these chambers the one to

the west, especially long and narrow, must have served as
a waiting-room for the public or the chorus.

Of the back wall of the *logeion*, the "scaenae frons,"
only the foundation walls of brick rubble remain *in situ*.
This was as usual liberally decorated ; many of the reliefs
in gypsum plaster with which it was adorned have been
found (Fig. 254).   The two lengthy halls behind the *scaenae
frons* must have been
connected with each
other in the upper floors
by arched openings, as
is taken for granted in
our reconstructed plan.
In   the   foundation —
above which the build-
ing is in large measure
ruined — the doorways
are not arranged for,
whereas in Babylonian
houses, such as in those
of Merkes, the door
openings   are   almost
without exception car-
ried right down to the
lowest course.

A   large   peristyle
with adjoining and al-
most uniform chambers
abuts on the stage at
the south.   The southern

FIG. 252.—View of the proscenium pillars.

row of these chambers is very largely destroyed, but of the
peristyle sufficient of the brick rubble foundations remain
to enable us to judge of the main part.   The peristyle had
a double nave at the south side, as is often the case with
palaestra-peristyles.   Fairly numerous remains still exist
of the columns that stood on these foundations ; they are
of burnt brick cut into circular forms, and some of them
that were roughly shaped were undoubtedly covered with
a fine whitewash that gave them a clearly cut outline.

On the east, by the side of the peristyle hall, there

X

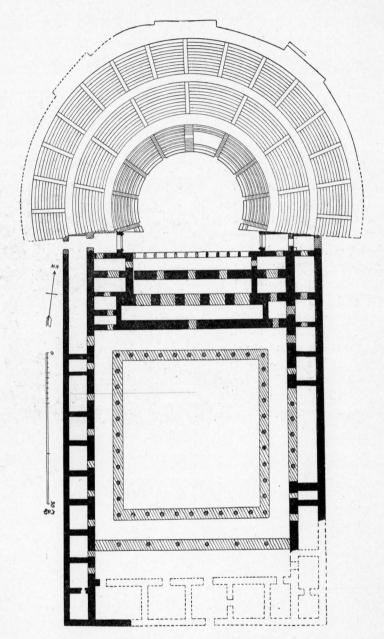

FIG. 253.—Plan of Greek theatre, restored.

opened out a long narrow *exedra*, which was also columned.
Both stage and peristyle stand on ancient ruined dwellings,
of which the mud-brick walls were brought to light in a
cross-cut we made through the central axis.

The plan, therefore, represents on the whole a combination of a theatre and of a palaestra. In any case the
Greek population of Babylon found here an indispensable

FIG. 254.—Gypsum decorations of Greek theatre.

centre for those amusements and intellectual interests
which they would have been most unwilling to abandon
in that remote metropolis of the East, on the development of which Alexander the Great had founded such
far-seeing plans.

The building, as it was first constructed, may well date
back to the time of Alexander himself, even though the
foundation inscription found here, which appears to refer
to a restoration, belongs to a later period.

THE NORTHERN MOUND OF HOMERA

ABOUT 16 metres in height, and with somewhat steep sides, the most northern of the mounds of Homera (*w* 13 on plan, Fig. 249) occupies

FIG. 255.—Section through the northern mound of Homera.

a dominating position above the whole of the adjacent surroundings, and forms a remarkable object from a very considerable distance. In order to discover its nature we carried a trench through it, from east to west, cutting the mound in half like an apple ; with the surprising result that the mound proved to contain no building such as we might have expected, judging from the Kasr. The entire mass from the top to 1 metre below zero consists of brick rubble, which has been intentionally and artificially heaped up. The layers (Fig. 255), which are alternately coarse and finer, are fairly horizontal at the base, but above they fall in the natural slope of about 45 grades towards the north-east. The mound must, therefore, have been gradually heaped up with débris thrown on it from the south-west.

The broken bricks have, for the most part, ancient asphalt or lime mortar clinging to them. Some of them also are unburnt, and the finer layers more especially contain much clay. The Nebuchadnezzar stamps have been found there, but no potsherds, a few Greek terra-cottas, and a fragment of a cylinder of Nebuchadnezzar with an inscription referring to the building of Etemenanki, the tower of Babylon. It is a duplicate of the cylinder : Neb. Hilp. iii. l. 18-24, and iv. l. 15-19 (M'Gee, *Zur Topographie von Babylon*, vi.).

Thus the mass of débris comes from a Babylonian building brought here in Greek times, and contains a document belonging to Etemenanki. At the ruins of Etemenanki the absence of débris had already struck us as remarkable. What is to be seen there at the present time—low banks round the deep trenches—is merely the result of modern digging by Arab brick robbers. Before this Arab disfigurement of the place, the site of the tower was completely level. At the Kasr and the hill of Babil, as elsewhere, the huge mounds of rubbish bear witness to the immensity of the ruins they represent. In Sachn we have the insignificant remains of a colossal building without débris, and in Homera a colossal mass of rubbish without a building, and we may therefore safely conclude with the greatest possible certainty that the débris of Etemenanki lies in Homera. This agrees admirably with the statement of Greek authors (Strabo, xvi. 1, 5), according to which Alexander the Great intended to replace the tower which had fallen in his time, and expended 600,000 days' wages on having the débris removed : " ἦν δὲ πυραμὶς . . . ἦν Ἀλέξανδρος ἐβούλετο ἀνασκευάσαι, πολὺ δ' ἦν ἔργον καὶ πολλοῦ χρόνου (αὐτὴ γὰρ ἡ χοῦς εἰς ἀνακάθαρσιν μυρίοις ἀνδράσι δυεῖν μηνῶν ἔργον ἦν), ὥστ' οὐκ ἔφθη τὸ ἐγχειρηθὲν ἐπιτελέσαι." The mass of rubbish that lies in Homera—the middle and southern groups also consist of exactly similar broken material — may be roughly estimated at 300,000 cubic metres, which corresponds well with the amount of wages quoted above. As the Euphrates flowed westward close to Etemenanki, and also between the Kasr and Homera, in the Greek period we can suppose that the transport was effected by water.

It may be supposed that the work of piling up débris

in this place would not be undertaken without some object.
The heaps might well have served good purpose in the
erection of new buildings, such as were undoubtedly planned
by Alexander. It is true that the northern mound was
never utilised, but we have already seen that the southern
one was used as the substructure for a theatre, and the
central group we will now observe more closely.

L

THE CENTRAL MOUND OF HOMERA

THE central group of Homera (*w* 21 on plan, Fig. 249),
which consists below of exactly the same débris as that we
have just described at the northern mound, differs greatly
from the latter in that at a height of 7.5 metres above zero
a platform is constructed, and that not by merely levelling
down a mound that already existed, but by actually piling
up materials to the requisite height and levelling them.
Upon this platform at the present time there is a layer of
earth, from 2 to 3 metres high, with some fragments of
brick and a few potsherds; no walls are to be seen in it.
It appears, therefore, that this top layer comes from quite
late and very inferior dwellings, for which the platform
itself was not constructed. The materials of which the
level of this platform consists are very much reddened, as
though they had been burnt. Indications of a great conflagration are to be found in blocks of mud brick smelted
together by a fierce fire, and bearing clear imprints of palm
and other wood. In many places the prints show the sharp
edges of good carpenter's work. All this is remarkable,
and we should like to find the explanation of it.

This may perhaps be found in the report given by
Diodorus (xvii. 115 [1]) of the funeral pyre Alexander the

---

[1] Αὐτὸς δὲ τοὺς ἀρχιτέκτονας ἀθροίσας καὶ λεπτουργῶν πλῆθος, τοῦ μὲν τείχους καθεῖλεν
ἐπὶ δέκα σταδίους, τὴν δ' ὀπτὴν πλίνθον ἀναλεξάμενός, καὶ τὸν δεχόμενον τὴν πυρὰν τόπον
ὁμαλὸν κατασκευάσας, ᾠκοδόμησε τετράπλευρον πυράν, σταδιαίας οὔσης ἑκάστης πλευρᾶς.
(2) εἰς τριάκοντα δὲ δόμους διελόμενος τὸν τόπον, καὶ καταστρώσας τὰς ὀροφὰς φοινίκων
στελέχεσι, τετράγωνον ἐποίησε πᾶν τὸ κατασκεύασμα.

Great caused to be erected to solemnise the funeral ceremonies of Hephaestion. In order to form a platform for this magnificently decorated wooden construction, he had part of the city wall of Babylon demolished, and used the brick materials thus obtained. The platform has perished very considerably on all sides, and the level surface that still survives is undoubtedly only a small part of the original, so that it is useless to endeavour to recover the traces of the construction in detail.

The place lies exactly opposite the Citadel, and was divided from it in the time of Alexander by the Euphrates. The magnificent pyre, which is said to have cost 12,000 talents, when seen from the Acropolis must have stood out in a most impressive manner against the eastern horizon.

LI

RETROSPECT

FROM the central position occupied by Homera we can command a peculiarly instructive view over the ruins of Babylon, and piece together and recall all that excavation has brought to light of the development of the city. In doing so, we will leave unnoticed the information obtained from written sources. They belong to a different kind of treatment.

The existence of Babylon in prehistoric times, before the fifth millennium, is proved by flint and other stone implements. It is impossible to carry excavations down to that depth, owing to the rise in the water-level (p. 261).

The earliest accessible ruins belong to the time of the first Babylonian kings (Hammurabi, *circa* 2500 B.C.), and lie yonder in Merkes (p. 240). The city, therefore, by that time included at least that region.

The same neighbourhood gave us the plan of houses of the time of the Kassite kings, Kurigalzu III. to Kudur-Bel (*circa* 1400–1249), Bel-nâdin-šum to Marduk-aplu-iddina II. (*circa* 1219–1154); and the strata above afforded those of the Assyrian, Neo-Babylonian, Persian, and Graeco-Parthian periods. All of these show that the division of the city into streets and blocks of houses remained practically unchanged throughout the course of centuries (p. 239 *et seq.*).

When the Assyrian kings ruled over Babylon they repaired mainly the great temple of Esagila, now under Amran, where the pavements of Esarhaddon (680–668 B.C.) and Sardanapalus (668–626 B.C.) still lie (p. 204). Sennacherib (705–681) had caused the Procession Street near Sachn to be paved.

On the Kasr, Sargon (710–705) built the wall of the Southern Citadel, with the rounded corner tower (p. 137). Sardanapalus restored Nimitti-Bel lying close to our point of observation, Homera, and Emach on the Kasr. At that time the great extension of the Southern Citadel itself was not built, nor yet that part of the Kasr that lay to the north of it, the mound of Babil and the outer city wall. All that belongs to the building period of the Neo-Babylonian kingdom (625–538 B.C.).

Nabopolassar (625–604) began with the western part of the Southern Citadel, built the Arachtu wall from the Kasr as far as Amran, and also the temple of Ninib (p. 229), and Imgur-Bel on the Kasr.

With Nebuchadnezzar (604–561) began the colossal rebuilding of the entire city, with the restoration of the temple of Emach on the Citadel, of Esagila, of Etemenanki, the tower of Babylon with its wide temenos, of the Ninib-temple in Ishin aswad, of temple "Z" and the earlier Ishtar temple in Merkes. He restored the Arachtu wall, constructed the earliest stone bridge over the Euphrates (p. 197) at Amran, the canal Libil-ḫigalla, that flowed round the Kasr on the north, east, and south, completed the Southern Citadel with his palace, and enlarged it towards the north in three successive extensions, in which the Procession Street was heightened and paved with stone, and the Ishtar Gate acquired its latest form, while both were decorated with the coloured enamelled frieze of animals. He built a new castle far out on the north and surrounded the city which he had enlarged in this fashion

with the great outer city wall, of which from Homera we
can see the white chain of mounds on the eastern horizon.

Of Nabonidus (555–538) we have more especially the
strong fortification wall on the banks of the Euphrates,
that has been excavated from Kasr to the Urash gate,
near the bridge at Amran (p. 200), and the Ishtar temple
in Merkes.

In the time of the Persian kings (538–331 B.C.), of
which Artaxerxes II. (405–358) has left us a memorial in
the marble building on the Southern Citadel (p. 127), the
great change must have occurred that essentially altered
the aspect of Babylon. The Euphrates, which until then
had only washed the west side of the Kasr, now flowed
eastward round the Acropolis. From this time dates
the plan of the city as it is described by Herodotus
(484–424 ? B.C.) and Ctesias, the physician of Artaxerxes.
The apparently wide bend of the river that then flowed
round the east of the Kasr we must now reconstruct in
imagination as we look across to the castle of Nebuchadnezzar from Homera.

Alexander the Great (331–323) set himself to prevent
the decline of Babylon, which was then beginning, and to
restore it to its former magnitude. The great tower
Etemenanki, the sanctuary of Bel, and a marked feature
of Babylon, was to have been rebuilt. The fallen masses
were carried away, and the débris lies here in the mounds
of Homera (p. 308), but the king died before he could
rebuild the tower.

From this time onward the burnt brick of the ancient
royal buildings was re-used for all manner of secular
buildings. The Greek theatre at Homera (p. 301) is built
of such material. Thus the pillared buildings of Amran
(p. 215 et seq.) and houses at Merkes, that are built of brick
rubble, belong either to the Greek (331–139 B.C.) or the
Parthian (139 B.C.–226 A.D.) periods, but to which of them
cannot be determined. At that time began the process of
demolishing the city area, which perhaps was now only
occupied by isolated dwellings, a process that certainly
continued throughout the Sassanide period (226–636 A.D.).

Amran alone was inhabited, and that only scantily, as

is shown by the uppermost levels there, which reach down as late as the Arab middle age (*circa* 1200 A.D.). When we gaze to-day over the wide area of ruins we are involuntarily reminded of the words of the prophet Jeremiah (l. 39): "Therefore the wild beasts of the desert, with the wild beasts of the islands, shall dwell there, and the owls shall dwell therein: and it shall be no more inhabited for ever; neither shall it be dwelt in from generation to generation."

LII

APPENDIX

HERODOTUS i. 178-187

178. Κῦρος, ἐπείτε τὰ πάντα τῆς ἠπείρου ὑποχείρια ἐποιήσατο, Ἀσσυρίοισι ἐπετίθετο. τῆς δὲ Ἀσσυρίης ἐστὶ μέν κου καὶ ἄλλα πολίσματα μεγάλα πολλά, τὸ δὲ οὐνομαστότατον καὶ ἰσχυρότατον καὶ ἔνθα σφι Νίνου ἀναστάτου γενομένης τὰ βασιλήια κατεστήκεε, ἦν ΒΑΒΥΛΩΝ, ἐοῦσα τοιαύτη δή τις πόλις. κέεται ἐν πεδίῳ μεγάλῳ, μέγαθος ἐοῦσα μέτωπον ἕκαστον εἴκοσι καὶ ἑκατὸν σταδίων, ἐούσης τετραγώνου· οὗτοι στάδιοι τῆς περιόδου τῆς πόλιος γίνονται συνάπαντες ὀγδώκοντα καὶ τετρακόσιοι. τὸ μέν νυν μέγαθος τοσοῦτόν ἐστι τοῦ ἄστεος τοῦ Βαβυλωνίου, ἐκεκόσμητο δὲ ὡς οὐδὲν ἄλλο πόλισμα τῶν ἡμεῖς ἴδμεν. τάφρος μὲν πρῶτά μιν βαθέα τε καὶ εὐρέα καὶ πλέη ὕδατος περιθέει, μετὰ δὲ τεῖχος πεντήκοντα μὲν πηχέων βασιληίων ἐὸν τὸ εὖρος, ὕψος δὲ διηκοσίων πηχέων· ὁ δὲ βασιλήιος πῆχυς τοῦ μετρίου ἐστὶ πήχεος μέζων τρισὶ δακτύλοισι.

179. Δεῖ δή με πρὸς τούτοισι ἔτι φράσαι, ἵνα τε ἐκ τῆς τάφρου ἡ γῆ ἀναισιμώθη καὶ τὸ τεῖχος ὅντινα τρόπον ἔργαστο. ὀρύσσοντες ἅμα τὴν τάφρον ἐπλίνθευον τὴν γῆν τὴν ἐκ τοῦ ὀρύγματος ἐκφερομένην, ἑλκύσαντες δὲ πλίνθους ἱκανὰς ὤπτησαν αὐτὰς ἐν καμίνοισι· μετὰ δὲ τέλματι χρεώμενοι ἀσφάλτῳ θερμῇ καὶ διὰ τριήκοντα δόμων πλίνθου ταρσοὺς καλάμων διαστοιβάζοντες ἔδειμαν πρῶτα μὲν τῆς τάφρου τὰ χείλεα, δεύτερα δὲ αὐτὸ τὸ τεῖχος τὸν αὐτὸν τρόπον. ἐπάνω δὲ τοῦ τείχεος παρὰ

τὰ ἔσχατα οἰκήματα μουνόκωλα ἔδειμαν, τετραμμένα ἐς ἄλληλα·
τὸ μέσον δὲ τῶν οἰκημάτων ἔλιπον τεθρίππῳ περιέλασιν. πύλαι
δὲ ἐνεστᾶσι πέριξ τοῦ τείχεος ἑκατόν, χάλκεαι πᾶσαι, καὶ σταθμοί
τε καὶ ὑπέρθυρα ὡσαύτως. ἔστι δὲ ἄλλη πόλις ἀπέχουσα ὀκτὼ
ἡμερέων ὁδὸν ἀπὸ Βαβυλῶνος· Ἴς οὔνομα αὐτῇ. ἔνθα ἐστὶ
ποταμὸς οὐ μέγας· Ἴς καὶ τῷ ποταμῷ τὸ οὔνομα. ἐσβάλλει δὲ
οὗτος ἐς τὸν Εὐφρήτην ποταμὸν τὸ ῥέεθρον. οὕτως ὦν ὁ Ἴς
ποταμὸς ἅμα τῷ ὕδατι θρόμβους ἀσφάλτου ἀναδιδοῖ πολλούς,
ἔνθεν ἡ ἄσφαλτος ἐς τὸ ἐν Βαβυλῶνι τεῖχος ἐκομίσθη.

180. Ἐτετείχιστο μέν νυν ἡ Βαβυλὼν τρόπῳ τοιῷδε, ἔστι δὲ
δύο φάρσεα τῆς πόλιος. τὸ γὰρ μέσον αὐτῆς ποταμὸς διέργει,
τῷ οὔνομά ἐστι Εὐφρήτης. ῥέει δὲ ἐξ Ἀρμενίων, ἐὼν μέγας
καὶ βαθὺς καὶ ταχύς· ἐξίει δὲ οὗτος ἐς τὴν Ἐρυθρὴν θάλασσαν.
τὸ ὦν δὴ τεῖχος ἑκάτερον τοὺς ἀγκῶνας ἐς τὸν ποταμὸν ἐλήλαται·
τὸ δὲ ἀπὸ τούτου αἱ ἐπικαμπαὶ παρὰ χεῖλος ἑκάτερον τοῦ
ποταμοῦ αἱμασιὴ πλίνθων ὀπτέων παρατείνει. τὸ δὲ ἄστυ αὐτό,
ἐὸν πλῆρες οἰκέων τριωρόφων τε καὶ τετρωρόφων, κατατέτμηται
τὰς ὁδοὺς ἰθέας, τάς τε ἄλλας καὶ τὰς ἐπικαρσίας τὰς ἐπὶ τὸν
ποταμὸν ἐχούσας. κατὰ δὴ ὦν ἑκάστην ὁδὸν ἐν τῇ αἱμασιῇ τῇ
παρὰ τὸν ποταμὸν πυλίδες ἐπῆσαν, ὅσαι περ αἱ λαῦραι, τοσαῦται
ἀριθμόν. ἦσαν δὲ καὶ αὗται χάλκεαι, φέρουσαι καὶ αὐταὶ ἐς
αὐτὸν τὸν ποταμόν.

181. Τοῦτο μὲν δὴ τὸ τεῖχος θώρηξ ἐστί, ἕτερον δὲ ἔσωθεν
τεῖχος περιθέει, οὐ πολλῷ τέῳ ἀσθενέστερον τοῦ ἑτέρου τείχεος,
στεινότερον δέ. ἐν δὲ φάρσεϊ ἑκατέρῳ τῆς πόλιος ἐτετείχιστο
ἐν μέσῳ ἐν τῷ μὲν τὰ βασιλήια περιβόλῳ τε μεγάλῳ καὶ
ἰσχυρῷ, ἐν δὲ τῷ ἑτέρῳ Διὸς Βήλου ἱρὸν χαλκόπυλον, καὶ ἐς ἐμὲ
ἔτι τοῦτο ἐόν, δύο σταδίων πάντῃ, ἐὸν τετράγωνον. ἐν μέσῳ δὲ
τοῦ ἱροῦ πύργος στερεὸς οἰκοδόμηται, σταδίου καὶ τὸ μῆκος καὶ
τὸ εὖρος, καὶ ἐπὶ τούτῳ τῷ πύργῳ ἄλλος πύργος ἐπιβέβηκε,
καὶ ἕτερος μάλα ἐπὶ τούτῳ, μέχρι οὗ ὀκτὼ πύργων. ἀνάβασις
δὲ ἐς αὐτοὺς ἔξωθεν κύκλῳ περὶ πάντας τοὺς πύργους ἔχουσα
πεποίηται. μεσοῦντι δέ κου τῆς ἀναβάσιός ἐστι καταγωγή τε
καὶ θῶκοι ἀμπαυστήριοι, ἐν τοῖσι κατίζοντες ἀμπαύονται οἱ
ἀναβαίνοντες. ἐν δὲ τῷ τελευταίῳ πύργῳ νηὸς ἔπεστι μέγας. ἐν
δὲ τῷ νηῷ κλίνη μεγάλη κέεται εὖ ἐστρωμένη καί οἱ τράπεζα
παρακέεται χρυσέη. ἄγαλμα δὲ οὐκ ἔνι οὐδὲν αὐτόθι ἐνιδρυμένον·
οὐδὲ νύκτα οὐδεὶς ἐναυλίζεται ἀνθρώπων ὅτι μὴ γυνὴ μούνη τῶν
ἐπιχωρίων, τὴν ἂν ὁ θεὸς ἕληται ἐκ πασέων, ὡς λέγουσιν οἱ
Χαλδαῖοι, ἐόντες ἱρέες τούτου τοῦ θεοῦ.

182. Φασὶ δὲ οἱ αὐτοὶ οὗτοι, ἐμοὶ μὲν οὐ πιστὰ λέγοντες, τὸν
θεὸν αὐτὸν φοιτᾶν τε ἐς τὸν νηὸν καὶ ἀμπαύεσθαι ἐπὶ τῆς κλίνης,
κατάπερ ἐν Θήβῃσι τῇσι Αἰγυπτίῃσι κατὰ τὸν αὐτὸν τρόπον,
ὡς λέγουσι οἱ Αἰγύπτιοι (καὶ γὰρ δὴ ἐκεῖθι κοιμᾶται ἐν τῷ τοῦ
Διὸς τοῦ Θηβαιέος γυνή, ἀμφότεραι δὲ αὗται λέγονται ἀνδρῶν
οὐδαμῶν ἐς ὁμιλίην φοιτᾶν), καὶ κατάπερ ἐν Πατάροισι τῆς
Λυκίης ἡ πρόμαντις τοῦ θεοῦ, ἐπεὰν γένηται. οὐ γὰρ ὦν αἰεί
ἐστι χρηστήριον αὐτόθι· ἐπεὰν δὲ γένηται, τότε ὦν συγκατα-
κληίεται τὰς νύκτας ἔσω ἐν τῷ νηῷ.

183. Ἔστι δὲ τοῦ ἐν Βαβυλῶνι ἱροῦ καὶ ἄλλος κάτω νηός,
ἔνθα ἄγαλμα μέγα τοῦ Διὸς ἔνι κατήμενον χρύσεον, καί οἱ
τράπεζα μεγάλη παρακέεται χρυσέη καὶ τὸ βάθρον οἱ καὶ ὁ
θρόνος χρύσεός ἐστι. καὶ ὡς ἔλεγον οἱ Χαλδαῖοι, ταλάντων
ὀκτακοσίων χρυσίου πεποίηται ταῦτα. ἔξω δὲ τοῦ νηοῦ βωμός
ἐστι χρύσεος. ἔστι δὲ καὶ ἄλλος βωμὸς μέγας, ἐπ' οὗ θύεται
τὰ τέλεα τῶν προβάτων· ἐπὶ γὰρ τοῦ χρυσέου βωμοῦ οὐκ
ἔξεστι θύειν ὅτι μὴ γαλαθηνὰ μοῦνα, ἐπὶ δὲ τοῦ μέζονος βωμοῦ
καὶ καταγίζουσι λιβανωτοῦ χίλια τάλαντα ἔτεος ἑκάστου οἱ
Χαλδαῖοι τότε ἐπεὰν τὴν ὁρτὴν ἄγωσι τῷ θεῷ τούτῳ· ἦν δὲ ἐν
τῷ τεμένεϊ τούτῳ ἔτι τὸν χρόνον ἐκεῖνον καὶ ἀνδριὰς δυώδεκα
πηχέων χρύσεος στερεός. ἐγὼ μέν μιν οὐκ εἶδον, τὰ δὲ λέγεται
ὑπὸ Χαλδαίων, ταῦτα λέγω. τούτῳ τῷ ἀνδριάντι Δαρεῖος μὲν
ὁ Ὑστάσπεος ἐπιβουλεύσας οὐκ ἐτόλμησε λαβεῖν, Ξέρξης δὲ ὁ
Δαρείου ἔλαβε καὶ τὸν ἱρέα ἀπέκτεινε ἀπαγορεύοντα μὴ κινέειν
τὸν ἀνδριάντα. τὸ μὲν δὴ ἱρὸν τοῦτο οὕτω κεκόσμηται, ἔστι δὲ
καὶ ἴδια ἀναθήματα πολλά.

184. Τῆς δὲ Βαβυλῶνος ταύτης πολλοὶ μέν κου καὶ ἄλλοι
ἐγένοντο βασιλέες, τῶν ἐν τοῖσι Ἀσσυρίοισι λόγοισι μνήμην
ποιήσομαι, οἳ τὰ τείχεά τε ἐπεκόσμησαν καὶ τὰ ἱρά, ἐν δὲ δὴ
καὶ γυναῖκες δύο· ἡ μὲν πρότερον ἄρξασα, τῆς ὕστερον γενεῇσι
πέντε πρότερον γενομένη, τῇ οὔνομα ἦν Σεμίραμις, αὕτη μὲν
ἀπεδέξατο χώματα ἀνὰ τὸ πεδίον ἐόντα ἀξιοθέητα· πρότερον δὲ
ἐώθεε ὁ ποταμὸς ἀνὰ τὸ πεδίον πᾶν πελαγίζειν.

185. Ἡ δὲ δὴ δεύτερον γενομένη ταύτης βασίλεια, τῇ οὔνομα
ἦν Νίτωκρις, αὕτη δὲ συνετωτέρη γενομένη τῆς πρότερον ἀρξάσης
τοῦτο μὲν μνημόσυνα ἐλίπετο, τὰ ἐγὼ ἀπηγήσομαι, τοῦτο δὲ τὴν
Μήδων ὁρῶσα ἀρχὴν μεγάλην τε καὶ οὐκ ἀτρεμίζουσαν, ⟨ἀλλ'⟩
ἄλλα τε ἀραιρημένα ἄστεα αὐτοῖσι, ἐν δὲ δὴ καὶ τὴν Νίνον,
προεφυλάξατο ὅσα ἐδύνατο μάλιστα. πρῶτα μὲν τὸν Εὐφρήτην
ποταμόν, ῥέοντα πρότερον ἰθύν, ὅς σφι διὰ τῆς πόλιος μέσης

ῥέει, τοῦτον ἄνωθεν διώρυχας ὀρύξασα οὕτω δή τι ἐποίησε
σκολιόν, ὥστε δὴ τρὶς ἐς τῶν τινὰ κωμέων τῶν ἐν τῇ Ἀσσυρίῃ
ἀπικνέεται ῥέων. τῇ δὲ κώμῃ οὔνομά ἐστι, ἐς τὴν ἀπικνέεται ὁ
Εὐφρήτης, Ἀρδέρικκα. καὶ νῦν οἳ ἂν κομίζωνται ἀπὸ τῆσδε τῆς
θαλάσσης ἐς Βαβυλῶνα, καταπλέοντες [ἐς] τὸν Εὐφρήτην ποταμὸν
τρίς τε ἐς τὴν αὐτὴν ταύτην κώμην παραγίνονται καὶ ἐν τρισὶ
ἡμέρῃσι. τοῦτο μὲν δὴ τοιοῦτο ἐποίησε, χῶμα δὲ παρέχωσε παρ'
ἑκάτερον τοῦ ποταμοῦ τὸ χεῖλος, ἄξιον θώυματος, μέγαθος καὶ
ὕψος ὅσον τι ἐστί. κατύπερθε δὲ πολλῷ Βαβυλῶνος ὤρυσσε
ἔλυτρον λίμνῃ, ὀλίγον τι παρατείνουσα ἀπὸ τοῦ ποταμοῦ, βάθος
μὲν ἐς τὸ ὕδωρ αἰεὶ ὀρύσσουσα, εὖρος δὲ τὸ περίμετρον αὐτοῦ
ποιεῦσα εἴκοσί τε καὶ τετρακοσίων σταδίων· τὸν δὲ ὀρυσσόμενον
χοῦν ἐκ τούτου τοῦ ὀρύγματος ἀναισίμου παρὰ τὰ χείλεα τοῦ
ποταμοῦ παραχέουσα. ἐπείτε δέ οἱ ὀρώρυκτο, λίθους ἀγαγομένη,
κρηπῖδα κύκλῳ περὶ αὐτὴν ἤλασε. ἐποίεε δὲ ἀμφότερα ταῦτα,
τόν τε ποταμὸν σκολιὸν καὶ τὸ ὄρυγμα πᾶν ἕλος, ὡς ὅ τε
ποταμὸς βραδύτερος εἴη περὶ καμπὰς πολλὰς ἀγνύμενος, καὶ οἱ
πλόοι ἔωσι σκολιοὶ ἐς τὴν Βαβυλῶνα, ἔκ τε τῶν πλόων ἐκδέκηται
περίοδος τῆς λίμνης μακρή. κατὰ τοῦτο δὲ ἐργάζετο τῆς χώρης,
τῇ αἵ τε ἐσβολαὶ ἦσαν καὶ τὰ σύντομα τῆς ἐκ Μήδων ὁδοῦ, ἵνα
μὴ ἐπιμισγόμενοι οἱ Μῆδοι ἐκμανθάνοιεν αὐτῆς τὰ πράγματα.

186. Ταῦτα μὲν δὴ ἐκ βάθεος περιεβάλετο, τοιήνδε δὲ ἐξ αὐτῶν
παρενθήκην ἐποιήσατο. τῆς πόλιος ἐούσης δύο φαρσέων, τοῦ δὲ
ποταμοῦ μέσον ἔχοντος, ἐπὶ τῶν πρότερον βασιλέων, ὅκως τις
ἐθέλοι ἐκ τοῦ ἑτέρου φάρσεος ἐς τούτερον διαβῆναι, χρῆν πλοίῳ
διαβαίνειν, καὶ ἦν, ὡς ἐγὼ δοκέω, ὀχληρὸν τοῦτο. αὕτη δὲ καὶ
τοῦτο προεῖδε· ἐπείτε γὰρ ὤρυσσε τὸ ἔλυτρον τῇ λίμνῃ, μνημό-
συνον τόδε ἄλλο ἀπὸ τοῦ αὐτοῦ ἔργου ἐλίπετο. ἐτάμνετο λίθους
περιμήκεας, ὡς δέ οἱ ἦσαν οἱ λίθοι ἕτοιμοι, καὶ τὸ χωρίον ὀρώρυκτο,
ἐκτρέψασα τοῦ ποταμοῦ τὸ ῥέεθρον πᾶν ἐς τὸ ὤρυξε χωρίον, ἐν
ᾧ ἐπίμπλατο τοῦτο, ἐν τούτῳ ἀπεξηρασμένου τοῦ ἀρχαίου ῥεέθρου,
τοῦτο μὲν τὰ χείλεα τοῦ ποταμοῦ κατὰ τὴν πόλιν καὶ τὰς κατα-
βάσιας τὰς ἐκ τῶν πυλίδων ἐς τὸν ποταμὸν φερούσας ἀνοικοδόμησε
πλίνθοισι ὀπτῇσι κατὰ τὸν αὐτὸν λόγον τῷ τείχεῖ, τοῦτο δὲ κατὰ
μέσην κου μάλιστα τὴν πόλιν τοῖσι λίθοισι, τοὺς ὠρύξατο,
οἰκοδόμεε γέφυραν, δέουσα τοὺς λίθους σιδήρῳ τε καὶ μολύβδῳ.
ἐπιτείνεσκε δὲ ἐπ' αὐτήν, ὅκως μὲν ἡμέρη γένοιτο, ξύλα
τετράγωνα, ἐπ' ὧν τὴν διάβασιν ἐποιεῦντο οἱ Βαβυλώνιοι· τὰς
δὲ νύκτας τὰ ξύλα ταῦτα ἀπαιρέεσκον τοῦδε εἵνεκα, ἵνα μὴ
διαφοιτέοντες τὰς νύκτας κλέπτοιεν παρ' ἀλλήλων. ὡς δὲ τὸ

τε ὀρυχθὲν λίμνη πλήρης ἐγεγόνεε ὑπὸ τοῦ ποταμοῦ καὶ τὰ
περὶ τὴν γέφυραν ἐκεκόσμητο, τὸν Εὐφρήτην ποταμὸν ἐς τὰ
ἀρχαῖα ῥέεθρα ἐκ τῆς λίμνης ἐξήγαγε· καὶ οὕτω τὸ ὀρυχθὲν
ἕλος γενόμενον ἐς δέον ἐδόκεε γεγονέναι καὶ τοῖσι πολιήτῃσι
γέφυρα ἦν κατεσκευασμένη.

187. Ἡ δ᾽ αὐτὴ αὕτη βασίλεια καὶ ἀπάτην τοιήνδε τινὰ
ἐμηχανήσατο. ὑπὲρ τῶν μάλιστα λεωφόρων πυλέων τοῦ ἄστεος
τάφον ἑωυτῇ κατεσκευάσατο μετέωρον ἐπιπολῆς αὐτέων τῶν
πυλέων, ἐνεκόλαψε δὲ ἐς τὸν τάφον γράμματα λέγοντα τάδε·

ΤΩΝ ΤΙΣ ᾽ΕΜΕΥ ῾ΥΣΤΕΡΟΝ ΓΙΝΟΜΕΝΩΝ ΒΑΒΥΛΩΝΟΣ
ΒΑΣΙΛΕΩΝ ᾽ΗΝ ΣΠΑΝΙΣΗ ΧΡΗΜΑΤΩΝ, ᾽ΑΝΟΙΞΑΣ ΤΟΝ
ΤΑΦΟΝ ΛΑΒΕΤΩ ῾ΟΚΟΣΑ ΒΟΥΛΕΤΑΙ ΧΡΗΜΑΤΑ. ΜΗ
ΜΕΝΤΟΙ ΓΕ ΜΗ ΣΠΑΝΙΣΑΣ ΓΕ ᾽ΑΛΛΩΣ ᾽ΑΝΟΙΞΗ. ῾ΟΥ
ΓΑΡ ᾽ΑΜΕΙΝΟΝ.

Οὗτος ὁ τάφος ἦν ἀκίνητος μέχρι οὗ ἐς Δαρεῖον περιῆλθε ἡ
βασιληίη. Δαρείῳ δὲ καὶ δεινὸν ἐδόκεε εἶναι τῇσι πύλῃσι
ταύτῃσι μηδὲν χρᾶσθαι καὶ χρημάτων κειμένων καὶ αὐτῶν τῶν
χρημάτων ἐπικαλεομένων μὴ οὐ λαβεῖν αὐτά. τῇσι δὲ πύλῃσι
ταύτῃσι οὐδὲν ἐχρᾶτο τοῦδε εἵνεκα, ὅτι ὑπὲρ κεφαλῆς οἱ ἐγίνετο
ὁ νεκρὸς διεξελαύνοντι. ἀνοίξας δὲ τὸν τάφον εὗρε χρήματα
μὲν οὔ, τὸν δὲ νεκρὸν καὶ γράμματα λέγοντα τάδε·

᾽ΕΙ ΜΗ ᾽ΑΠΛΗΣΤΟΣ ΤΕ ᾽ΕΑΣ ΧΡΗΜΑΤΩΝ ΚΑΙ
᾽ΑΙΣΧΡΟΚΕΡΔΗΣ, ᾽ΟΥΚ ᾽ΑΝ ΝΕΚΡΩΝ ΘΗΚΑΣ ᾽ΑΝΕΩΓΕΣ.

Αὕτη μέν νυν ἡ βασίλεια τοιαύτη τις λέγεται γενέσθαι.

DIODORUS ii. 7-10

7. Ὁ δὲ Νίνος τούς τε ἐν Βάκτροις παρέλαβε θησαυρούς,
ἔχοντας πολὺν ἄργυρόν τε καὶ χρυσόν, καὶ τὰ κατὰ τὴν
Βακτριανὴν καταστήσας ἀπέλυσε τὰς δυνάμεις. μετὰ δὲ ταῦτα
γεννήσας ἐκ Σεμιράμιδος υἱὸν Νιννύαν ἐτελεύτησε, τὴν γυναῖκα
ἀπολιπὼν βασίλισσαν. τὸν δὲ Νίνον ἡ Σεμίραμις ἔθαψεν ἐν
τοῖς βασιλείοις, καὶ κατεσκεύασεν ἐπ᾽ αὐτῷ χῶμα παμμέγεθες,
οὗ τὸ μὲν ὕψος ἦν ἐννέα σταδίων, τὸ δ᾽ εὖρος, ὥς φησι
Κτησίας, δέκα. διὸ καὶ τῆς πόλεως παρὰ τὸν Εὐφράτην ἐν
πεδίῳ κειμένης ἀπὸ πολλῶν σταδίων ἐφαίνετο τὸ χῶμα καθαπερεί
τις ἀκρόπολις. ὃ καὶ μέχρι τοῦ νῦν φασι διαμένειν καίπερ
τῆς Νίνου κατεσκαμμένης ὑπὸ Μήδων, ὅτε κατέλυσαν τὴν
᾽Ασσυρίων βασιλείαν. ἡ δὲ Σεμίραμις, οὖσα φύσει μεγαλ-
επίβολος καὶ φιλοτιμουμένη τῇ δόξῃ τὸν βεβασιλευκότα πρὸ

αὐτῆς ὑπερθέσθαι, πόλιν μὲν ἐπεβάλετο κτίζειν ἐν τῇ Βαβυλωνίᾳ,
ἐπιλεξαμένη δὲ τοὺς πανταχόθεν ἀρχιτέκτονας καὶ τεχνίτας, ἔτι
δὲ τὴν ἄλλην χορηγίαν παρασκευασαμένη, συνήγαγεν ἐξ ἁπάσης
τῆς βασιλείας πρὸς τὴν τῶν ἔργων συντέλειαν ἀνδρῶν μυριάδας
διακοσίας. ἀπολαβοῦσα δὲ τὸν Εὐφράτην ποταμὸν εἰς μέσον
περιεβάλετο τεῖχος τῇ πόλει σταδίων ἑξήκοντα καὶ τριακοσίων,
διειλημμένον πύργοις πυκνοῖς καὶ μεγάλοις, ὥς φησι Κτησίας ὁ
Κνίδιος, ὡς δὲ Κλείταρχος καὶ τῶν ὕστερον μετ᾽ Ἀλεξάνδρου
διαβάντων εἰς τὴν Ἀσίαν τινὲς ἀνέγραψαν, τριακοσίων ἑξήκοντα
πέντε σταδίων. καὶ προστιθέασιν ὅτι τῶν ἴσων ἡμερῶν εἰς τὸν
ἐνιαυτὸν οὐσῶν ἐφιλοτιμήθη τὸν ἴσον ἀριθμὸν τῶν σταδίων
ὑποστήσασθαι. ὀπτὰς δὲ πλίνθους εἰς ἄσφαλτον ἐνδησαμένη
τεῖχος κατεσκεύασε τὸ μὲν ὕψος, ὡς μὲν Κτησίας φησί, πεντήκοντα ὀργυιῶν, ὡς δ᾽ ἔνιοι τῶν νεωτέρων ἔγραψαν, πηχῶν
πεντήκοντα, τὸ δὲ πλάτος πλέον ἢ δυσὶν ἅρμασιν ἱππάσιμον.
πύργους δὲ τὸν μὲν ἀριθμὸν διακοσίους καὶ πεντήκοντα, τὸ δ᾽
ὕψος καὶ πλάτος ἐξ ἀναλόγου τῷ βάρει τῶν κατὰ τὸ τεῖχος
ἔργων. οὐ χρὴ δὲ θαυμάζειν εἰ τηλικούτου τὸ μέγεθος τοῦ περι-
βόλου καθεστῶτος ὀλίγους πύργους κατεσκεύασεν. ἐπὶ πολὺν
γὰρ τόπον τῆς πόλεως ἕλεσι περιεχομένης, κατὰ τοῦτον τὸν
τόπον οὐκ ἔδοξεν αὐτῇ πύργους οἰκοδομεῖν, τῆς φύσεως τῶν
ἑλῶν ἱκανὴν παρεχομένης ὀχυρότητα. ἀνὰ μέσον δὲ τῶν οἰκιῶν
καὶ τῶν τειχῶν ὁδὸς πάντῃ κατελέλειπτο δίπλεθρος.

8. Πρὸς δὲ τὴν ὀξύτητα τῆς τούτων οἰκοδομίας ἑκάστῳ τῶν
φίλων στάδιον διεμέτρησε, δοῦσα τὴν ἱκανὴν εἰς τοῦτο χορηγίαν
καὶ διακελευσαμένη τέλος ἐπιθεῖναι τοῖς ἔργοις ἐν ἐνιαυτῷ. ὧν
ποιησάντων τὸ προσταχθὲν μετὰ πολλῆς σπουδῆς, τούτων μὲν
ἀπεδέξατο τὴν φιλοτιμίαν, αὐτὴ δὲ κατὰ τὸ στενώτατον μέρος
τοῦ ποταμοῦ γέφυραν σταδίων πέντε τὸ μῆκος κατεσκεύασεν, εἰς
βυθὸν φιλοτέχνως καθεῖσα τοὺς κίονας, οἳ διειστήκεσαν ἀπ᾽
ἀλλήλων πόδας δώδεκα. τοὺς δὲ συνερειδομένους λίθους τόρμοις
σιδηροῖς διελάμβανε, καὶ τὰς τούτων ἁρμονίας ἐπλήρου μόλιβδον
ἐντήκουσα. τοῖς δὲ κίοσι πρὸ τῶν τὸ ῥεῦμα δεχομένων πλευρῶν
γωνίας προκατεσκεύασεν ἐχούσας τὴν ἀπορροὴν περιφερῆ καὶ
συνδεδεμένην κατ᾽ ὀλίγον ἕως τοῦ κατὰ τὸν κίονα πλάτους,
ὅπως αἱ μὲν περὶ τὰς γωνίας ὀξύτητες τέμνωσι τὴν καταφορὰν
τοῦ ῥεύματος, αἱ δὲ περιφέρειαι τῇ τούτου βίᾳ συνείκουσαι
πραΰνωσι τὴν σφοδρότητα τοῦ ποταμοῦ. ἡ μὲν οὖν γέφυρα,
κεδρίναις καὶ κυπαριττίναις δοκοῖς, ἔτι δὲ φοινίκων στελέχεσιν
ὑπερμεγέθεσι κατεστεγασμένη καὶ τριάκοντα ποδῶν οὖσα τὸ

πλάτος, οὐδενὸς ἐδόκει τῶν Σεμιράμιδος ἔργων τῇ φιλοτεχνίᾳ
λείπεσθαι. ἐξ ἑκατέρου δὲ μέρους τοῦ ποταμοῦ κρηπῖδα πολυτελῆ
κατεσκεύασε παραπλησίαν κατὰ τὸ πλάτος τοῖς τείχεσιν ἐπὶ
σταδίους ἑκατὸν ἑξήκοντα. ᾠκοδόμησε δέ καὶ βασίλεια διπλᾶ
παρ' αὐτὸν τὸν ποταμὸν ἐξ ἑκατέρου μέρους τῆς γεφύρας, ἐξ ὧν
ἅμ' ἔμελλε τήν τε πόλιν ἅπασαν κατοπτεύσειν καὶ καθαπερεὶ
τὰς κλεῖς ἕξειν τῶν ἐπικαιροτάτων τῆς πόλεως τόπων. τοῦ δ'
Εὐφράτου διὰ μέσης τῆς Βαβυλῶνος ῥέοντος καὶ πρὸς μεσ-
ημβρίαν καταφερομένου, τῶν βασιλείων τὰ μὲν πρὸς ἀνατολὴν
ἔνευε, τὰ δὲ πρὸς δύσιν, ἀμφότερα δὲ πολυτελῶς κατεσκεύαστο.
τοῦ μὲν γὰρ [εἰς τὸ] πρὸς ἑσπέραν κειμένου μέρους ἐποίησε τὸν
πρῶτον περίβολον ἑξήκοντα σταδίων, ὑψηλοῖς καὶ πολυτελέσι
τείχεσιν ὠχυρωμένον, ἐξ ὀπτῆς πλίνθου. ἕτερον δ' ἐντὸς τούτου
κυκλοτερῆ κατεσκεύασε, καθ' ὃν ἐν ὠμαῖς ἔτι ταῖς πλίνθοις
διετετύπωτο θηρία παντοδαπὰ τῇ τῶν χρωμάτων φιλοτεχνίᾳ τὴν
ἀλήθειαν ἀπομιμούμενα· οὗτος δ' ὁ περίβολος ἦν τὸ μὲν μῆκος
σταδίων τετταράκοντα, τὸ δὲ πλάτος ἐπὶ τριακοσίας πλίνθους,
τὸ δ' ὕψος, ὡς Κτησίας φησίν, ὀργυιῶν πεντήκοντα. τῶν δὲ
πύργων ὑπῆρχε τὸ ὕψος ὀργυιῶν ἑβδομήκοντα. κατεσκεύασε δὲ
καὶ τρίτον ἐνδοτέρω περίβολον, ὃς περιεῖχεν ἀκρόπολιν, ἧς ἡ
μὲν περίμετρος ἦν σταδίων εἴκοσι, τὸ δὲ μῆκος καὶ πλάτος τῆς
οἰκοδομίας ὑπεραῖρον τοῦ μέσου τείχους τὴν κατασκευήν. ἐνῆσαν
δ' ἔν τε τοῖς πύργοις καὶ τείχεσι ζῷα παντοδαπὰ φιλοτέχνως
τοῖς τε χρώμασι καὶ τοῖς τῶν τύπων ἀπομιμήμασι κατεσκευασμένα. τὸ δ' ὅλον ἐπεποίητο κυνήγιον παντοίων θηρίων ὑπάρχον
πλῆρες, ὧν ἦσαν τὰ μεγέθη πλέον ἢ πηχῶν τεττάρων. κατεσκεύαστο δ' ἐν αὐτοῖς καὶ ἡ Σεμίραμις ἀφ' ἵππου πάρδαλιν
ἀκοντίζουσα, καὶ πλησίον αὐτῆς ὁ ἀνὴρ Νίνος παίων ἐκ χειρὸς
λέοντα λόγχῃ. ἐπέστησε δὲ καὶ πύλας τριττάς, [ἐφ'] ὧν
ὑπῆρχον διτταὶ χαλκαῖ διὰ μηχανῆς ἀνοιγόμεναι. ταῦτα μὲν
οὖν τὰ βασίλεια καὶ τῷ μεγέθει καὶ ταῖς κατασκευαῖς πολὺ
προεῖχε τῶν ὄντων ἐπὶ θάτερα μέρη τοῦ ποταμοῦ. ἐκεῖνα γὰρ
εἶχε τὸν μὲν περίβολον τοῦ τείχους τριάκοντα σταδίων ἐξ ὀπτῆς
πλίνθου, ἀντὶ δὲ τῆς περὶ τὰ ζῷα φιλοτεχνίας χαλκᾶς εἰκόνας
Νίνου καὶ Σεμιράμιδος καὶ τῶν ὑπάρχων, ἔτι δὲ Διός, ὃν
καλοῦσιν οἱ Βαβυλώνιοι Βῆλον. ἐνῆσαν δὲ καὶ παρατάξεις
καὶ κυνήγια παντοδαπά, ποικίλην ψυχαγωγίαν παρεχόμενα τοῖς
θεωμένοις.

9. Μετὰ δὲ ταῦτα τῆς Βαβυλωνίας ἐκλεξαμένη τὸν ταπεινό-
τατον τόπον ἐποίησε δεξαμένην τετράγωνον, ἧς ἦν ἑκάστη

πλευρὰ σταδίων τριακοσίων, ἐξ ὀπτῆς πλίνθου καὶ ἀσφάλτου
κατεσκευασμένην καὶ τὸ βάθος ἔχουσαν ποδῶν τριάκοντα καὶ
πέντε. εἰς ταύτην δ᾽ ἀποστρέψασα τὸν ποταμὸν κατεσκεύασεν
ἐκ τῶν ἐπὶ τάδε βασιλείων εἰς θάτερα διώρυχα. ἐξ ὀπτῆς δὲ
πλίνθου συνοικοδομήσασα τὰς καμάρας ἐξ ἑκατέρου μέρους
ἀσφάλτῳ κατέχρισεν ἡψημένῃ, μέχρι οὗ τὸ πάχος τοῦ χρίσματος
ἐποίησε πηχῶν τεττάρων. τῆς δὲ διώρυχος ὑπῆρχον οἱ μὲν
τοῖχοι τὸ πλάτος ἐπὶ πλίνθους εἴκοσι, τὸ δ᾽ ὕψος χωρὶς τῆς
καμφθείσης ψαλίδος ποδῶν δώδεκα, τὸ δὲ πλᾶτος ποδῶν πεντεκαίδεκα. ἐν ἡμέραις δ᾽ ἑπτὰ κατασκευασθείσης αὐτῆς ἀπο-
κατέστησε τὸν ποταμὸν ἐπὶ τὴν προϋπάρχουσαν ῥύσιν, ὥστε
τοῦ ῥεύματος ἐπάνω τῆς διώρυχος φερομένου δύνασθαι τὴν
Σεμίραμιν ἐκ τῶν πέραν βασιλείων ἐπὶ θάτερα διαπορεύεσθαι
μὴ διαβαίνουσαν τὸν ποταμόν. ἐπέστησε δὲ καὶ πύλας τῇ
διώρυχι χαλκᾶς ἐφ᾽ ἑκάτερον μέρος, αἳ διέμειναν μέχρι τῆς
[τῶν] Περσῶν βασιλείας. μετὰ δὲ ταῦτα ἐν μέσῃ τῇ πόλει
κατεσκεύασεν ἱερὸν Διός, ὃν καλοῦσιν οἱ Βαβυλώνιοι, καθάπερ
εἰρήκαμεν, Βῆλον. περὶ τούτου δὲ τῶν συγγραφέων διαφωνούν-
των, καὶ τοῦ κατασκευάσματος διὰ τὸν χρόνον καταπεπτωκότος,
οὐκ ἔστιν ἀποφήνασθαι τὸ ἀκριβές· ὁμολογεῖται δ᾽ ὑψηλὸν
γεγενῆσθαι καθ᾽ ὑπερβολήν, καὶ τοὺς Χαλδαίους ἐν αὐτῷ τὰς
τῶν ἄστρων πεποιῆσθαι παρατηρήσεις, ἀκριβῶς θεωρουμένων
τῶν τ᾽ ἀνατολῶν καὶ δύσεων διὰ τὸ τοῦ κατασκευάσματος ὕψος.
τῆς δ᾽ ὅλης οἰκοδομίας ἐξ ἀσφάλτου καὶ πλίνθου πεφιλοτεχνη-
μένης πολυτελῶς, ἐπ᾽ ἄκρας τῆς ἀναβάσεως τρία κατεσκεύασεν
ἀγάλματα χρυσᾶ σφυρήλατα, Διός, Ἥρας, Ῥέας. τούτων δὲ τὸ
μὲν τοῦ Διὸς ἑστηκὸς ἦν καὶ διαβεβηκός, ὑπάρχον δὲ ποδῶν
τετταράκοντα τὸ μῆκος σταθμὸν εἶχε χιλίων ταλάντων Βαβυ-
λωνίων· τὸ δὲ τῆς Ῥέας ἐπὶ δίφρου καθήμενον χρυσοῦ τὸν
ἴσον σταθμὸν εἶχε τῷ προειρημένῳ. ἐπὶ δὲ τῶν γονάτων αὐτῆς
εἰστήκεσαν λέοντες δύο, καὶ πλησίον ὄφεις ὑπερμεγέθεις ἀργυροῖ,
τριάκοντα ταλάντων ἕκαστος ἔχων τὸ βάρος. τὸ δὲ τῆς Ἥρας
ἑστηκὸς ἦν ἄγαλμα, σταθμὸν ἔχον ταλάντων ὀκτακοσίων, καὶ τῇ
μὲν δεξιᾷ χειρὶ κατεῖχε τῆς κεφαλῆς ὄφιν, τῇ δ᾽ ἀριστερᾷ
σκῆπτρον λιθοκόλλητον. τούτοις δὲ πᾶσι κοινὴ παρέκειτο
τράπεζα χρυσῆ σφυρήλατος, τὸ μὲν μῆκος ποδῶν τετταράκοντα,
τὸ δ᾽ εὖρος πεντεκαίδεκα, σταθμὸν ἔχουσα ταλάντων πεντακο-
σίων. ἐπὶ δὲ ταύτης ἐπέκειντο δύο καρχήσια, σταθμὸν ἔχοντα
τριάκοντα ταλάντων. ἦσαν δὲ καὶ θυμιατήρια τὸν μὲν ἀριθμὸν
ἴσα, τὸν δὲ σταθμὸν ἑκάτερον ταλάντων τριακοσίων. ὑπῆρχον

δὲ καὶ κρατῆρες χρυσοῖ τρεῖς, ὧν ὁ μὲν τοῦ Διὸς εἷλκε τάλαντα
Βαβυλώνια χίλια καὶ διακόσια, τῶν δ᾽ ἄλλων ἑκάτερος ἑξακόσια.
ἀλλὰ ταῦτα μὲν οἱ τῶν Περσῶν βασιλεῖς ὕστερον ἐσύλησαν·
τῶν δὲ βασιλείων καὶ τῶν ἄλλων κατασκευασμάτων ὁ χρόνος
τὰ μὲν ὁλοσχερῶς ἠφάνισε, τὰ δ᾽ ἐλυμήνατο. καὶ γὰρ αὐτῆς
τῆς Βαβυλῶνος νῦν βραχύ τι μέρος οἰκεῖται, τὸ δὲ πλεῖστον
ἐντὸς τείχους γεωργεῖται.

10. Ὑπῆρχε δὲ καὶ ὁ κρεμαστὸς καλούμενος κῆπος παρὰ τὴν
ἀκρόπολιν, οὐ Σεμιράμιδος ἀλλά τινος ὕστερον Σύρου βασιλέως
κατασκευάσαντος χάριν γυναικὸς παλλακῆς. ταύτην γάρ φασιν
οὖσαν τὸ γένος Περσίδα καὶ τοὺς ἐν τοῖς ὄρεσι λειμῶνας ἐπιζητοῦσαν ἀξιῶσαι τὸν βασιλέα μιμήσασθαι διὰ τῆς τοῦ φυτουργείου
φιλοτεχνίας τὴν τῆς Περσίδος χώρας ἰδιότητα. ἔστι δ᾽ ὁ παράδεισος τὴν μὲν πλευρὰν ἑκάστην παρεκτείνων εἰς τέτταρα πλέθρα,
τὴν δὲ πρόσβασιν ὀρεινὴν καὶ τὰς οἰκοδομίας ἄλλας ἐξ ἄλλων
ἔχων, ὥστε τὴν πρόσοψιν εἶναι θεατροειδῆ. ὑπὸ δὲ ταῖς
κατεσκευασμέναις ἀναβάσεσιν ᾠκοδόμηντο σύριγγες, ἅπαν μὲν
ὑποδεχόμεναι τὸ τοῦ φυτουργείου βάρος, ἀλλήλων δ᾽ ἐκ τοῦ
κατ᾽ ὀλίγον ἀεὶ μικρὸν ὑπερέχουσαι κατὰ τὴν πρόσβασιν· ἡ δ᾽
ἀνωτάτω σῦριγξ οὖσα πεντήκοντα πηχῶν τὸ ὕψος εἶχεν ἐφ᾽
αὑτῇ τοῦ παραδείσου τὴν ἀνωτάτην ἐπιφάνειαν συνεξισουμένην τῷ
περιβόλῳ τῶν ἐπάλξεων. ἔπειθ᾽ οἱ μὲν τοῖχοι πολυτελῶς κατεσκευασμένοι τὸ πάχος εἶχον ποδῶν εἴκοσι δύο, τῶν δὲ διεξόδων
ἑκάστη τὸ πλάτος δέκα· τὰς δ᾽ ὀροφὰς κατεστέγαζον λίθιναι δοκοί,
τὸ μὲν μῆκος σὺν ταῖς ἐπιβολαῖς ἔχουσαι ποδῶν ἑκκαίδεκα, τὸ δὲ
πλάτος τεττάρων. τὸ δ᾽ ἐπὶ ταῖς δοκοῖς ὀρόφωμα πρῶτον μὲν
εἶχεν ὑπεστρωμένον κάλαμον μετὰ πολλῆς ἀσφάλτου, μετὰ δὲ
ταῦτα πλίνθον ὀπτὴν διπλῆν ἐν γύψῳ δεδεμένην, τρίτην δ᾽
ἐπιβολὴν ἐπεδέχετο μολιβᾶς στέγας πρὸς τὸ μὴ διικνεῖσθαι κατὰ
βάθος τὴν ἐκ τοῦ χώματος νοτίδα. ἐπὶ δὲ τούτοις ἐσεσώρευτο
γῆς ἱκανὸν βάθος, ἀρκοῦν ταῖς τῶν μεγίστων δένδρων ῥίζαις. τὸ
δ᾽ ἔδαφος ἐξωμαλισμένον πλῆρες ἦν παντοδαπῶν δένδρων τῶν
δυναμένων κατά τε τὸ μέγεθος καὶ τὴν ἄλλην χάριν τοὺς θεωμένους
ψυχαγωγῆσαι. αἱ δὲ σύριγγες τὰ φῶτα δεχόμεναι ταῖς δι᾽
ἀλλήλων ὑπεροχαῖς πολλὰς καὶ παντοδαπὰς εἶχον διαίτας βασι-
λικάς· μία δ᾽ ἦν ἐκ τῆς ἀνωτάτης ἐπιφανείας διατομὰς ἔχουσα
καὶ πρὸς τὰς ἐπαντλήσεις τῶν ὑδάτων ὄργανα, δι᾽ ὧν ἀνεσπᾶτο
πλῆθος ὕδατος ἐκ τοῦ ποταμοῦ, μηδενὸς τῶν ἔξωθεν τὸ γινόμενον
συνιδεῖν δυναμένου. οὗτος μὲν οὖν ὁ παράδεισος, ὡς προεῖπον,
ὕστερον κατεσκευάσθη.

STRABO xvi. 5-7.

5. Ἡ δὲ Βαβυλὼν καὶ αὐτὴ μέν ἐστιν ἐν πεδίῳ, τὸν δὲ κύκλον ἔχει τοῦ τείχους τριακοσίων ἑξήκοντα πέντε σταδίων, πάχος δὲ τοῦ τείχους ποδῶν δύο καὶ τριάκοντα, ὕψος δὲ τῶν μὲν μεσο- πυργίων πήχεις πεντήκοντα, τῶν δὲ πύργων ἑξήκοντα, ἡ δὲ πάροδος τοῖς ἐπὶ τοῦ τείχους ὥστε τέθριππα ἐναντιοδρομεῖν ἀλλήλοις ῥᾳδίως. διόπερ τῶν ἑπτὰ θεαμάτων λέγεται καὶ τοῦτο καὶ ὁ κρεμαστὸς κῆπος ἔχων ἐν τετραγώνῳ σχήματι ἑκάστην πλευρὰν τεττάρων πλέθρων· συνέχεται δὲ ψαλιδώμασι καμαρωτοῖς ἐπὶ πεττῶν ἱδρυμένοις κυβοειδῶν ἄλλοις ἐπ' ἄλλοις· οἱ δὲ πεττοὶ κοῖλοι πλήρεις γῆς ὥστε δέξασθαι φυτὰ δένδρων τῶν μεγίστων, ἐξ ὀπτῆς πλίνθου καὶ ἀσφάλτου κατεσκευασμένοι καὶ αὐτοὶ καὶ αἱ ψαλίδες καὶ τὰ καμαρώματα. ἡ δ' ἀνωτάτω στέγη προσβάσεις κλιμακωτὰς ἔχει, παρακειμένους δ' αὐταῖς καὶ κοχλίας δι' ὧν τὸ ὕδωρ ἀνῆγον εἰς τὸν κῆπον ἀπὸ τοῦ Εὐφράτου συνεχῶς οἱ πρὸς τοῦτο τεταγμένοι. ὁ γὰρ ποταμὸς διὰ μέσης ῥεῖ τῆς πόλεως σταδιαῖος τὸ πλάτος, ἐπὶ δὲ τῷ ποταμῷ ὁ κῆπος. ἔστι δὲ καὶ ὁ τοῦ Βήλου τάφος αὐτόθι, νῦν μὲν κατεσκαμμένος, Ξέρξης δ' αὐτὸν κατέσπασεν, ὥς φασιν· ἦν δὲ πυραμὶς τετράγωνος ἐξ ὀπτῆς πλίνθου καὶ αὐτὴ σταδιαία τὸ ὕψος, σταδιαία δὲ καὶ ἑκάστη τῶν πλευρῶν· ἣν Ἀλέξανδρος ἐβούλετο ἀνασκευάσαι, πολὺ δ' ἦν ἔργον καὶ πολλοῦ χρόνου (αὐτὴ γὰρ ἡ χοῦς εἰς ἀνακάθαρσιν μυρίοις ἀνδράσι δυεῖν μηνῶν ἔργον ἦν), ὥστ' οὐκ ἔφθη τὸ ἐγχειρηθὲν ἐπιτελέσαι· παραχρῆμα γὰρ ἡ νόσος καὶ ἡ τελευτὴ συνέπεσε τῷ βασιλεῖ, τῶν δ' ὕστερον οὐδεὶς ἐφρόντισεν. ἀλλὰ καὶ τὰ λοιπὰ ὠλιγωρήθη καὶ κατήρειψαν τῆς πόλεως τὰ μὲν οἱ Πέρσαι τὰ δ' ὁ χρόνος καὶ ἡ τῶν Μακεδόνων ὀλιγωρία περὶ τὰ τοιαῦτα, καὶ μάλιστα ἐπειδὴ τὴν Σελεύκειαν ἐπὶ τῷ Τίγρει πλησίον τῆς Βαβυλῶνος ἐν τριακοσίοις που σταδίοις ἐτείχισε Σέλευκος ὁ Νικάτωρ. καὶ γὰρ ἐκεῖνος καὶ οἱ μετ' αὐτὸν ἅπαντες περὶ ταύτην ἐσπούδασαν τὴν πόλιν καὶ τὸ βασίλειον ἐνταῦθα μετήνεγκαν· καὶ δὴ καὶ νῦν ἡ μὲν γέγονε Βαβυλῶνος μείζων ἡ δ' ἔρημος ἡ πολλή, ὥστ' ἐπ' αὐτῆς μὴ ἂν ὀκνῆσαί τινα εἰπεῖν ὅπερ ἔφη τις τῶν κωμικῶν ἐπὶ τῶν Μεγαλοπολιτῶν τῶν ἐν Ἀρκαδίᾳ "ἐρημία μεγάλη 'στὶν ἡ Μεγάλη πόλις." διὰ δὲ τὴν τῆς ὕλης σπάνιν ἐκ φοινικίνων ξύλων αἱ οἰκοδομαὶ συντελοῦνται καὶ δοκοῖς καὶ στύλοις. περὶ δὲ τοὺς στύλους στρέφοντες ἐκ τῆς καλάμης σχοινία περιτιθέασιν, εἶτ' ἐπαλείφοντες χρώμασι καταγράφουσι, τὰς δὲ θύρας ἀσφάλτῳ· ὑψηλαὶ δὲ καὶ αὐται

καὶ οἱ οἶκοι καμαρωτοὶ πάντες διὰ τὴν ἀξυλίαν· ψιλὴ γὰρ ἡ
χώρα καὶ θαμνώδης ἡ πολλὴ πλὴν φοίνικος· οὗτος δὲ πλεῖστος
ἐν τῇ Βαβυλωνίᾳ, πολὺς δὲ καὶ ἐν Σούσοις καὶ ἐν τῇ παραλίᾳ
[τῇ] Περσίδι καὶ ἐν τῇ Καρμανίᾳ. κεράμῳ δ' οὐ χρῶνται·
οὐδὲ γὰρ κατομβροῦνται. παραπλήσια δὲ καὶ τὰ ἐν Σούσοις καὶ
τῇ Σιτακηνῇ.

6. Ἀφώριστο δ' ἐν τῇ Βαβυλῶνι κατοικία τοῖς ἐπιχωρίοις
φιλοσόφοις τοῖς Χαλδαίοις προσαγορευομένοις, οἳ περὶ ἀστρονομίαν
εἰσὶ τὸ πλέον· προσποιοῦνται δέ τινες καὶ γενεθλιαλογεῖν, οὓς
οὐκ ἀποδέχονται οἱ ἕτεροι. ἔστι δὲ καὶ φῦλόν τι τὸ τῶν
Χαλδαίων καὶ χώρα τῆς Βαβυλωνίας ὑπ' ἐκείνων οἰκουμένη,
πλησιάζουσα καὶ τοῖς Ἄραψι καὶ τῇ κατὰ Πέρσας λεγομένῃ
θαλάττῃ. ἔστι δὲ καὶ τῶν Χαλδαίων τῶν ἀστρονομικῶν γένη
πλείω. καὶ γὰρ Ὀρχηνοί τινες προσαγορεύονται καὶ Βορσιππηνοὶ
καὶ ἄλλοι πλείους ὡς ἂν κατὰ αἱρέσεις ἄλλα καὶ ἄλλα νέμοντες
περὶ τῶν αὐτῶν δόγματα. μέμνηνται δὲ καὶ τῶν ἀνδρῶν ἐνίων
οἱ μαθηματικοί, καθάπερ Κιδηνᾶ τε καὶ Ναβουριανοῦ καὶ Σουδίνου.
καὶ Σέλευκος δ' ὁ ἀπὸ τῆς Σελευκείας Χαλδαῖός ἐστι καὶ ἄλλοι
πλείους ἀξιόλογοι ἄνδρες.

7. Τὰ δὲ Βόρσιππα ἱερὰ πόλις ἐστὶν Ἀρτέμιδος καὶ Ἀπόλ-
λωνος, λινουργεῖον μέγα. πληθύουσι δὲ ἐν αὐτῇ νυκτερίδες
μείζους πολὺ τῶν ἐν ἄλλοις τόποις. ἁλίσκονται δ' εἰς βρῶσιν
καὶ ταριχεύονται.

FLAVII JOSEPHI ANTIQUITATES X. 11

Παραλαβὼν δὲ τὰ πράγματα διοικούμενα ὑπὸ τῶν Χαλδαίων
καὶ διατηρουμένην τὴν βασιλείαν ὑπὸ τοῦ βελτίστου αὐτῶν, κυριεύ-
σας ὁλοκλήρου τῆς πατρικῆς ἀρχῆς, τοῖς μὲν αἰχμαλώτοις παρα-
γενομένοις συνέταξεν ἀποικίας ἐν τοῖς ἐπιτηδειοτάτοις τῆς Βαβυλωνίας τόποις ἀποδεῖξαι, αὐτὸς δ' ἀπὸ τῶν ἐκ τοῦ πολέμου
λαφύρων τό τε τοῦ Βήλου ἱερὸν καὶ τὰ λοιπὰ κοσμήσας φιλοτίμως,
τήν τε ὑπάρχουσαν ἐξ ἀρχῆς πόλιν ἀνακαινίσας καὶ ἑτέραν
καταχαρισάμενος πρὸς τὸ μηκέτι δύνασθαι τοὺς πολιορκοῦντας τὸν
ποταμὸν ἀναστρέφοντας ἐπὶ τὴν πόλιν κατασκευάζειν, ὑπερε-
βάλετο τρεῖς μὲν τῆς ἔνδον πόλεως περιβόλους, τρεῖς δὲ τῆς ἔξω,
τούτων δὲ τοὺς μὲν ἐξ ὀπτῆς πλίνθου καὶ ἀσφάλτου, τοὺς δὲ ἐξ
αὐτῆς τῆς πλίνθου. καὶ τειχίσας ἀξιολόγως τὴν πόλιν καὶ τοὺς
πυλῶνας κοσμήσας ἱεροπρεπῶς προσκατεσκεύασε τοῖς πατρικοῖς
βασιλείοις ἕτερα βασίλεια ἐχόμενα αὐτῶν· ὧν τὸ μὲν ἀνάστημα

καὶ τὴν λοιπὴν πολυτέλειαν περισσὸν ἴσως ἂν εἴη λέγειν, πλὴν ὡς
ὄντα μεγάλα καὶ ὑπερήφανα συνετελέσθη ἡμέραις πεντεκαίδεκα. ἐν
δὲ τοῖς βασιλείοις τούτοις ἀναλήμματα λίθινα ἀνοικοδομήσας καὶ
τὴν ὄψιν ἀποδοὺς ὁμοιοτάτην τοῖς ὄρεσι, καταφυτεύσας δένδρεσι
παντοδαποῖς ἐξειργάσατο, καὶ κατεσκεύασε τὸν καλούμενον κρεμαστὸν παράδεισον, διὰ τὸ τὴν γυναῖκα αὐτοῦ ἐπιθυμεῖν τῆς
οἰκείας διαθέσεως ὡς τεθραμμένην ἐν τοῖς κατὰ Μηδίαν τόποις.

Q. CURTI RUFI HISTOR. ALEX. V. I. 24-35

Ceterum ipsius urbis pulchritudo ac vetustas non regis
modo, sed etiam omnium oculos in semet haud inmerito
convertit. Samiramis eam condiderat, non, ut plerique
credidere, Belus, cuius regia ostenditur. Murus instructus
laterculo coctili bitumine interlito spatium XXX et duorum
pedum in latitudinem amplectitur: quadrigae inter se
occurrentes sine periculo commeare dicuntur. Altitudo
muri L cubitorum eminet spatio: turres denis pedibus
quam murus altiores sunt. Totius operis ambitus
CCCLXV stadia complectitur; singulorum stadiorum
structuram singulis diebus perfectam esse memoriae
proditum est. Aedificia non sunt admota muris, sed fere
spatium iugeri unius absunt. Ac ne totam quidem urbem
tectis occupaverunt—per LXXX stadia habitabatur—,
nec omnia continua sunt, credo, quia tutius visum est
pluribus locis spargi. Cetera serunt coluntque, ut, si
externa vis ingruat, obsessis alimenta ex ipsius urbis solo
subministrentur. Euphrates interfluit magnaeque molis
crepidinibus coercetur. Sed omnium operum magni-
tudinem circumveniunt cavernae ingentem in altitudinem
pressae ad accipiendum impetum fluminis: quod ubi
adpositae crepidinis fastigium excessit, urbis tecta corri-
peret, nisi essent specus lacusque, qui exciperent. Coctili
laterculo structi sunt, totum opus bitumine adstringitur.
Pons lapideus flumini inpositus iungit urbem. Hic quoque
inter mirabilia Orientis opera numeratus est. Quippe
Euphrates altum limum vehit, quo penitus ad fundamenta
iacienda egesto vix suffulciendo operi firmum reperiunt

solum : harenae autem subinde cumulatae et saxis, quibus pons sustinetur, adnexae morantur amnem, qui retentus acrius, quam si libero cursu mearet, inliditur. Arcem quoque ambitu XX stadia conplexam habent. XXX pedes in terram turrium fundamenta demissa sunt, ad LXXX summum munimenti fastigium pervenit. Super arcem, vulgatum Graecorum fabulis miraculum, pensiles horti sunt, summam murorum altitudinem aequantes multarumque arborum umbra et proceritate amoeni. Saxo pilae, quae totum onus sustinent, instructae sunt, super pilas lapide quadrato solum stratum est patiens terrae, quam altam iniciunt, et humoris, quo rigant terras : adeoque validas arbores sustinet moles, ut stipites earum VIII cubitorum spatium crassitudine aequent, in L pedum altitudinem emineant frugiferaeque sint, ut si terra sua alerentur. Et cum vetustas non opera solum manu facta, sed etiam ipsam naturam paulatim exedendo perimat, haec moles, quae tot arborum radicibus premitur tantique nemoris pondere onerata est, inviolata durat : quippe XX [pedes] lati parietes sustinet XI pedum intervallo distantes, ut procul visentibus silvae montibus suis inminere videantur. Syriae regem Babylone regnantem hoc opus esse molitum memoriae proditum est, amore coniugis victum, quae desiderio nemorum silvarumque in campestribus locis virum conpulit amoenitatem naturae genere huius operis imitari.

G. SMITH'S ESAGILA TABLET

See pp. 192-194

THE tablet was hurriedly transcribed by G. Smith on his journey to Nineveh, from which he was destined never to return, and his account of it remained our only source of information on the subject until V. Scheil discovered the text in private possession. It has now been fully edited by V. Scheil and M. Dieulafoy under the title *Esagil ou le temple de Bêl-Marduk à Babylone* in the *Mémoires de l'Académie des Inscriptions et Belles-lettres* (Paris, Picard, 1913). It is obvious that this important document, drawn up in the Seleucid era, is a first-hand authority and must now be taken into account in any fresh attempt to reconcile the data of the excavations with ancient inscriptions. Koldewey cannot be reproached for forming his conclusions from the only data before him, and no one could be more willing to modify his conclusions if necessary. Whether what has been laid bare by the excavator be recognisable as consistent with the temple buildings as they stood in Seleucid times, or must be referred to earlier ages, remains to be seen, and the excavator himself has the first right to be heard on this point.—[C. H. W. JOHNS.]

PUBLICATIONS OF THE GERMAN
ORIENTAL SOCIETY

Issued by J. C. Hinrichs'sche Buchhandlung,
Leipzig.

Assur

		M.	Cloth M.
Der Anu-Adad-Tempel . . .	1909	40	44
Keilinschriften historischen Inhalts .	1911	12	12.50
Die Festungswerke. 2 Bände . .	1913	135	147
Die Stelenreihen . . .	1913	45	50

Babylon

Die Tempel von Babylon und Borsippa .	1911	32	36
Die Hettitische Inschrift der Königsburg	1900	4 ⎫	
Die Pflastersteine von Aiburschabu .	1901	4 ⎬	22.50
Babylonische Miscellen . . .	1903	12 ⎭	
Die Inschriften Nebukadnezars II. im Wadi Brisā und am Nahr el-Kelb .	1906	20	22.50
Die Ausgrabungen von Jericho . .	1913	60	66
Kasr Firaun in Petra . . .	1910	16	19
Die Bauwerke von Boghazköi . .	1912	60	66
Die Ruinen von Hatra. 2 Bände .	1908, 1912	91	100
Die Ruinen von Ocheïdir . . .	1912	30	35
Nordmesopotamische Baudenkmäler altchristlicher und islamischer Zeit .	1911	50	58
Kirchen und Moscheen in Armenien und Kurdistan	1913	40	46

Abusir

Das Grabdenkmal des Königs Ne-user-re	1907	60	64
Priestergräber und andere Grabfunde vom Ende des alten Reiches bis zur griechischen Zeit vom Totentempel des Ne-user-re	1908	54	58
Griechische Holzsarkophage aus der Zeit Alexanders d. Gr. . . .	1905	35	37.50
Der Timotheos-Papyrus . . .	1903	12	15
Das Grabdenkmal des Königs Nefer-ir-ke-re	1909	30	34
Das Grabdenkmal des Königs Sahu-re: 1: Der Bau, 2: Die Wandbilder. 3 Tle.	1910, 1913	144	158
Das Hohe Tor von Medinet Habu . .	1910	25	29
Der Porträtkopf der Königin Teje .	1911	16	19

INDEX

THE END

Printed by R. & R. Clark, Limited, Edinburgh.

WORKS ON
ARCHÆOLOGY AND ANTIQUITIES

THE NINE MINOAN PERIODS. A Classification and Illustrative Sketch of the Successive Phases of Early Cretan Civilization from the Neolithic to the Beginning of the Iron Age. Together with an Address on the Minoan and Mycenæan Elements in Hellenic Life. By Sir ARTHUR J. EVANS, F.R.S. Illustrated. 4to. [*In the Press.*

KNOSSIAN ATLAS. Edited by Sir ARTHUR J. EVANS, F.R.S. Vol. I. The Wall Paintings, including coloured Lithographic Plates I.-XIII. from Drawings by E. GILLIÉRON, with Short Descriptive Sketch by the Editor (to which are appended Lumière Illustrations), and Notes on the Technique of the Frescoes by NOEL HEATON. 4to.
[*In the Press.*

THE CHURCH OF HEKATONTAPYLIANI IN PAROS. By H. H. JEWELL. With a Historical Note and a Note on the Inscriptions by F. W. HASLUCK, M.A. With Plans and Illustrations. Royal 4to. [*In the Press.*

ANCIENT ATHENS. By ERNEST ARTHUR GARDNER, M.A. Illustrated. 8vo. 21s. net.

SCULPTURED TOMBS OF HELLAS. By PERCY GARDNER, Litt.D. With thirty plates and eighty-seven engravings in the text. Super royal 8vo. 25s. net.

THE ACROPOLIS OF ATHENS. By Prof. MARTIN L. D'OOGE. Illustrated. 8vo. 17s. net.

THE RUINS AND EXCAVATIONS OF ANCIENT ROME. A Companion for Students and Travellers. By RODOLFO LANCIANI. Illustrated. Crown 8vo. 16s.

RUINS OF DESERT CATHAY. Personal Narrative of Explorations in Central Asia and Westernmost China. By Sir AUREL STEIN. Illustrated. 2 vols. Royal 8vo. 42s. net.

ACCIDENTS OF AN ANTIQUARY'S LIFE. By D. G. HOGARTH. Illustrated. 8vo. 7s. 6d. net.

MONUMENTAL JAVA. By J. F. SCHELTEMA, M.A. Illustrated. 8vo. 12s. 6d. net.

HERCULANEUM, PAST, PRESENT, AND FUTURE. By Sir CHARLES WALDSTEIN, Litt.D., Ph.D., and LEONARD SHOOBRIDGE, M.A. Illustrated. Imperial 8vo. 21s. net.

ANCIENT EGYPT. A Quarterly Journal. Edited by Prof. FLINDERS PETRIE, F.R.S. Quarterly Part, 2s. net; Yearly Subscription, post free, 7s. net.

LONDON: MACMILLAN AND CO., LTD.

HANDBOOKS OF
ARCHÆOLOGY AND ANTIQUITIES

EDITED BY

Professor PERCY GARDNER, Litt.D., of the University of
Oxford, and Professor FRANCIS W. KELSEY, of the
University of Michigan.

Extra Crown 8vo.

GREEK SCULPTURE. By Professor ERNEST A. GARDNER,
M.A. New Edition, with Appendix. Illustrated. Part I., 5s. Part II.,
5s. Complete in one vol., 10s.
APPENDIX separately. 1s. net.

GREEK AND ROMAN COINS. By G. F. HILL, of the
Coins Department of the British Museum. Illustrated. 9s.

THE ROMAN FESTIVALS OF THE PERIOD OF THE
REPUBLIC. By W. WARDE FOWLER, M.A. 6s.

A HANDBOOK OF GREEK CONSTITUTIONAL
HISTORY. By A. H. J. GREENIDGE, M.A. With Map. 5s.

THE DESTRUCTION OF ANCIENT ROME. A Sketch
of the History of the Monuments. By Professor RODOLFO LANCIANI.
Illustrated. 6s.

ROMAN PUBLIC LIFE By A. H. J. GREENIDGE, M.A.
10s. 6d.

CHRISTIAN ART AND ARCHÆOLOGY. A Handbook
to the Monuments of the Early Church. By W. LOWRIE, M.A.
Illustrated. 10s. 6d.

THE PRINCIPLES OF GREEK ART. By Professor PERCY
GARDNER, Litt.D. Illustrated. 10s. net.

LIFE IN ANCIENT ATHENS. The Social and Public Life
of a Classical Athenian from Day to Day. By Professor T. G. TUCKER,
Litt.D. Illustrated. 5s.

THE MONUMENTS OF CHRISTIAN ROME FROM
CONSTANTINE TO THE RENAISSANCE. By Professor ARTHUR
L. FROTHINGHAM. Illustrated. 10s. 6d.

GREEK ARCHITECTURE. By Professor ALLAN MAR-
QUAND. Illustrated. 10s. net.

GREEK ATHLETIC SPORTS AND FESTIVALS. By E.
NORMAN GARDINER, M.A. Illustrated. 10s. 6d.

ATHENS AND ITS MONUMENTS. By CHARLES H.
WELLER, of the University of Iowa. Illustrated. 17s. net.

LONDON : MACMILLAN AND CO., LTD.